Favourite Recipes of Old Prince Edward Island

Julie Watson

Nimbus Publishing Ltd

Nimbus Publishing Limited
PO Box 9301, Stn. A
Halifax, NS B3K 5N5
(902) 455-4286

Cover design: Arthur B. Carter, Halifax
Cover photo: John C. Watson, Vancouver
Printed and bound in Canada

Canadian Cataloguing in Publication Data
Watson, Julie V., 1943-
Favourite recipes from old PEI
Originally published under the title: Favourite recipes from old PEI kitchens. Willowdale, Ont.: Hounslow Press, 1986.
Includes index.
ISBN 1-55109-160-7
1. Cookery, Canadian—Prince Edward Island. 2. Prince Edward Island—Social life and customs. I. Title. II. Title: Favourite recipes from old Prince Edward Island.
TX715.6.W37 1996 641.59717 C96-950062-9

Canadä

Nimbus Publishing acknowledges financial support for our publishing activities from the Government of Canada through the Book Publishing Industry Development Program (BPIDP), and the Canada Council.

For the mothers who have influenced and enriched my life:

Vera Mather — my mom, who taught me to appreciate what is now and fight for my beliefs

Emma Hutchings — my grandmother, who encouraged me to follow my instincts and believed in my dreams

Reita Watson — my mother-in-law who shares her zest for life and is a doer

Hazel Falconer — who is the mother of a dear friend. Together they have introduced me to the values of Maritimers, the kinship of family and made my life much richer for having the honour to know them.

Acknowledgements

No project such as researching and assembling a book of this type can be successful without the help and support of a multitude of poeple. I would like to thank all who are mentioned in the text of this book along with the following who have made the creation possible.

I would especially like to thank Estelle Reddin, Assistant Professor of Home Economics at the University of Prince Edward Island who took time out from her busy schedule to sit and chat with me about the foodways of days gone by and imparted her enthusiasm for this fascinating subject to me. Students Anne Ellsworth and Joanne McKinnon (now McAdam) are also thanked for sharing the results of a summer project on historic foods which was done under the direction of Ms. Reddin.

Thanks also go to:

— Georges Arsenault, Professor in Acadian Studies, University of Prince Edward Island
— Orlo Jones and Linda Steel of The Prince Edward Island Museum and Heritage Foundation
— Anna Ivanis, Canadian Egg Marketing Agency
— Lynda Inman, Micmac Indian Village
— Ebury Press
— Gertrude Pendergast, Folklore Prince Edward Island
— Hazel Falconer and Helen Grant
— Chancellor Press, Mrs. Beeton's Book of Household Management
— Jackie Connolly, Carol and Russ Rogers, Debbie Gamble Arsenault
— Public Archives of Prince Edward Island

Introduction

When my publishers asked that I write a book of recipes and lore from "old Prince Edward Island kitchens," I was immediately excited. My love for delving into the past would be fully justified and I knew the experience would be one I enjoyed. My only problem with creating this book was the one that plagues me with all of my writing, I never want to end anything and keep finding new and interesting things to be included. My publishers can testify to this flaw in my nature, for they were the ones patiently awaiting the arrival of the manuscript!

Obviously the book did get done and I must credit my friends and family for that fact. They put up with my constant attention to the typewriter — and neglect of all other things. In my own defense I must say that I plodded on in spite of overwhelming events: a broken water pipe that doused the manuscript so that I had to retype it, a fall on the ice which put hand and arm into a cast, a husband who was diagnosed as diabetic and couldn't help me test recipes, a broken oven . . . I could continue the list until tears sprung to any reader's eyes, why we even had a fire!

But on to the important things that you will find on the following pages.

I became convinced while researching this book that the main reason yesteryear's cook was considered so good, so knowledgeable compared to the average cook of today, is simply that she had to cook. With only basic ingredients, utensils and facilities, the woman of a hundred (or even fifty) years ago had to provide meals that were nutritious and tasted good, several times each day.

She could not get a box of "instant" this or that down from the shelf nor turn to her freezer for prepared meals. It had to be done from scratch with only a few conveniences such as canned fruit available to help her along. And, those conveniences were a luxury, not to be used lightly. They were generally saved for special occasions such as social gatherings or the traditional holidays.

It was a case, with these women, of having to learn the basics of cooking. They had to know how things work—what to mix with what for the results they wanted.

While seldom acknowledged as such they were an important link in the chain of development, particularly in rural areas where feeding the working men was vital to success in the family business; whether it was a farm, fishing, mill or other enterprise. They had no fast food to turn to, no restaurant, no jar of peanut butter. Even a sandwich could not be made until they had baked the bread.

Coming from a family of working women who early on struck out for careers of their own, I often pause to regret that I did not have time to learn those basic skills at home. Until now I have found experimenting with food difficult and preferred to stay with the tried and true. One thing that writing this and my other cookbooks has done for me, is make me learn about food, and enjoy its preparation as much as eating it.

That knowledge is my publishers' gift to me. One that we invite you to share.

Table of Contents

A Brief Look at Island History 9

What was around back then 29

General Kitchen Knowledge 33

From the Butcher
- Pork 41
- Beef 53
- Lamb and Mutton 65
- Fowl 71

From the Fishmongers
- Fish 85
- Shellfish 107

From the Green Grocer and Garden
- Vegetables 129
- Fruits 201
- Dried Fruits and Nuts 247
- Herbs and Edible Wild Plants 251

From the Dairy 255

Eggs 267

From the Home Kitchen
Cakes 277
Filling for Cakes 281
Fancy Breads and Loaves 283
Cookies 291
Squares 299
Bread 305
Biscuits 313
Pastry 317
Puddings 319
Sauces 323
Those Special Olden Days 331
Yule Season 333

Index 341

This photo was taken from Matthew & MacLean's wharf in Souris about 1910 of a shipments of goods and foodstuffs arriving in P.E.I. The tall building in the upper right of the photograph was built by the Federal Government in 1904. It was the first artificial fish dryer in Souris and was operated by George E. MacFarlanek. It was advertised as a Patent Fish Dryer, but was not too successful. It burned down in 1918.

(Public Archives of Prince Edward Island photo accession no 2320 item 23-9)

A Brief Look at Island History

When attempting to encapsulate the history of Prince Edward Island, it is difficult to know where to begin, what to include and how far to go. I admit now to approaching this book with the plan to condense that past into three or four pages — after all, it's a small province, so how much could the past influence people, their lives and, in particular, what they ate? To find out one must read volumes, talk to dozens of people; then at some point, be able to say "stop" and work with the reams of material that have come forth.

. . . . .

Archaeological finds which include a spear-point in the North Tryon area and an "Ulu" (a ground slate tool for cutting and scraping — the name when translated means 'woman's knife') in the North Lake area lead the experts to believe that Debert Palaeo Indians visited this area as much as ten thousand years ago. At that time, the Island as it is today was nonexistent. The Northumberland Strait had not formed and the area was simply part of the mainland. It is speculated that early man, in his continual search for food, hunted the herds of caribou, then commonplace in the Maritimes, and perhaps seals and fish off the north coastal area.

Prehistoric man, it is certain, was nomadic. While our knowledge is limited, we do know that those early Islanders were known as the "Shellfish People".

More is known of the Micmac Indians, the inhabitants 'discovered' by visiting Europeans.

To understand what food stuffs are native to the Island, one simply has to look at the eating habits of the Micmacs in the 1500s. Nomads who roamed their tribal territory, they were primarily meat eaters, preying on herbivorous animals (and, we are told, observing a taboo against the meat of other meat eaters — the carnivores).

Their dietary calendar followed the seasonal supply provided by nature. In January the hunter tramped the ice for seal. In February and March he trapped and hunted beaver, rabbit, porcupine, moose, bear and deer. When fluttering clouds of waterfowls darkened the sky in spring, the Micmac took his harvest and later gathered eggs from the nesting pairs. From May until September food was easy to find. Fishing was good in the lakes and rivers, lobsters could be speared in tidal pools, clams and oysters plucked from shallow river estuaries. Fruits, leaves, wild vegetables and even some kinds of tender bark, as they came in season, supplemented the heavy meat diet.

In spring fiddleheads, the young tightly curled fronds of fern, were gathered and boiled. As summer lengthened, wild peas, lettuce, lily bulbs (eaten raw, baked or boiled) and other stalks and leaves were staples. A favourite vegetable, the wild potato, shaped and tasting more like a carrot, was found in marshes and the shadowy damp places at the edge of the forest. (I wonder if these later became known as the Jerusalem Artichoke?)

As summer waned into autumn there was the harvest of beech, hazel and witch hazel nuts to gather, after the first frosts dropped them from high branches. At this time of the year the Micmac speared fat eels, grown sluggish from the chilling waters and burrowing in the mud of the river bottom. Later when freeze-up came tommycod could be caught through holes chopped in the ice.

Waste was unknown to these people whose lives were dedicated to survival. Almost every part and piece of what they obtained from nature was used in an imaginative, resourceful, almost reverent way. Bones were cracked for their marrow—considered a delicacy; deer and moose intestines became sausage casings; scraps were used to make soup, then seasoned with wild mint and other herbs; milkweed pods, flowers and tender new leaves became broths and medicinal teas. In the sap of the maple and yellow birch the Micmac woman found her sweetenings, tapping the trees to gather sap for syrup and sugar which was carefully stored in birchbark containers.

The search for food was never ending, indeed it formed a lifestyle. The utilization of what they found became a blueprint for survival in their environment. The campsite was determined by the availability of a nearby source of clear, pure water, usually a small spring with a constant supply for cooking and drinking. The Micmac also refreshed himself in springtime with cool clear sap, drunk unboiled, straight from the tapped maple tree.

Strawberries, blueberries, blackberries, teaberries and cranberries appeared on the menu, eaten whole, crushed for juice, or dried and stored for winter use. "Tea" came from twigs of yellow birch, maple, spruce, hemlock and wild cherry which were broken and boiled in the cooking pot.

It was a well rounded diet, supplying all their needs and it all came directly from nature. Because he was a hunter, a fisherman, a gatherer, the Micmac ate few, if any grains. Bread was unknown to him. It was introduced by the first Europeans, and it signaled the beginning of the end of the Micmac's way of life. After tasting the wheaten bread of the French settlers, the Micmac began to trade furs for it. The independent life he had lived in harmony with nature began to erode, and the supremacy he held over his environment began to wane with an increasing dependency on the white man's food and ways.

The MicMac Village Encampment at Rocky Point offers today's visitor a glimpse back to the way of life of those early Micmacs. It is on their material and the booklet, *Abegweit Was Their Home,* that our information about that early lifestyle is based.

The Island, according to legend, was created by an Indian God who said it shall be the fairest of all earthly places. There are many variations of the legend, but the one I like most is that the God, calling his creation Minegoo, placed it among the stars and reserved it for his private habitation. After some meditation, however, he lifted the beautiful, bewitching island on his broad shoulders and set it in the Gulf of St. Lawrence, known to the Indians as the "Place of Laughing Waters". He gave it to the red men, for the clay was the colour of His people, but said, "I shall return each summer to Minegoo, just to lie among its green hillsides and listen to the music of the sea and forest."

Another legend, tells of Glooscap, the Indian God, taking his fiery paintbrush and colouring rocks and earth to Abegweit red — the gayest and most cheerful of colours—as he wanted a cheery home where he could go when he wished for a holiday.

Outside of such myths, the Micmacs called the island, Abegweit, meaning "(land) . . . cradled on the waves."

They were not the only ones to revere the beauty and plenty of the land in words.

By the 1500s, the Atlantic coast of the new world was attracting exploring ships and fishing vessels. The first written record of the Island was left by Jacques Cartier, who landed on the north-west shore July 1st, 1535.

"All this land is low and flat, the most delightful that may be seen, and full of beautiful trees and plains. The fairest that it may be possible to see."

He landed at four places and found the trees wonderfully fair and that there were cedars, pines, white elms, ash, willows and many other species of trees unknown to him, all without fruit. He described the lands where there were no woods as, *very fair and so full of peas, gooseberries, other small fruits and corn that it seemed to have been sown and cultivated there.* The land he described as the best quality that can be seen, and of great warmth, and that there were many turtle-doves, wood pigeons and other birds. He noted that there was nothing lacking save harbours. Cartier sailed along the north shore, not realizing that this was an Island, and missing the splendid harbours of the south side.

There is evidence that the Norsemen reached the new world many decades before Cartier. As well, fishermen from Brittany, Normandy and Northern Spain were active throughout the Gulf of St. Lawrence each summer. It is almost certain that the first white men to actually set foot on the Island were here for the purpose of drying fish and replenishing water supplies. One school of thought is that John Cabot discovered the island in 1497 or 1498. However, there is no documentation or evidence to substantiate the theory, so credit is commonly given to Cartier based on his written records—records that, incidentally, were lost until 1867 when his original account was discovered in Paris, France, the same year that Prince Edward Island hosted the Fathers of Confederation.

Whoever was actually the discoverer, it is fact that the lure that drew them to the region was the fish. Cartier's first trip to the Gulf of St. Lawrence confirmed the value of this vast new resource. The French began a very active fishing trade and by 1550, over 125 French fishing vessels were plying the waters between France and the Gulf. These early fishermen mastered the art of "green salting", that is salting the catch as soon as it was caught. Within 50 years this method of preservation had provided the foundation to a marketing organization for fish products.

Early writings tell us that the first white men to actually settle on the Island were two fishermen from Normandy who came to Isle Saint Jean (as we were then known) in 1719. Mathieu Turin along with his family of ten settled at East Point while Francois Douville and his family of 19 settled at St. Peter's Harbour. A number of farmers from Acadia (Nova Scotia) settled along the Hillsborough River and were joined by three boatloads of settlers from France.

Together, in 1720, they built the small village of Port Lajoie which was eventually relocated across the harbour to the place where Charlottetown now exists. These French colonists, whose descendants are known as Acadians, were commonly felt to be the first of the permanent settlers. Considering the distance and modes of travel available, one must assume they didn't know of the families located on the North Shore. They expanded across the Island, establishing settlements and fishing communities, such as the one to which Rene Rassicot, a Norman peasant, gave his name. Later it was anglicized to Rustico.

The French have always been known for their flair for living. They were the first to develop a "cuisine", and had a talent, even when very poor, for taking nothing and turning it into something. They gave their new homeland an eloquent legacy of folksong—ballads mingled with sharp-witted satirical verses; they brought with them such colourful ceremonies as the 'Blessing of the Fleet', that takes place to this day at several Acadian communities; and they gave to their villages unique names such as Souris (bearing witness to the time in the 1700s when a settlement was overrun by mice!).

Food production was of vast importance to these French settlers. One of the reasons for them being established here by the French government was to supply the beleaguered Fortress Louisbourg in Cape Breton, for in 1713 Newfoundland and Acadia had been ceded to Great Britain, with France still holding Cape Breton and St. Jean. French settlers came in considerable numbers, along with some Acadians seeking refuge under the flag they loved so well. Isle St. Jean then lay between French Cape Breton and Quebec.

The Island remained under French rule until 1758, and it was formally ceded to the British in 1763. At this time settlement was seldom, if ever, more than one farm deep from the shoreline anywhere and there was little reason for roads. Travel was mostly by canoes, the main thoroughfare, the Hillsborough River connecting the largest settlements of St. Peters and Port La Joie. In the 1750s, French settlers had been expelled from the Fundy area by the British, many of them swelling the Island's population to around 3,000. It was as much a refugee camp as a colony.

Then in 1758, the British, having taken the fortress of Louisbourg for the second and final time, rounded up French settlers here and deported them. There were only about 300 Acadians remaining by 1763, most of them in outlying areas.

In the early 18th century British interest had become directed toward the fishery; however, by the later half of the century this interest began to wane while that in agriculture surged ahead. The reason being, of course, that the necessities of life could be so easily and abundantly supplied by agricultural techniques. Few found it necessary to rely on the restless sea for their existence. By the time of the takeover of the Island, however, the fishing industry was regaining importance as an economic factor.

As well, there was pressure on the British Crown to award land on the Island to influential petitioners. In 1764, Samuel Holland arrived to do a survey. He divided the Island into 66 townships, or "lots", each of which was supposed to contain 20,000 acres: one small lot, nominally of 6,000 acres; and three town-sites with attached "Royalties," one in each County. In 1767 the British Board of Commissioners conducted a lottery in which the townships were awarded to petitioners. Each new proprietor agreed to pay quit-rents to the Crown and to settle his lot with 100 Protestant, non-British persons within 10 years.

However, the interest of most proprietors in their holdings was like that of the typical modern stockholder in his shares. Speculation was common. Many of the lots quickly changed hands, conditions of tenure were rarely honoured by the proprietors, rents went unpaid creating a landownership problem that would trouble the Island until after Confederation. The decree of Protestant, non-British persons was also ignored and, in the following years, pockets of Roman Catholic Highlanders grew up along side Protestant Scottish Lowlanders; Lowland Scots and English (also Protestant), French and Irish Roman Catholics.

Following the American War of Independence, the United Empire Loyalists moved north; and many of these loyal, energetic people made the Island their new home.

"Gentlemen have not always the making of good axemen," one writer said of the discouragement felt by the Loyalists in their new surroundings. The land was covered with dense, virgin forest that grew to the edge of the red sand beaches. Another writer of the late 1700s noted the reaction of a settler who arrived on the Island from the lush meadows of Annan. Viewing the giant maples and pines which had to be felled before his home could be built, the man sat down and wept.

From 1783 to the turn of the century, Loyalists from New England and others loyal to the British Crown settled in Prince Edward Island in increasing numbers. Some came directly from the new United States. Others, hearing of the rich soil, left the new

Loyalist strongholds in Nova Scotia and New Brunswick and felled enough of the forest to carve out a home. Loyal military regiments such as the Royal Nova Scotia Volunteer Regiment served briefly here from 1778 to 1782. Disbanded in 1783, they were offered grants on the Island. A total of 28 men, six women and four children accepted the offer of provisions for six months and land ranging from 500 acres for a lieutenant to 100 acres for a private in the Wheatley River area.

Writer, John W. Price, studied the Loyalist settlement and noted that:

> *"While the ship's rolls and census documents of the era often list the Loyalist women only as adjuncts of their husbands or fathers, their contribution was just as important as that of the men. Some Loyalist women were raised with all the comforts of urban New England and had to adapt overnight to the harsh realities of the frontier."*

Others came from less comfortable circumstances. One is recorded as having bought her own fare from Scotland; another was sent to P.E.I. at 16 in the hope that she might find a husband. For men and women alike the harsh reality revolved around clearing trees, building a home and attempting to gather enough food to last the family until the next harvest.

Like the Acadians, the Loyalists became an integral part of Island development. They were joined by another ethnic group perhaps unexpected in P.E.I., the Lebanese.

The Lebanese were particularly noted as tradesman. In the early days they walked the clay roads as pedlars, selling from packs on their backs. Writer, Ronald Gilbert, says they sold tea, sugar and clothing door to door, spending the night in farm homes in exchange for a pair of mittens or silk stockings.

> *"When they saved enough money they'd buy a horse and wagon to make their rounds; eventually many invested in small general or grocery stores. Today, the pedlars' sons and grandsons are affluent businessmen, lawyers, politicians."*

Settlement at first followed the patterns set by the French, along shorelines. But as more people came seeking land it gradually moved inland. Transportation began with an east-west pattern—up the Hillsborough and along the North Shore. The Island's first ferries operated across the mouths of the north shore bays and estuaries. The first interior roads connected Charlottetown to

Malpeque and St. Peters. By the 1850s the Island's basic road network was complete.

Many changes had been made by the British. Upon takeover in 1758, it became known as Island of St. John and was annexed to Nova Scotia. The French village of Port Lajoie became Fort Amherst. In 1769, the Island was granted a separate government no longer administered from Nova Scotia. Since the Island government was to be financed by quit-rents from the proprietors, and since they continued to evade their financial responsibilities, landownership remained a hotly contested issue.

When the first British census was taken in 1798, the population was found to be 4,372. In 1799 our name was changed to Prince Edward Island, after an heir to Britain's throne, and three counties were formed: Kings, Queens and Prince, governed from the capital city of Charlottetown, named to honour Queen Charlotte, consort of King George III.

Steady immigration continued for almost 100 years, with the majority of people coming from the British Isles. To understand why people flocked to this land, one must visualize the situation they were leaving behind. By the 18th century, Britain was in the midst of an agricultural revolution. The old open-field system of farming had given way to large enclosed estates, and newly invented machines were putting farm labourers out of work. The country people flocked to cities by the thousands only to find no way of making a living. Promises of free land, just an ocean voyage away, must have seemed like a miracle in an era where great landowners ruled over all.

Those early settlers were a determined lot—rugged, strong and full of hope for a new life in a new land. They had to compete with a totally new and strange environment, which must have seemed very hostile when winter winds blew and hoards of mice invaded field and home. Even harder to bear was the politicizing and changes of government which took place.

In many ways they were worse off than the earlier French who had arrived with more skills. Rev. Wm. H. Warren, in an article in the Prince Edward Island Magazine, cited an example of the differences in skills. The French had dyked the marsh lands along their settlements and, consequently, had abundance of pasture and grass to feed their livestock in winter.

"In view of the difficulty of clearing the upland, the Acadian settler cast up sea walls. It was hard work, but he soon formed

a smooth area from which he could make a living; and later he could clear the uplands and so make his farm. The English neglected the dyke-lands and the embankments gradually broke down and disappeared."

Still, we must recognize that these people had been misled in their homeland, and many arrived on our shores ill equipped. Not only did they need to build their homes, but there was a dearth of the building material they were most used to—stone. Food, clothing, furniture and utensils, almost all had to be made. The homemaker, through all the political upheaval and uncertainty, had to concern herself with the care and welfare of her family, a never-ending task that filled her every day. She not only cooked and made clothes; she also had to forage or grow much of what went onto the table. She had to preserve the summer bounty for the cold days of winter, using a vast store of knowledge which few can imagine today. Think of it. How many of us could even begin to make vinegar, sweetener, yeast, cheese, butter, turn wilderness into a garden and care for livestock. Those endless hours of toil are not something I envy the women who first settled Prince Edward Island.

There are aspects of their life one could envy, however, particularly on the social side of things.

In 1806 John Stewart Esq. published *An Account of Prince Edward Island in the Gulph of St. Lawrence, North America.* He tried to describe every aspect of life and the things that affected it with the object of:

"Making the Colony better known among those who are interested in its prosperity; or on whose judgement and determination its future prospects depend."

He resided here many years and was able to describe many aspects of life in those years.

"The amusements which Charlotte Town can yet afford are only such as may be expected in a young country thinly inhabited: in Spring, Summer and Autumn, shooting, fishing, riding and sailing; water parties are frequently made, when each family taking their dish en pic nic a marquee is pitched at some of the many charming spots on the banks of the adjoining rivers, and many hours are thus pleasantly spent. In winter there is some shooting, but it is often attended with more fatique than most people would think it

worth, as it is generally necessary to use snow-shoes whenever we go off the roads in the forest. Driving carioles is a favourite amusement at this season, they go with great rapidity when the roads are well beaten: but the rivers in fine weather when snow is not too deep on the ice afford the best field for this diversion. There is an assembly once a fortnight in winter, which commences with the Queen's birthday, and the party is numerous enough to be very happy. Private theatricals were attempted for two winters, but some of the party being only temporary residents, that amusement has been given up for the present."

Of course, similar activities took place all over the Island, albeit often on a much smaller scale. Almost all either featured food, or a gathering at someone's home, after invigorating outdoor activities to partake of some delightful repast.

Another, less favorable report was soon to be written. In 1822 *A Series of Letters, Descriptive of Prince Edward Island* was published by one Walter Johnstone, a native of Scotland who:

*"Went out (to Canada) for the express purpose of surveying Prince Edward Island, and collecting information on the subject of Emigration. During two summers and one winter, he was assiduously engaged in the prosecution of this object; and the small volume presented to the public, will be found to contain a full and particular account of the Climate, Soil, Natural Productions and Mode of Husbandry adopted in the Island; together with sketches of scenery, manners of the Inhabitants, etc. etc.; the whole being intended for the guidance of future Emigrants, particularly as to what Implements and Necessaires it may be proper to provide themselves with before crossing the Atlantic."**

He was not, it seems, particularly impressed with efforts to farm the land and, in fact, seemed surprised that the settlers were able to survive at all, considering the methods being used to produce food and develop the land.

He did, however, see hope for the future of the Islander, even if his viewpoint was slightly prejudiced towards the better things left at home in Scotland.

*Taken from the book Journeys to the Island of St. John edited by D.C. Harvey published by the MacMillan Company of Canada Ltd., Toronto, 1955.

"But better views are beginning to be entertained and adopted, and oat and barley mills are loudly called for everywhere (the Island had, he said been wrongly designated wheat country); and I may assert, without the fear of contradiction, that whenever the Dumfries-shire mode of agriculture, of living, of feeding cattle and pigs, is adopted, there will be nothing to hinder the settlers from enjoying all those comforts as to food, which a Scotch farmer, or his family, wished to look for forty or fifty years ago. I mean a breakfast and supper of good oatmeal, a dinner of potatoes and pork, or beef and mutton, with potatoes and barley soup. Their oats, barley, and potatoes, are superior in their quality to almost any in Scotland. They might also have a cask of good home-brewed beer to treat a friend with, and plenty of whisky of the same manufacture.

But me thinks I hear you, or rather the women in Scotland, saying, when they read this, "What! is there no tea there!" I assure you it is dear, and often dearer, than at home; that is, the right kind, and less to pay it with. But as such as cannot be content with what is mentioned above, they should not come here. I must also observe, a few years must be spent in persevering industry before these plans can be fully adopted, or these comforts expected, after entering upon a new farm here."

letter dated September 13, 1821

In some ways Islanders of the era were better off than those who settled in Upper Canada, for they were closer to direct shipping to Europe, the Southern United States and the Caribbean Islands. Citrus fruit, oranges and lemons, were obtainable by the 1860s. Molasses had been long available, then sugar cane gradually replaced it and the home-produced maple sugar.

By the mid-1800s the American markets were stimulating the Island fishing industry, and the 1861 census showed 89 established fishing settlements. The main fish products were dried cod, salt herring, gaspereaux, mackerel and fish oil. The greatest harvest during the period was mackerel, chiefly taken by American vessels for their home markets. The cod fishery remained steady but was usually not of first importance. Indeed, the Island has never been considered a good area for "making" dried cod. The strong sunshine tended to "burn" the fish; as well, the cod-fishing areas of the north shore were continually plagued by blowing sand which

183 II° GUILIELMI IV. Cap. 2.

CAP. II.

An Act to prevent the Destruction of Oysters, by burning the same, for the purpose of converting the Shells thereof into Lime.

Penalty for burning Oysters, for the purpose of making lime of the shells.

WHEREAS large quantities of Oysters are wantonly destroyed by persons burning them when making Lime from the Shells: For remedy whereof—Be it enacted, by the Lieutenant Governor, Council and Assembly, That from and after the Twenty-fourth day of *March*, One thousand eight hundred and thirty-two, no person or persons shall use or destroy any Oysters taken from any of the rivers, bays or creeks of this Island, by burning the same for the purpose of converting the shells thereof into lime, under a penalty not exceeding Five Pounds, and costs of prosecution.

II And be it enacted, That upon complaint of a

Islanders did eventually come to appreciate the true value of the oyster, as is seen in this extract from a Royal Gazette dated 1832.

(Public Archives of PEI Accession 2320)

ground into the drying fish.

Lobsters were very plentiful, easily caught with dip nets, poles, or simply by picking from the rocks.

The first fish cannery on Prince Edward Island, owned by John Cairns, a Scotsman, opened in Charlottetown in 1857. In the Tuesday, March 22, 1858, issue of the *Islander* (the newspaper of the day) the following advertisement appeared:

"Prepare for lent — as the season draws near, the subscriber considers it a duty he owes to the public to make known that he has on hand a very superior article of fresh oysters, mackerel and lobsters. These have been carefully prepared and hermetically sealed by Cairns and Romans (a business partner) and will be found as well flavored as if just taken from their native element. Try them and judge yourself. Owing to a large cash outlay connected in getting up this delicious preparation, the terms of sale will be invariably cash on delivery by wholesale or retail."

During the first half of the 19th century many Islanders managed to acquire title to their lands so that, by the time of Confederation, about half of the lots were in freehold tenure.

Purchases by the provincial government after Confederation made landownership possible for the former tenants by lease purchase agreements. Land had been cultivated and farms tended to be prosperous (in some areas more so than others because of the land and skill of the owner). A pattern developed with mixed farms predominating throughout the central north shore region and specialization more common in other areas—as we still see today.

It was at Charlottetown, in 1864, that the most important events in Canada's history began when the project of a confederation of the British North American Provinces took shape. The leading public men of Quebec and Ontario (at that time Lower and Upper Canada) met at Charlottetown and joined there a Conference of the Maritime Provinces discussing Maritime Union. The larger project easily eclipsed the lesser, and the larger Provinces united on July 1, 1867. Prince Edward Island once again refused to come into the union.

Cobbett wrote of Prince Edward Island as "a rascally heap of sand, rock, and swamp, in the horrible Gulf of St. Lawrence," "a lump of worthlessness that bears nothing but potatoes." He was not the first writer nor the last that ignorantly maligned our fair inheritance. Each of the provinces in its turn has had the finger of scorn pointed at it, and the tongue of detraction wagged against it; but each and all must continue to prosper while a genial sun smiles on a fertile soil tilled by the hands of free men.

Picturesque Canada, 1882, one of the earliest tourist guides, noted that:

> *"Prince Edward Island was among the earliest of the colonies to establish a system of public education, which has been carried on with increasing efficiency; and the result is that the little Province has sent forth into the world more than its proportion of men of mark and learning. The people are sober, religious and industrious."*

With the local economy flourishing, Islanders had been able to see few benefits in joining the other provinces in 1867. The 1800s were the great years of wooden shipbuilding. Hundreds of magnificent sailing vessels were constructed in shipyards throughout the Island. Money was enriching the coffers of many an Island entrepreneur. Very large crops of oats and potatoes were being exported, the fishing industry was enhanced by the growth of fish and lobster canneries and times were good. Stubbornly, Islanders resisted Confederation, many viewing it as a threat to self-

Stanhope Beach Lodge on the Island's north shore is remembered as being largely self sufficient even in the 1920's. Bread was baked every day, butter was homemade during the winter by the caretaker's wife and stored in crocks in the cellar, the cows on the farm supplied milk and cream year-round. The garden kept the hotel in vegetables, the hen house produced eggs and chickens, and fish and seafood were bought from Covehead and Tracadie fishermen. Meat and groceries were brought from Auld's Mill (an Auld still ownes and operates the Lodge), potatoes and berries were purchased from local people.

Many of those traditions continue today, bread and cakes are baked daily, fish and seafood are obtained from local fishermen and the owner even cultivates their own mussels. One thing that has changed is the availability of liquor. During 1927 when prohibition was in full swing, thought was often given to how the hotel obtained its supplies. A possible explanation may be that the caretaker's nephew was "capitaine du navire Bluenose" and signed a shipping manifest for a consignment of "liqueurs divers, destination Haute Mer, High Sea (Sic)". That does not explain however, how the cargo got past the Mounties who regularly watched Covehead Harbour.

Back in the mid 1800s Angus and Sally MacMillan founded what is considered to be the oldest resort on the Island. Today their great great grandson, Gerald Auld owns and operates the resort.

determination.

By the 1860s Prince Edward Island was becoming recognized as a tourist retreat as well. *Picturesque Canada, 1882* pointed out the virtues of the province but also focused on the heart of the problem that was to force their capitulation to pressures to join Confederation.

"There is no more salubrious summer resort in all America than Prince Edward Island. The sea-bathing is delightful; for the waves coming in curving, laughing, dancing over long reaches of shining sands warmed by the summer sun. The sea-breeze is never far away; and if you go to the northern coast you may enjoy it in its coolest perfection when the waves are edged with angry foam, 'white as the bitter lip of hate.' The scenery is never grand except when great gales beat upon the exposed coast, hurling the waters of the Gulf upon the trembling land; but though not grand or sublime, it is ever lovely, ever suggestive of comfort, peace and plenty; a smiling heaven and a happy people. In the depths of winter there is isolation; but even then there are compensations. What more exhilarating than sports on the ringing ice of those rivers and harbours! And the sleighing never fails. The silver thaw is seen here in a degree of perfection never, perhaps, attained elsewhere. Often, in one night, the grim dull forest are transferred into groves of crystal, each branch and twig bending gracefully under its brilliant burden. Ice half an inch thick forms on the boughs. The sun shines on the scene and it becomes indescribably brillant. The coasts of P.E. Island are almost entirely free from the fog which is so troublesome on the Atlantic coast of Nova Scotia and Cape Breton. Sometimes it hangs on the far off horizon eastward, as if longing for orders, usually refused, to invade these pleasant shores.

We have said that Prince Edward Island is isolated; but there is coming and going in the very heart of winter. The telegraph flashes its daily messages under the waters of the Strait and the ice-boat carries passengers and mails from shore to shore. It is said that the Indian name for the Island is (or was) Epayguit, "Anchored on the Wave." The point of crossing by ice-boat is from Cape Traverse in P.E.I., to Cape Tormentine in New Brunswick, where the distance is about nine miles. The standard ice-boat is 18 feet long, 5 feet wide, and 2 feet 2 inches deep. Its frame is oaken; it is planked with cedar, and the planks are covered with tin. It has a double keel which serves for runners, and four leather straps are attached to each side. The crews are hardy, powerful, and courageous men, equally ready to pull, or row, or swim if need should arise. There is often open water half the distance, and this is regarded as the easiest crossing. The passage usually occupies three and a half hours. Occasionally when the ice is bad and the tide strong in the wrong direction the struggle continues for nine or ten hours. Only once in thirty years has a serious accident occurred. In 1855 a violent snow-storm swept down suddenly on the boat. The men lost their way. After battling with the fury of the elements from Saturday until Tuesday, they finally landed about forty miles out of their course, one of the passengers having meanwhile perished.

We advise our readers to visit this garden of the Sea Provinces in summer."

Land transport was also debilitating the will of Government as mounting railway debts and promises by the federal Government of continuous communication with the mainland forced Islanders to reconsider. On the first of July, 1873, Prince Edward Island cast her lot with the other provinces and joined Confederation.

Economic prosperity was heightened at the end of the century by the booming fox industry which began in 1896 when Charles Dalton and Robert Oulton first selected and bred rare silver-black foxes. Breeding spread, prices soared, and fox ranching made many Islanders wealthy until that industry, too, declined when the bottom fell out of the fur market in 1930.

The result of the financial success of first the shipbuilder, then the fox breeder, is evidenced in the fine stately homes such as the one preserved at the Green Park Heritage Site. The prosperity was reflected in the kitchen. Often time there was a summer and a winter kitchen so that in summer the heat from cooking did not invade the house, while during the winter the heat would disperse to the living area. At the Yeo House in Green Park this is evidenced by the location of the den used by the head of the house; its door opened directly into the kitchen. Of course, these wealthy families enjoyed the full benefits of kitchen help and probably a maid.

In July 1912 The Canadian Magazine published an article exploring the contrasts existing between the Maritime Provinces "as touching common customs and usages are many and varied":

"The Prince Edward Islander of the present is perhaps more nearly related to the people of the mother land than others of the east, as he represents the partly-fused descendant, only one or two generations removed from old-time conditions. He is hardy, industrious, intelligent, loyal to Britain, and just

as loyal to his Island home. Force of stubborn facts compels him to admit that it may not be the largest Province of the Dominion, but in all other respects he claims for its equality. In many respects his claims are well founded and, in any case, the thought is one that does credit to his patriotic instincts. A school boy, on being asked to name the large islands of the world in order, is said to have replied: "The Island, the British Isles, and Australia." This may not be an in apt illustration of the school boy's thought. But the rising generation is experiencing a widening horizon, and his patriotic pride now begins to embrace the whole Dominion. If, in the past, he has been somewhat insular and more British than Canadian, it is from no fault of his. The Island, as to population, courts higher education more than the sister provinces. Politics and the learned professions generally appeal to him, and in them he excels. The ministry and college professorships are callings greatly to his liking, and these he often fittingly adorns."

Unfortunately, there are few glowing dissertations about the women of the province. However, there are a few insights into Island life.

While other areas measure wood by the yard (Nova Scotia) and cord (New Brunswick) Prince Edward Island computed unsawn timber by the ton, probably a survivor from ship-building days. Shingle measurements all through Canada, and indeed North America, were in compact bunches of four to the thousand.

"For some reason this is not the method pursued on the Island, where considerable trade is carried on in fir shingles. Here they are put up in larger bunches of three to the thousand. Lime productions here again differed. Considerable lime is manufacturing for agriculture, almost wholly from imported stone, with coal as fuel."

I particularly enjoyed their commentary on Island roads and transport:

"We notice some peculiarities in the country roads. Here as a general thing: they are laid out with a surveyor's compass and run perfectly straight in the direction desired and generally at right angles with themselves. The country has been spoken of as one of straight highways and crooked railways. While the highways pursue their course regardless of hill or dale, it has been said of the railway, 'the larger hills

were avoided and the smaller ones were gone around.' In the other Provinces the tendency is in the opposite direction. While the highways twist and turn in all directions, the railroads, where possible, pursue an unswerving course.

It is, however, on the winter roads and the method of using them that the most striking contrasts appear. In the mainland provinces, as in most other civilized countries where runners are used in the winter, the snow roads are broken with and for a span of horses. This system is never employed on Prince Edward Island. The roads are invariably broken for a single track. As a consequence, they are invariably bad and next to impossible for a span of horses. This seems to be a matter of surprise in a country where horses abound. Such clinging to an unnecessary custom can only be explained by the stubbornness of established custom. A matter so easily remedied should not be permitted to remain, since a change would save a great deal of inconvenience and much profanity."

The topic of agriculture closed the comparisons:

"As a rule, the Islander uses much more farm machinery and farms generally more scientifically and profitably than his neighbors across the little strip of water. Everywhere with him wheat takes prominent places in the rotation of farm crops. He supplies most of his own needs in this respect. One old man, by reason of the partial failure of his crops, had occasion to buy a barrel of flour at the local store. This he took home in the shades of a dark night lest his neighbors might learn of the fact, and his reputation suffer in consequence. Buckwheat, so plentiful in New Brunswick, is a minus quantity in Prince Edward Island, not being grown even for stock purposes. Here the pancake, so dear to the heart of the New Brunswicker, can hardly be had for love or money. Customs and habit again."

For all the complaint about winter roads, things were changing. The automobile had arrived, granted as a summer vehicle for the first few years, but it had arrived. In fact, the first automobile assembled in Canada was built right in our own Charlottetown. The steam-driven car was designed by Rev. Father Belcourt of Rustico. Parts were built to his specifications by a foundry in Pittsburgh in 1859, then shipped to Charlottetown in sections and assembled by White's Carriage Shop on King Square. Sometime later the good Father, while going down a long hill in South Rustico, found himself with no brakes and wrecked his creation—probably becoming the first victim of an automobile accident as well. Father Belcourt was undoubtedly ahead of his time. By 1904 auto sales were still slow, but the novelty was catching on. They were sold, manufactured and even operated as transport for beach outings.

By 1913 Islanders decided that they must accept the auto. A petition by about 500 electors was granted by the Government-in-Council to allow automobiles to operate in Summerside. There was no road between Summerside and Charlottettown, so cars would be loaded on the train for the journey. At that time they were also loaded onto flat-bed rail cars for crossing the Strait, as the ferries were simply not set up for automobiles.

Things soon changed both on the roads, in commerce and in the home. A new era was beginning. One of electricity, telephones, and easier transportation changed the whole way of life for Islanders—subtly, to be sure, but changed nonetheless.

The fishing industry certainly reflected the changes for us. In the 1870s the supply of lobsters along the Canadian coast seemed inexhaustible. A canner writing in 1873 of the supply for his factory stated:

> *"The heavy gale of last August drove more lobsters ashore within five miles of my packing house than I could make use of during the whole summer. They formed a row from one to five deep, and I should estimate them at an average of 1,000 lobsters to every two rods of shore."*

Another writer, commenting on the abundance of lobsters:

> *"In spite of their increased commercial value, it is nevertheless a fact that in some of the northern parts of the Gulf of St. Lawrence good marketable lobsters are used to manure the fields."*

By 1883 the value of the fishing industry was nearly two million dollars. Five million pounds of lobster was packed in 1882 and each little cove had a lobster factory. By the turn of the century lobster had become the leading fisheries product, contributing 59 per cent of the production by 1904. In the same era, oyster production reached its peak; and from 1876 to 1910 the Island produced 867,226 barrels of oysters. But then a rapid decline began and oysters almost disappeared in some areas.

When gasoline-powered fishing boats were introduced in 1910, the effect was revolutionary. No longer was the fisherman dependent on the vagrant wind or power of his own arms. Few sails were left by 1915. His field of operations was increased; so was the landed pounds of fish. By the turn of the century, there were more than 200 "factories," or small canneries, around the Island. The impact affected more than the fishermen. Those canneries provided jobs and most of the workers were daughters of fishermen (paid wages of 40 to 50 cents per day). Soon came the introduction of the sanitary tin can, which could be sealed by a machine and need not depend on slow hand-soldering.

Prior to the first World War, the chief market for canned lobster was Great Britain. After the war, the United States market came into prominence. In 1924, the first shipment of live lobster was made by rail from the Maritimes to the U.S.; the first from the Island followed in 1927 (from Tignish Fisheries Ltd.). These markets received a severe setback by the ravaging depression of the 1930's. The purchasing power of the public dropped so low that a luxury like lobster was in small demand. Beans, codfish and stew meat were the normal diet. Following the depression the marketplace improved. However, World War II was just around the corner.

With airmen from all over the world training here in Prince Edward Island, our hugh portion of the population volunteering to fight (the highest ratio in the country), and the influx of war brides and new immigrants, the Island was about to face its first radical changes in decades. Not only did technology burst forth after the war, but new cultures joined us bringing many exciting changes to our Island.

Many, many wonderful tales, both fact and legend, about Prince Edward Island, which has as rich a heritage as any other place one could be. Too many to tell here. All I can do is urge readers to delve into the richness of the past. But later. For now, let's turn to the kitchen and see just how those grand women of the Island fed their families the very best that they could muster. How I wish for a journey back to those genteel times—but I wonder, could I sit at the table and hold my tongue and not tell of the wonderful things that were ahead for the whole family, but particularly for the women?

Descending into a dark cold cellar, ice, cut in the winter and delivered for ice boxes, refrigerators, freezers . . . what I wonder is around the next corner?

What was around back then

Farm Improvements

The dear old homestead of the past,
Has witnessed many a drastic change;
The woods are disappearing fast,
Through which the schoolboys loved to range.

The farmer used to walk for miles
Behind the plough in furrows true;
Now on a tractor seat he sits,
An iron steed to see him through.

Now in his car he rides to town,
Long gone, is that old fashioned rig;
He drives back home with growing mash—
Imagine! shopping for a pig.

The old time hen—now up to date,
Has no great use for oats or wheat;
Her tastes have changed—strange though it seems—
He brings her home a laying treat.

The fatted calf—still fatter grows,
On linseed cake with all the frills,
O sorry day—a sad, sad tale,
When water dries up in the rills.

Midst life's vicissitudes and cares,
He shops for stock and sows his seeds;
Tho' with their high falutin' tastes
They still fill in our many needs.

For with an egg—or better—two
And bacon frying in the pan
For breakfast—and a roast at noon,
That's good enough for any man.

Through weather rough or weather fine
He'll smile and say—things might be worse;
A man of courage and of deeds,
Tho' all the stock drag at his purse.

Golden Moments
Coined in the mint of time
by John of "The Lilacs"
an Island poet 1946

As I began collecting recipes for this book, I had more than one occasion to wonder whether products mentioned were available in the pre-World War II days. So, playing super-sleuth, I decided to do a little checking and was amazed at what I found.

Our good friends, Carol and Russ Rogers, who live where an inn was located many years ago started me off in my search. When stripping walls to put up new wallpaper, they found a Sinclair & Stewart Ltd. (of Summerside) Catalogue—dated 1874. Advertised in the catalogue were many items that are part of our life in the 1980s: Campbell's Tomato Soup was 15 cents a tin; assorted flavors of Jello — 3 for 25 cents; Kellogg's Corn flakes or Pep — 2 for 24 cents; All-bran was more expensive at 2 for 45 cents; Bakers Cocoa — 48 cents for a 1-pound tin; Bakers chocolate — 25 cents for a half-pound package and Knox Gelatine — 25 cents.

One puzzler which still hasn't been solved appeared with the listings of evaporated (dried to us) fruits. The usual peaches at 25 cents a pound; apricots at 30 cents; apples at 18 cents; dates at 12 cents; figs at 13 cents and prunes at 15 cents were listed with dromedary at 25 cents a package. According to Collins Dictionary a dromedary is a one-humped camel. Can't see them packaging those for a quarter!

Also listed were raisins, currants, walnuts, oatmeal ($3.75 for a 90-pound bag of rolled oats, $4.15 for 98 pounds, ground), shredded coconut, ginger, rice, corn syrup, all manner of fresh vegetables (including corn) in almost as varied a selection as we find today. Tinned fish and vegetables, including pumpkin, at 2 for 25 cents, were listed.

By 1912 The Canadian Magazine listed vacations in cooler latitudes which brought cruise ships to P.E.I. They also advertised such products as HP Sauce, Worcestershire sauce, E.D. Smith's Jams and Jellies, Magic Baking Powder, Labatt's Ale, Stout and Lager and Bovril. Puffed Wheat was 10 cents except in the far west. Even candy-coated Chicklets had appeared.

By 1932, Delmonte was on the shelves along with Heinz, who offered up several varieties of Oven Baked Beans and spaghetti in cans. In fact, canned goods were very popular because they stored so easily. On April 1, 1932 the *Guardian* advertised 21 flavours of Campbell's Condensed Soup "Sunshine Health Flavour" from the Campbell Soup Company in New Toronto, Ontario—all at 12 cents a can. That same day, Koop's Limited offered weekend roasts cut from "Choice Easter Beef" at 16 cents a pound. Sugar-cured picnic hams were 14 cents a pound. In fish, fresh stocks of scallops, halibut, cod, haddock, salmon, smelts along with smoked finnan haddie and dry cod were to be had. Fleishmann's Yeast, Chase & Sandborn's Coffee, Cream of Wheat, French's Mustard, molasses (of course), Quick Quaker Oats, Tums, Lifesavers, Dentyne and Wrigley's gum. It all led me to realize that checking out each food mentioned was probably a waste of time. We may have improved our packaging techniques, and introduced frozen food; but really, things haven't changed all that much.

Why, by the 30s, even controls were creeping in:

"It is well recognized principle of retail merchandising that the discriminating housewife prefers quality in everything she buys. This fact is born out by the increased demand for branded beef, which is quite general throughout the dominion. . . . . It is also interesting to note that practically all the better-class butcher shops and retail stores are featuring branded beef in the meat departments as a quality feature in attracting trade to the store."

Guardian
Charlottetown
April 5, 1932

Cooking by Guess Work

She guessed the pepper, the soup was too hot!
She guessed the water, it dried in the pot!
She guessed the salt, and what do you think?
For the rest of the day we did nothing but drink.

She guessed the sugar, the same was too sweet;
And by her guessing she spoiled the meat.
What of the moral? 'Tis easy to see;
A good cook measures and weights to a T.

A wartime cookbook
locally printed
belonging to Mrs. Douglas Gallant
North Rustico.

"The early settlers often helped one another by working together at cropping, or harvesting and other big jobs such as building a barn or a house. Such days of co-operative work were called Frolics. There was the building frolic when the rafters of a building went up; the stumping frolic and the threshing frolic. On those days all worked very hard, long hours. The women came also to help cook the big meals for their men. And then at night they would have a party. Someone would play the fiddle, and there would be dancing and a happy social evening.

Women had their frolics too. These were mat hooking, weaving, knitting and quilting frolics. All blankets were woven at home on a huge loom housed usually in an outbuilding or unfinished room over the kitchen ell. Many women could take the wool off the sheeps' backs and put it on the backs of their families. They could shear the sheep, wash and card the wool, spin it into yarn to be knit or woven into cloth. After a web of cloth was finished in the loom, there was a thickening or "fulling" frolic when the cloth was spread on a big table to be kneaded by the women. They maintained a rhythm by singing as they worked.

Later on, as the population increased and the people prospered, halls were built and dances and socials became popular. The basket or pie social was one where all the girls and women in the district filled baskets with the best lunch they could prepare or baked a special pie. They were beautifully decorated and sold by auction to the highest bidder. These socials were favorite means to raise money for worthwhile community projects."

Folklore Prince Edward Island by
James and Gertrude Pendergast

General Kitchen Knowledge

When hearts are light and spirits gay
You almost hear the table say:
"These people give me hearty cheer,
I'm very glad they're round me here."
If food is wholesome, linen white,
China and silver polished bright,
With pride the table spreads its leaves,
Glad to dispense what it receives.
With friends in loving converse near
The table speaks for all to hear.
It says as plain as table can:
"Draw round me all, I'm spread for man."

— *Table Talk*

What's in a Pinch?

One of the problems that today's cook has to cope with when using old recipes is knowing just what some of the measurements mean. A perfect example is the "pinch". Apparently back in 1932 it was also questionable, for in the Charlottetown *Guardian* on June 29th of that year, the subject was dealt with on the page entitled *Woman's Realm ÷ Social and Personal ÷ Fashions ÷ Literature:*

"Many a tasty dish would be just a little tastier, and many a sad stew would be just a little less sad if cooks would make some effort to standardize their 'pinch'," said Max Werder, Assistant Victualling Superintendent of the Canadian National Steamships, in a recent issue of hints to housewives.

Mr. Werder advises all cooks to measure their fingers and

weigh their 'pinch' capacity so that a 'pinch of salt' or a 'small pinch of cayenne pepper' will become terms with some meaning. He says the former amount should be a quarter of an ounce and the latter a sixteenth of an ounce."

Weights and Measures — Old to New

All measurements should be made level or flat.

1 small pinch	1/16 teaspoon
1 large pinch	1/8 teaspoon
3 teaspoons	1 tablespoon
1 saltspoon	1/4 teaspoon
1 rounded tablespoon	2 tablespoons
1 dessertspoon	2 teaspoon
4 tablespoons	1/4 cup
1 wineglass	1/4 cup
1 gill	1/2 cup
2 cups	1 pint
2 pints	1 quart
4 quarts	1 gallon
8 quarts	1 peck
4 pecks	1 bushel
16 ounces	1 pound

And on to Metric

The chart below shows the approximate replacement measure to be used as a guideline only. Remember, metric measures are not interchangeable with standard measures. When cooking with standard recipes, use standard measures; with metric recipes, use metric measures.

Volume Measures

Symbols are for liter — L
milliliter — mL

1 mL	approximate replacement	1/4 tsp
2 mL	approximate replacement	1/2 tsp
5 mL	approximate replacement	1 tsp
15 mL	approximate replacement	1 tbsp
30 mL	approximate replacement	1 oz
50 mL	approximate replacement	1/4 cup or 2 oz
75 mL	approximate replacement	1/3 cup or 3 oz

125 mL	approximate replacement	½ cup or 4 oz
175 mL	approximate replacement	⅔ cup or 5 oz
200 mL	approximate replacement	¾ cup or 6 oz
250 mL	approximate replacement	1 cup or 8 oz
500 mL	approximate replacement	2 cups or 16 oz
1000 mL	approximate replacement	4 cups or 32 oz
1 L	approximate replacement	4 cups or 32 oz
1.2 L	approximate replacement	5 cups or 40 oz
1.5 L	approximate replacement	6 cups or 48 oz
1.6 L	approximate replacement	7 cups or 56 oz
2 L	approximate replacement	8 cups or 64 oz

Mass (Weight) Measures

Symbols are for kilogram — kg
gram — g

250 g	approximate replacement	½ pound
500 g	approximate replacement	1 pound
1000 g or 1 kg	approximate replacement	2 pounds

Length Measures

Symbols are for centimeter — cm
millimeter — mm

10 mm or 1 cm	approximate replacement	⅜ inch
13 mm or 1.3 cm	approximate replacement	½ inch
2.5 cm	approximate replacement	1 inch
5 cm	approximate replacement	2 inches
15.3 cm	approximate replacement	6 inches
30 cm	approximate replacement	12 inches

Temperature Measures

Symbol for Celsius — °C

100°C	approximate replacement	200°F (Fahrenheit)
140°C	approximate replacement	275°F
150°C	approximate replacement	300°F
160°C	approximate replacement	325°F
180°C	approximate replacement	350°F
190°C	approximate replacement	375°F

200°C	approximate replacement	400°F
220°C	approximate replacement	425°F
230°C	approximate replacement	450°F

About Measuring

- to measure flour spoon lightly into measuring cup. Level off with straight edge of knife
- to measure brown sugar, spoon into measuring cup and pack it down with back of a knife.

Equivalents

This handy table will save you measuring time:

- 1 pound butter equals 2 cups
- butter the size of a hazelnut equals 1 rounded teaspoon
- butter the size of a walnut equals 1 rounded tablespoon
- butter the size of an egg equals ¼ cup
- 2 tablespoons butter, sugar or salt equals 1 ounce
- 4 tablespoons flour equals 1 ounce
- 4 cups flour equals one pound
- 3 cups cornmeal equals one pound
- 1 cup whipping cream equals 2 cups, whipped
- 2 cups solid meat equals one pound
- 1 square bitter chocolate equals 1 ounce
- 1 ounce chocolate equals ¼ cup cocoa
- 1 ounce grated chocolate equals one square or 5 tablespoonfuls
- 1 4-ounce package of nuts equals 1 cup, chopped
- 1 pound walnuts or pecans in shell equals ½ pound shelled
- 1 cup walnuts or almonds shelled equals ¼ pound
- 1 cup pecans shelled equals ⅓ pound
- ⅓ cup blanched, chopped almonds equals 1 ounce
- 1 cup raisins equals six ounces

Sugar

Using older recipes we often see sugars with unfamiliar names. We have defined some of them below:

Caster (or Castor) Sugar — a very fine crystalline sugar — best for cakes, sifted over for decoration and in meringues

Confectioner's Sugar — icing sugar or powdered sugar

Demerara Sugar — a brown sugar with large crystals and fine flavor. Available in specialty shops

Golden Syrup — a uniquely British product, pale yellow with a thick honey-like consistency. Quite unlike molasses. Used to be specially brought in, now available in some supermarkets
Lump sugar — sugar cubes
Powdered Sugar — icing sugar
Preserving Sugar — pure refined sugar in large white crystals or irregular lumps used for jams, jellies and marmalades. We commonly use white granulated sugar in its place.
Treacle — a rather vague term that has been used to cover everything from golden syrup to molasses. Treacle Tart is usually made with Golden syrup.
When a recipe calls for a sugar you are unfamiliar with, substitute regular granulated white sugar in half the called-for amount, then taste and add until it suits you. Sugar was sometimes obtained in chunks and pounded as needed.

Sugar Equivalents

- 1 pound of icing sugar equals 3¾ cups, sifted
- 2 cups granulated sugar equals 1 pound
- 2⅔ cups brown or powdered sugar equals 1 pound

Household Hints from the Late 1800's and Early 1900's

- To clean mud from clothing — use a corn-cob to rub the mud from the clothing, then brush well.
- To remove the smell of onions from the breath — parsley eaten with vinegar will destroy the unpleasant breath caused by eating onions.
- To destroy odor of burning lamp wicks (oil lamps) — boil new lamp wicks in vinegar and then thoroughly dry them. There will then be no odor from them when burning.
- To clean lamp chimneys — rub them with a piece of newspaper upon which a little kerosene has been poured. This is better than soap and the chimney will not be so likely to crack. Or, hold chimney over the steam from a boiling kettle, then wipe it inside and out with a soft muslin cloth.
- To exterminate bed bugs — use kerosene oil freely wherever the bugs are found.
- To polish patent leather — orange juice will be found to be a good polish for patent leather.

— To loosen screws — hold a red hot poker on the head of a rusty screw for two or three minutes, and it may be easily removed with a screw driver.
— To clean blackened silver — add a teaspoonful of ammonia to a cup of water and use a little of this to make a paste with whiting. Apply the paste to the silverware with a soft chamois and polish it, using another chamois to dry.
— To get rid of flies — it is said that you will not be troubled with many flies if you keep geraniums growing in the house. Then why not have more flowers and fewer flies?
— Mosquitoes and flies — apply to the face and hands a mixture of six parts of sweet oil, one part pennyroyal and one part creosote, and you will prevent bites of mosquitoes and flies. Do not let it get in the eyes.
— To remove scorches from cloth — spread over the scorched places a mixture of the juice of two onions, two ounces of Fuller's earth and one-half pint of vinegar. These ingredients should be mixed, thoroughly boiled and cooked before using.
— To remove mildew — dip the article in sour buttermilk; lay it in the sun to whiten and wash in clean water. Another method is to apply a mixture of soap, starch, salt and the juice of a lemon. Use half as much salt as starch.
— Fire kindler — soak corn-cobs in kerosene oil; when needed put a cob in the stove, set fire to it and put on the fuel.
— To remove paint spots from windows — dissolve an ounce of salsoda in a pint of soft water. Use it hot. Tie flannel on a stick, dip into the liquid and apply until the paint is softened; then wash off with hot water.
— Grafting wax — melt together two pounds of rosin and a half pound each of tallow and beeswax. Mix thoroughly, cool in cold water and work until it is pliable.
— Care of coffee pots — if you would have good coffee, always keep the inside of the pot clean. Boil it out once in a while with soap, water and wood ashes and scour it thoroughly.
— The teakettle — in localities where there is lime in the water, it is well to keep an oyster or egg shells in the teakettle to receive the lime deposits.
— To drive away fleas — sprinkle a few drops of lavender about the beds and other places they infest.
— To remove bad smells from clothing — articles of clothing or any other articles which have bad smelling substances on them may be freed from the smell by wrapping them up lightly and

burying in the ground for a day or two.

— To remove the smell of fresh paint — mix chloride of lime in water, sprinkle hay with it and place in the room.
— Icy windows — rub the glass with a sponge dipped in alcohol, and the windows will be kept free from ice. Alcohol is also good to polish them with.
— Water-proof paper covering jars — used in preserving, etc. — brush the paper over with linseed oil and hang over a line until dry.
— To remove tight glass stoppers — wet a cloth in hot water and wrap it around the neck of the bottle. Another way is to wind a cord once around the neck of the bottle and saw back and forth a few times until the neck is heated and expands.
— To remove tar — scrape off all the tar possible and then thoroughly wet the place with either melted lard or good salad oil and let it remain for 24 hours; if woolen or silk, take out the grease with either spirits of wine or ether; if cotton or linen, wash out in strong warm soap suds.
— Black ink, copying or writing fluid — rain water, one gallon; brown sugar, one-eighth pound; gum arabic, one-eighth pound; powdered nutgalls, three-eighths pound; clean copperas, one-eighth pound; bruise and mix then let stand for 10 days, shaking occasionally; strain. If not used as a copying ink, one-fourth of the sugar or gum is needed as it will then flow more freely. This ink is fine for records and deeds for it may be read hundreds of years hence.

Cures and Remedies

Pumpkin seed — for tapeworms, eat a lot of shelled seeds at night. One of the best remedies known for tapeworms. They are also good for suppression of urine.

Strawberry — persons who suffer from kidney or bladder troubles should frequently eat strawberries when they are in season; and, at other seasons, they should use a syrup made from the berries. Strawberries are a very valuable remedy for either kidney or bladder troubles. Strawberry leaf tea with alum is good for sore mouth.

Thyme — used to make a toothpaste, antiseptic, tonic; to treat hysteria, painful menstruation, colic, etc.

Ginseng — at one time cultivated on the Island. Good for pain in the bones from colds, debility, weakness from excessive venery, gravel and is a good restorative. It improves the appetite, strengthens the stomach and invigorates the system.

From the Butcher

Pork

From the first sailings across the Atlantic until the present day, Pork has played a very important role in the kitchens of Islanders. So valued was livestock to the early settler that life and limb would be risked for them.

"I think it was on the third Sunday we lost one of our pigs and knew not how, on the fourth another on the fifth another on the sixth we lost the Sow. It being in the After noon several saw her fall over board. There was a great Swel and but little wind the Vessel rol very mutch and her feet Slipping could not save herself. Our Capt being inform of the misfortune came on deck when we could see her swim remarkable well at a considerable distance from the Vessel. I believe half a mile. The mate whose name was Johnson an Excelent Swimer said if the Capt would order the Ship about he would fix a rope to him and Swim after her. This being done we soon came near her and we haul her in again."

In the excitement one John Compton fell from his viewpoint in the loft.

"When the mate had made the rope fast to the Sow we then haul'd her up. She seemd not the Worst for it and Continued very well afterward."

Poor Mr. Compton did not fare quite so well. After securing the safety of the sow the mate swam to rescue him, however, the gentleman was very sick afterwards and bedridden for several weeks.

Thos. Curtis: Voyage to the
Island of St. John's, 1775

Preserving Pork for Winter

"My father would kill a pig. This was in the 30s, 40s and 50s, my mother spent a full day frying the pork. Then it was poured into bottles, fat and all, and sealed. This kept perfectly all winter. During the winter, you took out what you needed, warmed it up, and dinner was ready. This tasted delicious."

/ R.W.

Pigs were an important addition to any farm because of their ability to look after themselves. They could root in the woods for enough food to keep healthy and, in fact, had to be fenced out of the garden. Their sizable litters meant that pig was a faster-growing, easier-to-keep animal than either cattle or sheep. And since both of those animals had other uses, pig was most valuable for its meat.

The meat could be salted and packed in strong brine to keep through the winter. It could be cured in smokehouses to make ham or bacon, and it also kept well stored in fat. Virtually every part of the pig could be used: headcheese, jellied hock, sausages, streaky bacon all come from secondary portions of the pig.

Pork Hocks in Jelly

Clean hocks well by scrubbing with a bristle brush, then soak in a salt brine overnight. Put hocks in a large cast iron pot and cover with boiling water. Simmer until tender then remove the lean meat and cast aside skin, gristle and bones. Layer meat closely in a loaf pan or mold, sprinkling occasionally with salt and pepper. When the liquor from the cooking has cooled, skim off the fat; then pour just enough into the mold to cover the meat. Press by placing a weight on meat until set (just a couple of hours in the refrigerator). Serve sliced with a chutney, pickle or sauce.

Head Cheese

Made in a similar way except the head is used along with the hocks. Cook until the flesh comes from the bones. Put lean meat through a meat grinder or chopper and press with weights to remove liquid (there will be fat in it). Use fat-free liquor as above after mixing meat with a little summer savory or sage, salt and pepper to taste.

Pork Scrapple

I'm not just sure of the origin of this dish; but I was told that, when made this way, it comes from the United States, somewhere around Pennsylvania. Apparently, it would be made after killing a hog; and any combination of pork meat could be used.

1¼ pounds pork (meat scraps, steak, liver, kidney, heart—today's cook is most likely to buy a cheaper chop)
3 cups water
½ cup cornmeal
1 onion or celery stick chopped fine (optional)
salt and pepper
¼ cup flour
½ tsp sage
¼ tsp ground allspice
flour
1 tablespoon shortening

Boil the meat until tender in water flavoured with salt and pepper. Remove lean meat and cut into pieces. Strain liquor and chill so that fat can be removed. Mix cornmeal, the quarter cup flour and spices in a saucepan and stir in 1 cup of the liquor. Stir over medium heat, until thick. Measure out another 1½ cups liquor and after stirring meat into cornmeal mixture, add liquor gradually, stirring well. Bring to a boil, reduce heat and simmer without covering for half an hour. Grease a loaf pan that is 9 × 5 × 3 inches and spread mixture evenly in it. Chill overnight or longer. Invert mold; slice scrapple half an inch thick. Dredge in flour then brown in hot spider (frying pan) to serve.

Pork Cake

Every so often you come across a recipe that not only sounds intriguing but also gives a picture of ingredients that were available at comparatively modest cost. This is one such, dates from the early 1900s:

> *"One pound fat pork, 1 pound seeded raisins, 1 pound seeded dates, 1 pound currants, 1 pound figs, 1 teaspoonful cinnamon, 1 teaspoonful ground cloves, 2 cups molasses, 1*

cup sugar, 1 teaspoonful soda, 8 cups flour, 1 pint of hot water poured over the flour and let cool. Mix all together and bake."

Pâté from "Up West"

2 pounds lean pork
2 pounds lean veal
3 tbsp minced onion
1½ tsp dried dill (or 1 tbsp fresh, minced)
1 bay leaf
⅛ tsp dried thyme
2 cloves garlic, halved
pinch nutmeg
dry red wine
⅓ cups dry sherry
¼ tsp salt
⅛ tsp black pepper
8 pieces lean bacon
20 stuffed green olives, sliced

Slice the pork and veal into very thin strips and arrange in layers in a large glass dish. Combine onion, dill, bay leaf, thyme, garlic, nutmeg, and enough red wine to cover the meat slices in the dish. Refrigerate this for one full day (24 hours). Drain well then finely mince about one quarter of both the pork and veal by putting it through a meat grinder. Season the meats with the sherry, salt and pepper. Turn oven to 350°F. Line a loaf pan with bacon, placed side by side and hanging over the edge of the dish. Arrange a layer of drained meat slices over the bacon, then a layer of minced meat and half the sliced olives. Continue layering, finishing with olive slices. Fold the end of the bacon over the top. Put the loaf pan in a larger dish of water and bake for 1½ hours. While cooking find a strip of wood or plate with which you can press the pâté. Place it (if you are using wood, cover it!) on the pâté after taking it from the oven and set a four-pound weight on top. By cooling, pressed, you make a firm loaf of pâté that slices nicely. Chill before serving.

Note: This recipe differs from the traditional Acadian Pâté but is still delicious. It works best if you can buy the meat in one piece of each so that you get nice strips when you cut it.

Acadian Pork Tourtière

1½ pounds lean ground pork
1 small onion, minced
½ cup boiling water
1 garlic clove, chopped
1½ tsp salt
¼ tsp mace
¼ tsp black pepper
¼ tsp sage
pinch ground cloves
3 medium potatoes
Pastry (for a two-crust, deep, nine-inch pie)

Mix together in a heavy saucepan the pork, onion, water and seasonings. Cook over low heat, stirring constantly, until meat loses its pink colour and the liquid is down to about half. Cover and cook 45 minutes longer. Meanwhile, boil and mash potatoes. Mix mashed potatoes into cooked meat mixture. Set aside to cool.

Preheat oven to 450°F. Roll out half the pastry and line pie plate. Fill with the cooled meat mixture. Roll out the remainder of the dough and cover the pie. Seal and flute edges; slash top crust. Bake in 450°F oven for ten minutes, then reduce heat to 350°F and bake 30-40 minutes longer. Serves 6-8.

School Children's Choice Chops

"I can recall as we kids would come home for our noon meal (no cafeteria, no place nearby for cokes, bars or hamburgers), though it meant walking five or six blocks (no busing, and practically no parents drove cars) we were always assured of home cooking.

After doffing my coat and tam I'd run to the kitchen and open the oven door to see what mother prepared for dinner. (Everyone ate dinner at noon in those days.) If we were lucky we kids would enjoy the following recipe.

For our family mother would get eight to ten pork chops, lean and she would cut away all fat, then brown them in a skillet on top of the stove (wood and coal stove, incidentally). In a large oblong baking pan she would first grease the bottom and lay the chops in rows; then she added a couple of carrots, thinly sliced, also a small turnip cut up in small pieces, one large or two small onions, sliced; and two large potatoes, peeled and thinly sliced. Seasoning would consist of 1 tsp each of salt, pepper, summer savory and a dash of Worcestershire sauce. One cup of water would be poured over all.

She would give the meal about an hour or so to cook in a slow oven. When cooked I would add about a quarter cup of tomato sauce or a few dashes of ketchup.

Naturally, a couple of helpings of this appetizing meal would set us up for the walk back to school and afternoon class until 3 p.m. If we were lucky, when we got back home mom would have a batch of molasses cookies (see index) baked, piled up on a large platter in the kitchen."

/ J.C.

About Cured Pork

Cured meat, such as smoked ham or salted pork, were frequently used before the days of refrigeration; and many an Islander recalls the flavourful hams that used to be served with scalloped potatoes or corn casserole.

Verna's Baked Ham

1 ham, 8-10 pounds
½ cup brown sugar
½ tsp mustard
¼ cup flour
3 tbsp vinegar (or water)
2 tbsp whole cloves

Soak ham in cold water overnight. Boil 1 hour and drain. Remove rind and cover with paste made of brown sugar, mustard, flour and vinegar. Stick in cloves. Bake in a slow oven (250°F) for four hours.

Joan's Baked Ham

Soak and scrub the ham. Make a thick paste of rye flour and water. Spread all over the ham. Set on rack in pan in hot oven to bake paste, then lower temperature, let bake about four hours at 250°F. Make a hole in the paste and pour in a cup of hot cider or liquid from the pan, repeat twice if needed. Bake one hour longer, remove crust intact, and skin. Brush with beaten yolk of egg, sprinkle with brown sugar and rye bread crumbs and brown. Save crust and use to keep left-over ham moist.

Beer Glazed Ham Slices

6 slices of ham (about ¾″ thick)
2 tbsp butter
1 tbsp cornstarch
1 tsp dry mustard
¼ tsp ground ginger
¼ tsp ground cloves
1 bottle regular beer or ale
½ cup light brown sugar, firmly packed

In a large skillet lightly brown the ham in the butter then remove and keep warm. Mix together the cornstarch, mustard, spices; then stir in ¼ cup beer until smooth. Pour this and the remaining beer into skillet, add sugar. Stir constantly until smooth and thick. Return ham to sauce, reduce heat, cover and simmer until ham is heated, basting with sauce from time to time.
Serves 6.

Devilled Ham Squares

Cut bread in slices one-third inch thick, then in squares or substantial fingers of nice size for serving. Spread lightly with butter, then with a layer of devilled ham. Put in a moderately quick oven to heat thoroughly and serve with hot tomato sauce.

Tomato Sauce

2 cups canned tomatoes
¼ cup water
2 tbsp chopped onion
3 cloves
⅛ tsp chopped parsley
4 tbsp butter
⅓ cup flour
1 tsp salt
¼ tsp pepper

Cook together the tomatoes, spices, water and herbs, for 20

minutes. Strain through sieve—there should be about 2 cups liquid; if necessary add a little water or vegetable stock to make up the quantity. Melt the butter and blend in the flour, cooking it until brown but taking care not to burn it. Add the salt and pepper and gradually add the tomato stock until the sauce thickens smoothly.

Lillian's Split Pea Soup with Salt Pork

Wash a pint of split peas and cover with tepid water, adding a pinch of soda; let remain overnight to swell. In the morning put them in a kettle with three quarts of cold water, adding half a pound of lean salt pork cut into slices; also a teaspoonful of salt and a little pepper. Cook slowly for three hours, stirring occasionally or until the peas are dissolved, adding a little more boiling water to keep up the quantity as it boils away. Strain through a colander. Serve with small squares of toasted bread. If not rich enough, add a small piece of butter. An excellent choice for cooking on the wood stove.

Sausages

Prince Edward's most famed citizen, Lucy Maud Montgomery, the creator of Anne of Green Gables, numerous other books, short stories and poems, once wrote of her love for sausages. The author in the book, The Alpine Path, told the story of her early life and the beginning of her career as a writer. During a visit to her Grandfather Montgomery's farm at Park Corner, Lucy Maud, about five years old, had the only serious illness of her life—an attack of typhoid fever.

> *"The night before I took ill I was out in the kitchen with the servants, feeling as well as usual, 'wide-awake and full of ginger', as the old cook used to declare. I was sitting before the stove, and cook was 'riddling' the fire with a long, straight bar of iron used for that purpose. She laid it down on the hearth and I promptly caught it up, intending to do some 'riddling' myself, an occupation I much liked, loving to see the glowing red embers fall down on the black ashes."*

Unfortunately, Lucy Maud grasped the wrong end of the poker, burning herself badly. The next day she woke with a violent headache and, a few days later, was diagnosed as having typhoid fever.

Lucy Maud Montgomery, authoress who took Prince Edward Island into the hearts of readers all over the world with her Anne of Green Gables novels.

"Typhoid fever patients were not dieted so strictly during convalescence in those days as they are now. I remember one day, long before I was able to sit up, and only a short time after the fever had left me, that my dinner consisted of fried sausages—rich, pungent, savory, home made sausages, such as are never found in these degenerate days. It was the first day that I had felt hungry, and I ate ravenously. Of course, by all the rules of the game, those sausages should have killed me, and so cut short that 'career' of which I am writing. But they did not. These things are fated. I am sure that nothing short of pre-destination saved me from the consequences of those sausages."

Lucy Maud Montgomery
the Alpine Path

Sausages were a great favorite in days past and were the basis for many family dishes.

Upside Down Sausage Cornbread

8 sausages, fried to a golden brown and drained well
1 cup cornmeal
2 cups buttermilk
1⅓ cups all-purpose flour
½ tsp baking soda
2 tsp baking powder
½ tsp salt
¼ cup granulated sugar
⅓ cup lard
1 egg
½ tsp vanilla

Fry the sausages until evenly browned and drain well. Grease well a 9-inch round cake pan (deep). Arrange the sausages in a pinwheel design in the bottom of the pan. Meanwhile, soak the cornmeal in the buttermilk for about 10 minutes. Sift together the flour, baking soda, baking powder, salt and sugar. Cut in the lard with a pastry blender until the consistency of coarse oatmeal with a few larger pieces. Beat egg and vanilla together and stir into cornmeal mixture. Add to dry ingredients all at once, stirring just to moisten. Pour into pan being careful not to disturb the sausages. Bake in a 425°F oven for 30-35 minutes or until cornbread tests done with a toothpick. Serve warm with butter and maple syrup.

Sausage Toast

Fry six link sausages; remove the skins and mix with a grating of good cheese, such as Parmesan, and a tablespoonful of mixed mustard; spread the mixture on hot buttered toast. Excellent for luncheon.

Sausage Pudding From Malpeque

1 lb sausage meat
2 tbsp gravy (or stock)
1 tsp chopped parsley
2 rashers (strips) bacon
4 oz bread crumbs
1 tbsp Tomato Catsup or other sauce
1 oz dripping (to grease the dish)
salt and pepper
mashed potatoes (have them cooking to serve with the pudding)

Chop the bacon and mix it with the bread crumbs, parsley and catsup. Add the sausage meat and mix all together with the gravy and a seasoning of salt and pepper (to taste). Press this into a well greased baking tin and bake for half an hour in a hot 450°F oven. Turn out and surround with a wall of mashed potatoes and serve at once on a hot dish. Serves 4.

M.C.

Toad in a Hole

Brown your favourite sausages well—drain away all fat. Prepare Yorkshire Pudding (see index). Grease a pan, lay in the sausages; pour over the Yorkshire Pudding mixture and bake as directed.

Sausage Stuffing

Sausage always played an important part in my family Christmas. Sausage meat, well browned, broken into bite-size pieces and drained was added to the stuffing for the turkey. As well, Nanny, my grandmother, would make Pigs in a Blanket (Sausage Rolls) as a special treat.

Pigs in a Blanket

Sausages of your choice (small, thin ones are best) or sausage meat

pastry (flaky or puff pastry is best)
1 egg (beaten with 1 tsp water)

There are two ways of making sausage rolls; you can cut rectangles of rolled pastry to roll around a sausage. Seal the joint with a little water and brush lightly with a beaten egg for glaze.

Or, roll the pastry into a long strip, then roll out sausage meat into a long thin strip on a floured board. Place the sausage meat on the pastry, brush the edges with water, fold over, and seal. Put onto an ungreased cookie sheet after you have cut roll into pieces of the size you desire, with the joint down. Make slits on the top of each. Brush over with beaten egg.

Bake at 450°F; check after 10 minutes. Since the sausage has to be thoroughly cooked and the pastry should be golden brown, it may be necessary to reduce the heat for a few minutes more cooking.

Cool before eating.

Beef

Early writings do not mention the consumption of beef as often as they do the smaller domestic animals. Being so big and hard to ship, they were slower gaining a place as a source of food. Many of the animals were too valuable a source of milk, breeding and even pulling a wagon or plow, to end up on the table. It wasn't too many years, though, before beef took its place on the table.

Norma's Beef in a Pot (Pot Roast)

There is a school of thought that quite a number of people of German descent settled on the Island. At the time when the Scots settled the Orwell area, for example, many men had come off ships from the old country and found wives in the new land. Those women could well have come from German settlements on the mainland. The clue is in recipes which have been handed down, for many of them have a "flavour" that is more German than Scottish.

5 lbs of a lesser cut of beef, for the best cuts will not hold up with cooking
drippings or olive oil
8 onions, in chunks
2 carrots, in chunks
1 parsnip (optional—I prefer this dish without)
1 stalk celery root, with leaves, chopped
6 cloves garlic, crushed
30 peppercorns, cracked
12 oz ale or beer
bouquet garni to taste

2 bay leaves
⅓ cup currant jelly
1 tsp. Bovril Broth and
  Seasoning Base
cornstarch

Brown the meat on all sides using drippings in a hot pan (use the pot in which you will be cooking the pot roast). Remove the meat, reduce the heat to medium and cook the carrot, celery, onions and garlic, stirring, until just soft. Return the meat. Add peppercorns, beer, bouquet garni, bay leaves, currant jelly and Bovril. Simmer for 2-3 hours, then remove meat and vegetables. Strain off the liquid and carefully pour off all fat by allowing the liquid to settle first. Measure liquid. You should have about three cups (if necessary boil it down until you have three cups). Now is the time to put your personal stamp on this dish. Take a little of the liquid in a spoon and taste it. You may want to add a little salt, sugar or even Bovril. Mix part of the liquid with cornstarch and whisk it into the remainder with a fork to make a lovely shining sauce. Slice the meat onto a hot platter; surround with vegetables. Pour a little of the sauce over all, sprinkle with parsley and serve with potatoes or hot biscuits. The lady who gave me the recipe serves her's with bannock—a blending of Scottish and German fare. German fare.

Planked Steak

Many old cookbooks included recipes for various meats and fish cooked on wood. I even found one that called for nailing meat to a board and cooking by the fire. That seems a little impractical, for I'm sure with luck like mine the fat covered board would catch fire and my dinner would go up in smoke. The following is delicious and not as risky.

Broil a 1¾-inch thick porterhouse, sirloin or crosscut of rump steak for 5 minutes by placing in a preheated oven. Cook on a greased rack as near the flame or element as possible. Turn after 2 minutes. Butter a plank to place the steak on, trim off the edges of steak, 1-2 inches from the edge of the plank. With a pastry bag and tube filled with well-mashed potatoes, arrange an artistic border around the steak. Place in hot oven and bake until potatoes are browned and steak is cooked, then spread with butter, season with salt and pepper, garnish and serve by placing the plank directly on a hot mat on the table. (A hot mat is a protective, thick-padded place mat to hold serving dishes and protect the table from scorching.)

Dill Steak Rolls

Very thinly cut steak
paprika
dill pickles
bacon

Sprinkle steak with paprika, roll around dill pickle, wrap in bacon and broil. When cooked the dill flavor permeates the meat.

Spiced Beef

We first experienced spiced beef in the home of friends who brought a fairly large piece of meat out of the refrigerator, cut off several thin slices and slowly browned them in a frying pan for lunch. It was delicious, and is the second recipe below. Beef used to be "cured" this way to both add to its tenderness and flavour and preserve it for a longer time.

10 lbs beef, round or rump
½ cup coarse salt
3 tbsp saltpeter
2 tbsp sugar
2 tsp celery salt
2 tbsp cinnamon
1 tsp cayenne
4 bay leaves

Mix salt and spices and rub all into every side of the beef. Place meat in a bowl and add bay leaves. Cover and refrigerate. Rub any salt mixture and brine that falls into bowl into beef for 14 days. To cook, rinse beef under cold water; tie beef firmly in a large piece of cheesecloth or muslin. Place in boiling water to cover and simmer for three hours. Allow to cool in brine overnight.

Carol's Spiced Beef

Carol tells us that, in the days before refrigeration, this was prepared by hanging the meat in a cold cellar with a bowl underneath to collect juices to use for basting. She treats hers in a bowl for a week, then hangs to dry. Then it is kept in the refrigerator and sliced as needed.

When buying your beef choose a well-shaped rump, short rib or sirloin tip that is lean. Also works well with ham or venison.

2 tbsp salt
3 tbsp brown sugar
2 tsp cinnamon
½ tsp ground cloves
1 tsp allspice
¼ tsp pepper
¼ tsp saltpeter

Mix well. Rub into meat. Put in a bowl; cover and place in the refrigerator. Keep turning and basting with juices for one week. Roll up and tie (in cheesecloth or a sugar sack) and hang to dry.

Fillet of Beef

5 lbs fillet of beef
salt and pepper
¼ cup butter
1 cup each peas, carrots and
potatoes

(The original recipe calls for potatoes and carrots to be cut into fancy shapes and then all three served around the meat as a garnish. I would think most cooks would prepare more potatoes for this quantity of meat and serve separately as is suggested by the mashed potatoes.)

Wipe fillet; remove fat and skin. Fold thin end over and fasten with skewer or string. If not larded (marbled), put chunks of butter on upper side, season with salt and pepper. Place in a roasting pan, with one cup hot water, in hot oven from ¾ to 1 hour, depending on size, basting 3 or 4 times, adding hot water if necessary. Remove skewers or string and set fillet aside. Thicken gravy in pan, add Kitchen Bouquet (or Bovril broth and seasoning base) and strain. Reheat fillet in sauce.

Serve the meat on a hot platter surrounded by peas and fancy cut carrots and potatoes or mashed potatoes with the gravy in a hot bowl with ladle.

For a variation baste with 1 cup thick sour cream when nearly done. After making gravy, simmer fillet in it for a few minutes.

Shepherd's Pie

Originally Shepherd's Pie was made with leftover meat from a roast that had been put through a meat grinder. It was simply a way to use up the leftovers, by putting ground meat and leftover vegetables in a dish, adding leftover gravy, topping with mashed potatoes and placing in the oven to bake. It was a childhood favourite of mine. This recipe is a more elaborate creation, more modern, and perhaps as good.

1 cup fine soft bread crumbs
1½ lbs ground beef
2 whole eggs
1 tsp salt
2 tbsp dry mustard
¼ cup finely diced green pepper
1 medium onion, finely chopped
⅓ cup ketchup
3 large potatoes, cooked and mashed
¼ cup milk
1 tbsp butter
2 eggs, separated
⅓ cup grated cheddar cheese
salt and pepper to taste

Mix bread crumbs with meat. Combine 2 eggs, salt, 1 tbsp mustard, green pepper, onion and ketchup; blend into meat mixture. Lightly pack into 10-inch casserole. Bake at 350°F for 15 minutes. Combine mashed potatoes, milk, butter, remaining mustard, egg yolks and half of the grated cheese. Beat egg whites until stiff; fold into potato mixture and season with salt and pepper. Swirl onto hot meat mixture and sprinkle with remaining cheese. Continue baking 45 minutes or until topping is tipped with brown. Serves 6.

Cornish Pasties

Another "meal" which came from the British Isles is Cornish Pasties. Referred to by some as meat pies, these were first created by women to send off with their husbands who could not get home from sea or field, yet needed a substantial meal. Originally, they were quite large, as a plate was often used as the guide for cutting

Cornish Pasties, fruit cakes and turnovers traditional fare for the hardworking family.

pastry circles. Today we make them much smaller. Pasties could easily be packed in a lunch in the days before plastic bags, for they are quite durable. They are usually made of finely chopped beef or lamb (leftovers at times, I suspect), but we have used ground beef.

Pastry:
4 cups flour
⅛ tsp salt
1½ cups butter
8-10 tbsp cold water

Combine flour, salt and butter until it looks like coarse meal. Add water (starting with 8 tablespoons) until it forms a ball without crumbling. Wrap and refrigerate at least one hour. Roll out about ¼-inch thick on floured board. Cut into 6-inch rounds. Fill as directed with the following:

Filling:
1 lb ground beef
¾ cup diced carrots (dice them fine)
1 cup very finely chopped onions
1½ cups diced potatoes (also fine)
1½ tsp salt
½ tsp pepper
1 egg, lightly beaten

(I like to add ½ tsp celery salt and cut salt to 1 tsp.) Combine beef, carrots, onions, potatoes, salt and pepper. Place about ¼ cup of mixture on half of each pastry round. Moisten edges with cold water. Fold pastry in half to cover meat; seal the edges with the tines of a fork. Place on a greased cookie sheet; brush with a beaten egg. Cut two slits in the top to let steam escape. Bake in a preheated 400°F oven for 15 minutes; reduce heat to 350°F and bake 30 minutes longer or until brown. Serve hot or at room temperature.

Mrs. Gallant's Fricassee

A traditional way to use up leftover meat from a roast with this large family. Serves 7, so half it if you wish.

4-5 cups lean meat cut from a roast and chopped to small pieces
6 cups raw potato, diced
2 cups onion, chopped
left-over gravy or juices from roast (see note)

dripping
½ tsp summer savory
salt and pepper to taste

Note: If you have saved the dripping from the roast, remove the fat from the top and add the jellied meat juices at the bottom to your fricassee.

Brown onion in dripping (or butter). Add the rest of the ingredients and cold water to cover. Cover the pot and cook over a low heat for 30-45 minutes or until potatoes are done and you are ready to serve. Stir from time to time while cooking. Mrs. Gallant adds left-over peas or carrots towards the end of cooking, if she has them.

Ox-tail

A standby meat product not often used today, the ox-tail requires long, slow moist cooking for tenderness. The hearty taste of an ox-tail stew makes one forget that it is an economical meal. Simmered with onions, carrots and spice or garlic, it is delicious; add parsley and a rich red wine and it's glorious. Ox-tails, of course, are not the tails of oxen, but rather of beef cattle.

Ox-tail Soup

This recipe comes to us from the old Settlement Cookbook, dated 1928.

3 lbs lean beef
2 ox-tails
6 qts water
1 tbsp salt
1 large onion, diced
¼ cup celery root, diced
1 tsp parsley root, diced
2 tbsp fat
1 tbsp flour
3 carrots (small to medium, left whole)

Have the ox-tails split and cut into small pieces and fry them lightly in the fat. Put meat and ox-tails in soup kettle; pour over the water and salt and let it come slowly to a boil, then cook slowly but steadily 4 hours or longer. Add the vegetables. Boil 1 hour longer and reduce stock by nearly one half. Strain. Heat 1 tablespoon fat in a spider (frying pan); add a tablespoon flour; brown and gradually pour in one cup of the soup stock. Stir this into the remaining stock and return the carrots, cut into small pieces, and the rest of the meat and vegetables. Serve hot with croutons.

Liver and Onions with Brown Gravy

Organ meats such as liver were highly prized by early cooks and should not be overlooked as often as they are today. The nutritional value of liver is widely documented—its delightful taste is not.

The secret to having an enjoyable meal of liver is to buy good liver. I always ask the butcher to cut me some of his best, nothing tough or full of sinew.

Looking back at my childhood and remembering how I fought not to eat liver and onions, I am frankly mortified. I recall well the day I discovered that I actually liked it. Too stubborn to admit I had been wrong, I continued to put my poor parents through many hours, I'm sure, of wishing they had any child but me. I used to sit in my chair, refusing to eat while all the time my mouth was watering and I longed for the liver on my plate. I used to satisfy myself by having extra gravy on my potatoes—delicious it was, too.

Slice onions thin and place in pan to lightly brown in butter. Use about two good-sized cooking onions to one pound of beef liver and 2-3 tbsp. butter. While onions are cooking until tender, dredge the liver in flour. Remove onions and, if necessary, add shortening to medium hot pan. When it is sizzling add the liver and cook 2-3 minutes on each side until nicely browned. Remove the liver and keep warm while you make a rich brown gravy in the same pan using Bisto Gravy Mix. Either return liver and onions to gravy to warm, or serve directly and smother with gravy and onions. Serve with mashed potatoes and peas.

Note: Early cooks used to brown salt pork or bacon in the pan first, then onions and liver. Just drain off most of the fat to cook the onions, adding a little only if needed.

Liver Loaf

1 lb beef or pork liver
1 small onion
5 slices bacon

1 tbsp bacon fat
1 tbsp flour
¼ tsp salt
⅓ cup Carnation Milk, diluted
  with
⅓ cup liquor from liver
⅔ cup bread crumbs
1 egg, slightly beaten

Buy liver in one piece. Wash and skin if necessary. Simmer 45 minutes without adding water. Remove large veins. Chop liver and onion fine. Dice bacon fine, fry out the fat. Drain on absorbent paper. Prepare the sauce of fat, flour, salt and milk. Combine all ingredients, mixing thoroughly. Form into a loaf, place in greased pan. Bake in moderate oven (350°F) 45 minutes. Pour ¼ cup around loaf to keep moist.

To Corn or Pickle Beef, Tongue or Goose Meat

10 lbs brisket or rump (or
  tongue or goose)
1 cup brown sugar
ginger and a little garlic
¾ tbsp saltpeter
salt and pepper

Salt well on all sides; add pepper and the rest, dissolving saltpeter in a little water. Place in a stone jar; cover with plate and weight down with a stone to allow juice to draw over night. Add cold water to cover and leave in brine 10 days, turning meat every other day.

To Cook Corned Beef (good for store-bought corn beef as well)

1 corned beef
water to cover (cold)
6 bay leaves
1 tsp whole pepper
1 tsp cloves
1 onion, sliced

Wash and if salty, soak in cold water over night. Place in kettle with seasonings and let simmer slowly until tender (2-4 hours). Then remove from liquid.

To Cook Corned Tongue

As above. Remove from cooking liquid; peel off the outer skin; cut off root and let cool in the brine. May be sliced cold or served hot with a sauce or gravy.

My mother always separates the lean meat, places it in a pudding bowl, covers with some of the gelatine left in the pan (or mixes up a packet by the directions), covers with a plate and presses in the refrigerator. It makes a lovely moist meat that slices well. She doesn't corn her tongue, but simply boils it first.

Mustard sauce is nice served with ham, or corned beef. (See index.)

Boiled Dinner

The boiled dinner is almost as much an Island institution as salt fish or potatoes, particularly in rural or fishing homes where the men can't keep to a strict schedule. When they do come in for a meal, they want it fast and lots of it. Although the recipe says to cook the vegetables one hour, it will not hurt them to simmer for a longer time.

Boiled dinner can be prepared using ham, cottage roll, corned beef, beef, even fish. My husband particularly likes a ham, simmered with cabbage on the wood stove all day long, especially when he comes in from a cold day of shoeing horses or riding. You can vary what you put in according to what you have on hand.

4 lb corned beef
1 small cabbage
3 large carrots
6 medium onions
6 small parsnips
6 medium potatoes
1 small turnip

Wash meat quickly in cold water. If very salty, soak one-half hour in cold water, or let come to a boil; then drain. Place meat in a kettle, with boiling water to cover. Let cook 3 to 5 hours or until tender. Two hours before serving, add carrots, cabbage and turnips cut in quarters and, one hour before serving, add parsnips, onions and potatoes. Serve attractively arranged on a platter.

Corned Beef Hash with Eggs

2 cups diced cooked potatoes
1½ cups chopped corned beef
⅓ cup cream
3 tbsp melted butter
½ tsp salt
pepper
6 eggs
paprika
1 small onion, chopped fine(if desired)

Blend potatoes, beef and onion. Add cream and half of butter. Add salt and pepper. Blend mixture and place in buttered baking dish. Make 6 inserts in top. Bake 20 minutes in 400°F oven. Reduce heat to 350°F. Add the eggs and cover with teaspoon of cream and dot with butter. Bake until egg is cooked. Add dash of paprika to serve.

Note: This recipe dates from the 1930s. The reference to blend means simply to mix, not to place in a blender.

Dripping

Dripping (or rendered fat)—the fat that is left after roasting or cooking meat was a mainstay in the kitchen in days gone by. I grew up thinking there is nothing on God's earth that tastes quite so good as a toasted dripping, Marmite or Bovril, turkey and lettuce sandwich on Boxing Day. I still feel that way and, quite frankly, anticipate my Boxing Day treat even more than Christmas dinner.

After cooking roast beef or turkey pour off the fat and let set. Fat and gelatine will separate — the flavor is almost all in the jelly at the bottom. Be sure to use both in your sandwich, spreading on hot toast; next spread on just a little Marmite, then some slices of turkey and lettuce and a sprinkle of salt and pepper.

Dripping (or rendered fat) from strongly flavoured meats such as bacon, pickled meat and ham may be used for warming up potatoes, seasoning vegetables, browning fish or leftover meat. Goose, duck, turkey or chicken fat is good for spreading sandwiches, and for making pastry.

To the early Island cook, butter was a luxury to be used to its best advantage. Dripping was valued for cooking.

Lamb and Mutton

In my family lamb, or mutton, was served with regularity and was always delicious. It came as quite a surprise to me to find so many people immediately "turned off" at the idea of eating this meat. This prejudice has been explained in several ways. Some said it was once associated with being a poor man's meat, and thus it became a matter of pride in the family not to have it appear on the table (which might explain the recipe for Mock Venison which follows). To my mind the main reason for any aversion people have developed towards this fine meat comes from poor cooking methods. My husband and I have frankly deceived many of our friends by inviting them over for a "Sunday Roast" without letting them know we were serving lamb. We have never had anyone say they didn't like it after tasting it.

Lamb 'n' Ham Savory

Take some mutton chops, either from the loin or neck; trim them neatly and put them with chopped parsley, butter, pepper and salt in a stew-pan over a slow fire. After browning, place the chops, with some good brown gravy, into the baking dish and add slices of raw ham. Cover with the lid, but first fill with mashed potatoes to the brim. Bake two hours in a slow oven (250°F), then the cover may be taken off, and the chops will be found tender and succulent.

Lamb Chops Cooked with Mint Sauce

This is a good recipe for your crock pot as it likes to slow cook. Line chops on a rack in baking dish (they can lodge against one another). Brush with mint sauce and cook in a slow oven (225°F) for 3 hours. If they seem to be drying at all, baste with more mint sauce. This gives a tangy meat, very tender.

A genuine Irish Stew

Purchase lamb sufficient for your family and eliminate first step.

Cut two pounds of chops from the best end of a neck of mutton, and pare away nearly all the fat. A portion of the breast may be cut into squares and used, but a neck of mutton is the best joint for the purpose.

Take as many potatoes as will amount, after peeling, to twice the weight of the meat. Slice them and eight large onions. Put a layer of mixed potatoes and onions at the bottom of the stew-pan. Place the meat on this and season it plentifully with pepper and lightly with salt. Pack closely and cover the meat with another layer of potato and onion. Pour in as much water or stock as will moisten the top most layer; cover the stew pan tightly, and let its contents simmer gently for three hours. Be careful not to remove the lid, as this will let out the flavour.

Lamb and Rosemary

This is a very old recipe from a treasured family cookery book.

2 lbs breast of lamb (lean)
sprig of Rosemary
1 bay leaf
salt and pepper
2 oz fresh butter
¼ pt stock (a consommé cube melted in ¼ pt hot water can be used)

Use some of the butter to grease a baking dish that is just large enough to take the meat. Put the rosemary and the bay leaf in this. then the joint, first sprinkling it well with salt and pepper. Pour the stock into the dish, and spread the remainder of the butter over the joint. Cover with buttered paper, and bake for three quarters of an hour at 450°F. Remove the paper and brown the meat well. Place it on a very hot dish; skim as much fat as possible from the gravy. Strain over the joint and serve.

Lamb Curry

¼ cup drippings
2 lbs neck of lamb, diced (or buy stewing lamb)

1 onion, minced
½ tsp salt
Juice of ½ lemon
water or soup stock (use a
  bouillon cube if desired)
3 tbsp flour
2 tsp curry powder
boiled rice

Brown the lamb and onions in the dripping. Add the seasonings and soup stock or water to cover. Simmer until tender or bake in a casserole two hours. Thicken the gravy with the flour and curry powder stirred smooth in ¼ cup cold water. Serve in a border of boiled rice.

Baked Stuffed Lamb Chops

4 lamb loin chops about one
  inch thick
½ lb mushrooms, diced
4 tbsp butter
2 tbsp minced onion
½ tsp summer savory
¼ tsp salt
⅛ tsp pepper
3 slices white bread, cubed

Sauté onion, mushrooms and seasonings in butter until vegetables are tender. Remove from heat and stir in bread. Mix well to combine (if necessary add ¼ cup water). Preheat broiler. Slice chops through to bone cutting horizontally so that you have a slit to place stuffing in (you can use 8 thin chops and fasten together with skewers or toothpicks). Place chops on a rack in the broiling pan. Broil 10-15 minutes until cooked as desired. Carefully turn once during cooking time. Remove any toothpicks before serving. Serves 4.

Mock Venison

As game became scarce, it became more valued and, as a result, imitations were introduced to the family menu. Remember that mutton, like fish, was a poor man's food. How roles have reversed today!

"Place mutton in an earthen dish; add small onion sliced and cover with hot water and vinegar that has been boiled. Let

stand 24 hours. Drain and dry meat; season with salt, pepper, a bit of pulverized thyme between the fingers and a teaspoonful of caraway seed. Roast in oven until tender."

Rabbit

Dare we say, as much fun to hunt as it is to eat. Only, I suppose if one didn't have the worry of a family to feed. Rabbit is now "farmed" and readily available.

You Fool 'em Rabbit

This is a great way to introduce those who can't stand the thoughts of eating a bunny, to rabbit meat. Just don't mention what kind of meat it is and no one will know.

2 rabbits, prepared for cooking
  and cut in serving pieces
potato stuffing (see index)
6 tbsp flour
salt and pepper to taste
1/3 cup coarse dry bread crumbs
2 1/2 tbsp butter

Place meat in a large kettle, cover with water and simmer until tender (about 45 minutes). Cool, then remove all lean meat from the bones, cutting into pieces not bigger than one inch. Reserve the stock. Spread a layer of potato stuffing on the bottom of a well-greased casserole and cover with meat. Mix the flour with two cups of the stock until thoroughly blended. Gently pour half over the meat. Salt and pepper to taste, then repeat with a second layer and top with stuffing. Sprinkle with bread crumbs and dot the top with butter. Bake 40-50 minutes in a preheated 350°F oven. When the top is golden brown, serve.

Rabbit Bondinettes

(Also good with chicken or veal.)

To every pound of finely minced meat add one-quarter pound of mashed potatoes; season with salt and pepper, and moisten with a gravy made from the bones of the cold meat (or use left-over gravy). Press the minced meat into well-buttered cups and bake for 20 minutes. Turn out on a dish; pour a little browned gravy round and stick a sprig of parsley into each bondinette.

Hasenpfeffer

After the rabbit has been in salt water for several hours, rinse with clear water. Boil until tender in water containing an onion in which are stuck about a dozen cloves. When tender take from liquor; roll in flour and fry brown in skillet, using equal quantities of butter and lard. Just before removing from skillet, sprinkle over a little cinnamon and about 1 tablespoonful of vinegar (more or less to suit taste). Cook closely; let smother for a few minutes; remove rabbit; put flour in skillet and brown in remaining grease; add liquor in which the rabbit was cooked to make a nice gravy; pour over rabbit.

Rabbit Supreme from Russ

Cut a dressed young rabbit in serving pieces. Sprinkle pieces generously with salt and pepper, then roll in flour and brown on both sides in hot butter or a mixture of butter and dripping. Cover brown meat with a thick layer of thinly sliced onions; sprinkle with salt; add one cup of freshly soured cream; cover with a tight lid; simmer for one hour (or until very tender). Remove to platter, allowing the sauce to cover each serving, and arrange small pan-browned potatoes around the meat. If desired this rabbit may be baked in a slow oven, 325°F.

Fowl

Goose, Duck, Chicken, Turkey and Game Birds

In the following recipes we are assuming that you will be obtaining your fowl ready to cook; in other words, plucked and cleaned. If you should wish to do these two steps yourself, we strongly suggest you refer to *Mrs. Beeton's Book of Household Management.* Originally published between 1851 and 1861 as a series of magazine supplement, and then in book form in 1861, Mrs. Beeton's is undoubtedly one of the most widely known reference books for the homemaker ever printed.

Published in England it has turned up enough times in my research to convince me that many women immigrating from the "old country" brought the book along as one of their most valued possessions. I know that even in the 1950's, my own family carried a Mrs. Beeton's when they came to settle in Canada. It was quite exciting to me to discover that the old book has been reprinted in its entirety in 1984, proving the timelessness of such good sound household advice as Isabella Betton gave her readers.

> *"What moved me, in the first instance, to attempt a work like this, was the discomfort and suffering which I had seen brought upon men and women by household mismanagement. I have always thought that there is no more fruitful source of family discontent than a housewife's badly cooked dinners and untidy ways. Men are now so well served out of doors,—at their clubs, well-ordered taverns and dining houses, that in order to compete with the attractions of these places, a mistress must be thoroughly acquainted with the theory and practice of cookery, as well as be perfectly conversant with all the other arts of making and keeping a comfortable home."*
>
> *Isabella Beeton*

Chicken Paprika

1½ cups cooked chicken, at least
four slices
2 tbsp fat
1 large sliced onion
1 tbsp paprika
1 egg yolk, beaten with
1 cup sour cream
salt and pepper to taste

Sauté onion in hot fat until golden brown. Add chicken and paprika. Cook 5 minutes. Add egg yolk/sour cream mixture, salt and pepper. Simmer very slowly for 10 minutes. Serves 3-4.

This is nice served with Mushroom Croquettes and rice or noodles.

Chicken Roll

1½ to 2 cups chopped cooked
chicken
2 cups flour
4 tsp baking powder
¾ tsp salt
3 tbsp butter or shortening
⅔ cup milk
2 tbsp melted butter
¼ cup finely chopped stuffed
olives
1 tbsp minced green pepper
2 tbsp chicken broth
1 tbsp sherry
2 tbsp milk
Left-over chicken gravy, or
condensed tomato or
mushroom soup plus 1 tbsp
sherry (optional)

Sift flour with baking powder and salt; cut in butter or shortening. Gradually add milk to make a soft dough. Roll lightly into an 11- × 4-inch rectangle, ½-inch thick. Brush with melted butter. Mix chicken, olives, green pepper, chicken broth and sherry. Spread on dough. Roll like you would a jelly roll. Seal edges with dampened fingers. Brush with milk. Bake on greased shallow pan in hot (425°F) oven 25 minutes or until done. Serve with gravy, or soup, mixed with 1 tbsp sherry as a sauce. Serves 3-4.

Chicken n'Corn Scallop

1 1-lb can cream-style corn
1 cup milk
1 egg
1 tbsp flour
6 green onions and tops, chopped
6-8 chicken drumsticks
30 saltine crackers
¼ cup butter
½ cup sliced mushrooms, fresh or canned

In a large shallow baking dish combine the first five ingredients, mixing well. Generously sprinkle drumsticks with paprika and arrange over the corn. Dash with seasoned salt if desired. Crumble crackers over the top and dot with the butter. Bake at 350°F until chicken is tender (about an hour), then place the mushrooms in the center and return to the oven to heat them through.

Chicken Sandwich

1 cup finely chopped cooked chicken
Mayonnaise to moisten mixture
salt
pepper
¼ cup pimiento olives chopped fine (optional)
2 hard boiled egg yolks, mashed
celery salt

Use thin slices of bread spread with creamed butter, then add chicken mixture. Garnish with lettuce, if desired.

Documentation tells us that the first chicken cannery in Canada was located in Murray Harbour, P.E.I. Samuel Prowse, who went on to become a senator, built a factory in 1897 where both chicken and lobster were canned. Prior to 1913 they also made their own cans.

Stuffed Chicken or Game Bird

Stuff a chicken with bread cubes, chopped onion and sorrel leaves. Spread fresh sage leaves over the bird to roast.

Chickens were highly valued by early farmwives—not for the meat as much as the eggs. There were other fowl, such as geese, to give meat, but as long as a hen was laying she certainly would not be killed for meat. The result was that a lot of old tough birds made it to the stew pot. They would be cooked long and slow for a nice tender meal.

Old Fashioned Chicken Pie

Cook a chicken (about 6 pounds) in 1 quart of water with a sprinkle of salt and pepper, until it is ready to fall off the bones. Cool and remove meat. Strain the broth and then thicken by mixing six tablespoonfuls flour with cold broth, adding a small amount of broth at a time. Cook over low heat, stirring constantly until thick. Make a regular pie crust and line the bottom and sides of a large casserole with it, being sure it is not rolled too thin. The chicken, left in fairly large pieces can be laid in pastry with thickened gravy poured over all. Lay pastry on top, flute the edges together and slash the top to allow steam to escape. Bake at 425°F for 40 minutes and serve hot. Serves 8-10 people.

Note: I like to add a thinly sliced carrot to the chicken for the appearance and flavour it gives.

Acadian Chicken Ragoût with Dumplings

1 chicken, about 5 pounds, cut into pieces
4-5 tbsp butter
8 cups hot water
1 tsp salt
¼ tsp pepper
1 large onion, chopped fine
1 large carrot, sliced
1 clove
1 bay leaf
pinch thyme
1 clove garlic, crushed

Dumplings:
2 cups flour
4 tsp baking powder
salt
2 eggs
1 cup milk

Brown the chicken on all sides in butter. Use a large skillet or cast-iron pot so that you can add all other ingredients (except dumplings). Bring to a boil and simmer, covered, for about two hours. The chicken should be tender. Prepare the dumplings by beating the eggs with the milk, sifting together dry ingredients, then beating all together until the batter is light and smooth. Remove the cooked chicken and set where it will keep hot. Drop spoonfuls of the batter into the liquid. Cover and boil over a medium heat for 10 minutes. Place the chicken on a hot platter; place the dumplings around it, and pour the hot liquid over top. Enough for six hungry workers.

Chicken in Oatmeal

The Scottish, it seems, fry just about everything in oatmeal. Trout is delicious, as is this chicken.

2 — 3 lbs chicken, cut in pieces
1½ cups flour
1 tsp poultry seasoning
4 cups rolled oats
2 eggs, beaten
⅓ cup milk
dripping (or oil) for frying
black pepper to taste

Rinse and pat dry the chicken. In one pie plate combine flour and poultry seasoning; in another place the rolled oats. Beat eggs lightly with the milk. Meanwhile, have dripping heating in a cast-iron pan. Dredge the chicken in flour; shake; dip in egg and roll in oats until covered. Fry until golden brown all over. Have the oven hot (325°F) and as the chicken is done place it in oven. (Be careful not to break the crust on the chicken.) Bake in the oven for 20-30 minutes, until cooked through. Season with pepper before serving if desired.

Glazed Chicken Liver Pâté

Spooned into an earthenware crock or terrine or a pretty crystal bowl, pâté can be served as a late night snack when entertaining, on a buffet or with a pre-dinner drink.

½ cup onion, chopped fine
¼ cup butter
1 lb chicken livers, with
membranes removed
3 hard-cooked eggs
1 package cream cheese (8 oz)
¼ cup parsley, chopped
¾ tsp salt
black pepper

Sherried Aspic (recipe follows)
pimiento
gherkins

In a large skillet, sauté onions in butter until soft. Remove with slotted spoon and set aside. Sauté livers in pan until cooked, about 10 minutes. Place onions, livers, eggs and cream cheese into a food processor and process — until smooth. Or, place ingredients, a little at a time, into blender and blend until smooth. (See note below.) Stir in parsley, salt and pepper. Pile mixture into a 3-cup crock or bowl that is pretty enough to place on the table. Cover and refrigerate. Meanwhile, prepare the Sherried Aspic below. Decorate pâté with pimiento cutouts and gherkin slices. Spoon chilled, slightly thickened Aspic over. Refrigerate until firm. Garnish if desired to serve.

Note: Pâté in French means a savory pie, however, it has come to be applied to a paste made from minced meat or fish which is served in a crock or bowl instead of a crust. The old way to prepare it was tedious for the homeowner as the meat was minced and put through a sieve. The eggs and cream cheese here serve to replace flour, eggs and white sauces that were used as binders. Many of the old-style pâtés were sealed while hot and then given time to mature before eating. If sealed hot with a layer of fat, they would keep, like potted meats, for several weeks.

Sherried Aspic

½ cup beef broth

2 tsp unflavored gelatin
1 tbsp dry sherry

In a small saucepan, sprinkle gelatin over broth; let stand to soften for 5 minutes. Heat over a low heat, stirring to dissolve gelatin. Remove from heat. Stir in sherry. Pour into a small bowl and chill until slightly thickened. Use as directed above.

Soup Made From Chicken or Turkey Carcass

Break the carcass in 5 or 6 pieces; add any left-over gravy and all scraps of skin, dressing, etc. Add left-over giblets, if any. Add 1 carrot, 1 onion and 2 tbsp. rice. Cover with cold water; bring to boiling point and simmer for three hours. Strain. Add additional seasonings if necessary. If soup is too thick, add a little rich cream or milk. Serve very hot, with croutons.

My Mother's Turkey Delight

While the thoughts of left-over turkey dismayed many of my friends, it was just the opposite in my house. We actually looked forward to leftovers more than the big turkey dinner—at least I did. We would always enjoy one meal with meat and left-over vegetables, warmed in mom's great gravy and never had to face dry turkey for sandwiches.

When cooking the turkey, mom would carefully drain all the drippings into a bowl. The carcass would be stripped of all meat, either that night or the next day and the meat jellied. First, all of the white fat would be taken from the top of the dripping, (which had been in the refrigerator), and the jelly from the bottom placed in a saucepan. While it was slowly melting over low heat, the meat was packed into a bowl as tightly as possible. She chose a bowl in which the meat could be pressed by placing a weighted plate on top. If there was enough jelly from the bird to cover the meat, fine; if not, she stretched by adding a little water and used envelopes of gelatine to thicken it. She poured the liquid over the meat, placed the weighted plate on top and put the whole thing in the fridge. A large jar filled with water or cans made good weights. As soon as it was set, the meat was ready to slice. It stayed moist and had much more flavour than plain turkey.

Turkey with Curry Sauce

Nice for a buffet; lay meat out on a large platter and pour sauce over all—a nice way to use up left-over turkey or chicken.

1 lb meat sliced from a roast turkey
1 small onion, sliced thin
2 tbsp dripping
½ tbsp curry powder (or to taste)
¼ tsp turmeric
¼ cup all-purpose flour
2 cups chicken stock
1 tbsp cranberry jelly
⅔ cup sour cream

Fry onion until transparent; add curry powder and turmeric and keep over heat for a few more minutes. Blend in the flour, then stir in the stock gradually and bring to a boil. Cover and simmer for 20 minutes. Remove and stir in the cranberry jelly. Rub through a sieve. When cold stir in the cream.

Turkey Potato Hash

1 large turkey breast, boned and minced
6 tbsp butter
4 cups potatoes, cooked and diced
1 small onion, chopped fine
pinch nutmeg
pinch summer savory or sage (according to taste)
salt and pepper
3 tbsp heavy cream

Fry turkey in half of the butter until it is an opaque white. In a bowl mix the turkey, potatoes, onion, cream and spices. Cook this mixture in the rest of the butter in a cast-iron pan until crusty and brown. Try to only turn once. Serve immediately.

Hashed Goose

"The remains of cold roast goose

2 onions
2 oz butter
1 pt boiling water
1 dessertspoonful flour
pepper and salt to taste
1 tablespoonful port wine
2 tablespoonfuls of mushroom
ketchup (sauce)

Cut up the goose into pieces of the size required. The inferior joints, trimmings, &c, put into a stewpan to make the gravy; slice and fry the onions in the butter of a very pale brown; add these to the trimmings, and pour over about a pint of boiling water; stew these gently for ¾ hour, then skim and strain the liquor. Thicken it with flour, and flavour with port wine and ketchup, in the above proportion; add a seasoning of pepper and salt, and put in the pieces of goose; let these get thoroughly hot through, but do not allow them to boil and serve with sippets of toasted bread."

Mrs. Beeton's
Book of Household Management
1861

Francois Fricassed Goose

back, wings, neck, gizzard and
heart of goose
salt, pepper and ginger
½ onion, sliced
clove of garlic, minced
2 tbsp fat
2 tbsp flour
1 cup goose broth
1 tsp chopped parsley
1 piece celery root (or stalk of
celery)

Season meat well with salt, pepper, ginger and, if desired, rub with a little garlic. Let stand overnight. Then place in a kettle with boiling water to cover; let simmer slowly several hours; add onion and celery; let boil 2 hours and when meat is tender remove from kettle; reheat and cover with the following sauce:

Heat the fat; add flour and then 1 cup of the hot goose broth; let boil until smooth; season to taste; add the chopped parsley and serve hot with dumplings or potatoes.

Goosemeat, Preserved in Fat

Some geese, particularly wild ones, are too fat to roast well. The tendency to fat is probably the main reason that some people claim to truly dislike goose and duck. This is one reason why, in our family we usually cook goose or duck on a spit.

Render the fat of the goose (see below); remove and cut the skin into small pieces. The scraps, when brown, shriveled and crisp can be served hot or cold. When the fat is nearly done (or clear), add the breast and legs of goose, previously salted, and boil in the fat until tender and browned. Place meat in crock and pour the clear, hot fat over it to cover. Cool. Covered with a plate and stone, it will keep in a cool, dry place for months. When ready to serve, take out meat; heat, and drain off fat.

To Render Goose Fat (or Duck or Beef)

Cut the fat into small pieces. Put in a deep iron kettle and cover with cold water. Place on a stove uncovered; when the water has nearly evaporated, set the kettle back and let fat fry out slowly. When the fat is still and scraps are shriveled and crisp at the bottom of the kettle, strain the fat through a cloth into a stone crock; cover and set it away in a cool place. The water may be omitted and the scraps slowly rendered out on back of stove or in a moderate oven. For beef fat take cold fat, cut in squares or grind. When fat is rendered out, pour in crock. To every four pounds of beef fat, allow 1 pound of butter; let dissolve in the hot fat. The butter may be omitted.

About Roasted Ducks

Being on the flyaway for ducks and geese meant many of these fine birds graced the table in spring and fall. We are fortunate enough to have neighbours who raised ducks and geese, some of them free-range, so that we get a sample of old-fashioned goodness when we buy from them. I usually cook these fattier birds on a spit or at least on a rack to drain away as much of their fat as possible.

Two old recipes follow.

Roasted Ducks

2 fine young ducks
Sage and onion forcemeat (stuffing)

Dripping
Butter
Flour

Pluck, singe and empty the ducks; scald the feet and skin. Cut off the neck and pinions (the latter at the first joint) and skewer all firmly. Fill with sage and onion stuffing (see below). Roast before a clear, brisk fire; frequently baste with butter and dredge with flour to make the breast look frothed before serving. Serve with good brown gravy in the dish and apple sauce in a tureen. Geese are roasted in the same way.

Sage and Onion Stuffing

6-8 large onions
½ pt bread crumbs
1 heaped tablespoonful of fresh
sage leaves, finely chopped
1 oz butter
salt, pepper and sugar to taste

Peel and cut onions in quarters; put in cold water with a pinch of salt and of sugar and boil them until half done. Drain, dry and chop them and add an ounce of butter to each half a pint. Cook without letting them take colour in a clean saucepan for 10 minutes. Add an equal measure of bread crumbs, finely chopped sage, salt and pepper to taste, and if desired, a few grains of nutmeg. A little parsley is thought an improvement by many. The boiling and sweating of the onions will be found an improvement over the ordinary method. Do not omit a tiny pinch of sugar. Sufficient for a goose or a couple of ducks.

Duck with Burgundy Sauce

1 duck
Salt and pepper
1 gill of good burgundy
A little cayenne
A little grated lemon rind
A small piece of brown roux
about the size of a walnut
(see below)
1 pt of good gravy

Do not stuff the duck, but roast in the usual fashion; then, before sending to table, cut it across in several places. Into these furrows, sprinkle a dash of cayenne, lemon rind (finely grated), and a pinch of salt and white pepper. Heat the burgundy, but do not let it boil, then pour slowly over the bird. Thicken the gravy with the roux, and pour around, but not over. Cover for a few minutes, then baste the bird over with the gravy and wine, and send to the table piping hot. The cover which is placed over it, even for these few minutes, should be heated beforehand.

Roux

The most popular and most generally adopted thickening is effected by mean of roux. Literally the word roux means 'russet' but, in the culinary sense, it is a mixture of flour and butter cooked or blended to certain degrees, to white, brown or fawn colours. The quantity of flour and butter employed are used in equal proportions. If made beforehand in large or small quantities, it should be kept in covered jars where it will keep good for months. A tablespoon is usually found sufficient to thicken a pint of liquid. Stock roux must always be kept in jars, well covered, in a cool place, ready at hand.

If the roux is used in a cold state (stock roux), it may be mixed with cold or hot stock; but as soon as mixed, it must be stirred constantly over the fire until boiling or, if mixed hot, the liquid should be poured by degrees into the roux away from the fire and then stirred over the fire until it boils.

Special precaution must always be exercised in making a sauce with a roux thickening, that the temperature be lowered or, in other words, that the roux be allowed to cool a little before the liquid stock or gravy be added. This will prevent the sauce from getting lumpy and will do much towards making a sauce perfectly smooth. All roux must be stirred constantly during the process of blending (frying) or roasting.

White Roux — a mixture of flour and butter cooked in a stew pan on a moderate fire without allowing it to attain any color (equal amounts of flour and butter).

Blond or Fawn Roux — as above, cooked until it has acquired a light blond or fawn color.

Brown Roux — This is the so-called stock roux, which can be prepared in large quantities to be used cold as required. It is made in exactly the same manner as the foregoing (melt butter; stir in flour), with the exception that it is fried longer until it becomes a darker colour, a chestnut brown or russet brown. It is best to finish the roux in a slack oven, for the slower the process the better the blending and the finer the aroma of the sauce will be.

Roux is the basis of White and many other Sauces.

To Roast Grouse

Pluck the grouse; clean the inside and wipe thoroughly both inside and out with a damp cloth. Game birds should never be washed. Mix half an ounce of fresh butter with a saltspoonful of black pepper, half a teaspoonful of salt and a few drops of lemon juice, and place inside each bird. Truss the birds as for roasting and dredge the outside with ordinary flour. A slice of fat bacon should be wrapped over the breast of each bird.

Roast before the fire, or in the oven, and baste frequently. Remember that grouse should be just sufficiently cooked without being under or overdone. Twenty-five to 30 minutes is allowed for cooking, according to the size of the bird. Gravy, browned bread crumbs, and bread-sauce are served with roast grouse. This dish should be garnished with crisp watercress (if available).

If preferred, while the roasting is going on, a thick slice of buttered toast may be made and soaked in the dripping pan so that, as soon as the grouse are ready, they can be laid on it and served on a very hot dish. This toast may be further improved in flavour if the livers are boiled for a few minutes, then cut up and pounded in a mortar with a little cayenne, salt and butter, until made into a smooth paste, then spread on the toast.

To Roast Pigeons

This recipe was found, handwritten, among the files in the Public Archives of P.E.I. While few of us wish to roast pigeons, we do have access to Cornish Game Hens which are just a little bigger.

> *"Fill them with parsley clean washed and chopped and some pepper and salt rolled in butter fill the body tie neck end close so that nothing can run out put a skewer through the legs and have a little iron on purpose with six hooks to it and on each hook hang a pigeon fasten one end of the string to the chimney and the other end to the iron this is what we call the poor mans spit flour them baste them with butter and turn them gentle for fear of hitting the bars they will roast nicely*

and be full of gravey take care how you take them off not to lose any of the liquor you may melt a very little butter and put into the dish your pigeons oght to be quite fresh and not two much done this is by much the best way of doing them for then they will swim in their own gravy and avery little melted butter will do

To [Driefs] a Goose with Onions on Cabbage

salt the goose for a week then boil it. it will take an hour. you may either make onion sauce as we do for ducks, or cabbage boiled, chopped and stewed in butter, with alittle pepper and salt lay the goose in the dish and the sauce over it, it eats very good with either."

Note: With no punctuation, old-style script and spelling, and worn paper this presents a challenge!

Noodles for Soup

1 cup flour (sifted), or more as needed
2 eggs
Pinch salt

Beat eggs lightly. Slowly add sifted flour and salt. Knead well, then chill 30 minutes or longer. Roll in thin sheets; place on cloth until quite dry but not brittle. Roll; cut very fine. Have broth nicely seasoned and boiling. Drop in noodles; cook 5 to 10 minutes.

Souffled Crackers

To serve with soup

Soak soda crackers in ice water for 8 minutes; remove, taking care not to break them; drain; place on a cookie sheet. Brush with melted butter, and bake in a very hot (450°F) oven until puffed and browned—about 20 minutes. Serve very hot with a sprinkling of paprika over them.

From the Fishmongers

Fish

The life's blood of Islanders since earliest man set foot on this red clay soil, fish, and fishing have been an integral part of day-to-day living.

We are most fortunate to have a variety of fish to satisfy all fish lovers. From the delicate taste of hake or sole to the more meaty cod or haddock or the flavourful trout, smelt or salmon.

For the purpose of cooking, fish can be generally broken down into two types: white and the others. White fish are considered 'lean' and are generally interchangeable in recipes. They include haddock, hake, sole, turbot, cod, flounder, swordfish and pollock (Boston Blue). These lean fish will dry out faster than the fatty species such as mackerel and thus must be moist cooked or basted during cooking.

Pickled Fish

1 pt vinegar
1 pt water
Salt to taste
20 peppercorns
18 allspice
5 bay leaves, broken up
4 slices lemon
5 slices onions

Boil vinegar and water ½ hour with salt, pepper, allspice, bay leaves and 4 slices of onion. Add lemon slices, cook 5 minutes, then remove. Simmer the fish in this liquor until you can pull out a fin. Cook only a few small fish or slices of fish at one time. Pick fish as cooked into a stone crock with one or more raw sliced onion between layers. Pour over the hot liquid with seasonings. Cover and keep in a cool place. In a few days the liquid will form a jelly around the fish. This liquid, is enough for ½ gallon of fish. Will keep several weeks.

To Serve with Fish

White fish poached or steamed is delicious served with a sauce or relish.

"A well seasoned sauce and a dash of paprika is a necessary accompaniment to serve with fish. A fat fish should have a sharp acid sauce. A lean fish requires a rich sauce to give flavor to the fish. A tart relish, a well seasoned coleslaw or pickled beets are appetizing. Boiled fish requires a sauce with a rich flavor and a note of color. Serve a hot Hollandaise, and egg or a hot cheese sauce. Serve Mayonnaise salad dressing with cold boiled fish. For fried, baked or broiled fish, serve Tartar Sauce, Chili Sauce or Hot Hollandaise Sauce."

early Watkins Cookbook

Cream Sauce

2 tbsp butter
2 tbsp flour
1 cup chicken stock
Little salt
Little paprika
2 egg yolks
⅓ cup cream
1 tbsp lemon juice
Celery salt
Onion seasoning
Red pepper

Melt butter; add flour; blend well. Add chicken stock and cream, stirring constantly. Bring to boiling point; remove from fire. Add beaten egg yolks and seasonings.

Browned Butter Sauce

(This is especially good if you add toasted thin-sliced almonds)

1/3 cup butter
1 tsp lemon juice
salt and pepper
paprika
1 tbsp Worcestershire sauce, if desired
celery salt

Brown butter in pan, stirring well. Add seasonings.

White Fish

As previously mentioned, white fish is usually completely interchangeable in recipes. You may have favourite fish, or economics may influence your shopping.

Don't hesitate to try white fish boiled, and smothered with a white sauce—the most common way it was served in days past. Firm fleshed cod and haddock are best.

Hake Casserole

Today known also as the Basquelle, Hake are a wonderful fish with snow-white flesh, that is sweet and delicate, somewhat less bland in flavour than cod.

1 1/2 tbsp butter
1 cup onion, chopped
1 1/2 cups celery, chopped
salt and pepper to taste
1/4 cup butter
1/4 cup flour
2 cups milk
1 1/3 pounds hake fillets
1/4 cup fine cracker crumbs

Melt butter in frying pan; add onion and celery; sauté until limp, but not brown. Add salt and pepper to taste. While this is cooking melt 1/2 cup butter in pot, when completely melted, add flour and stir until flour and butter are blended. Gradually add milk. Stir until sauce begins to thicken. Place fillets in the bottom of a deep casserole dish; layer onions and celery; pour sauce over and top with cracker crumbs. Bake 30 minutes at 350°F.

Haddock

"At breakfast time, my mother suggested that I go down to the east shore and get a haddock from one of the incoming fisherman for our evening meal. Gasoline type engines allowed the catches to be brought directly to the hard sandy beach where tables were provided for the cleaning and boning of cod and a larger species of fish known as hake. An occasional haddock or two would usually be found amongst the catch and being not as amenable to the curing process as either cod or hake, one had little difficulty in obtaining this delicacy from any of the fishermen. Many of the youngsters in the community, whose families were not engaged in fishing, practiced this method of obtaining a fish, for free. The first boat to arrive was belonged to Alexander MacKenzie—fortunately, there were some haddock in the catch, one of which he cleaned and boned while I waited. The thought of a morning swim hastened my steps homeward. After placing the fish in a copper-bottomed boiler partly filled with cold water from our well, I picked up my "homemade" bathing suit and returned to the cove to find my friends already splashing waist-deep in the water—two or three being in the water all-together. During periods of high tide, an occasional crab could be spotted crawling on the hard bottom of this sand-ribbed beach and a loud yell would indicate that one had made contact with a youngster's foot—a startling, but relatively harmless occurrence."

Prince Edward Island — the way it was
A glimpse back to 1914 by author
Whitman Cecil Daly

Stuffed Haddock

4-5 lb haddock, dressed
1 tsp salt
½ cup butter
¾ cup celery, chopped
¼ cup onion, chopped fine
3 cups cracker crumbs

2 tbsp lemon juice
1 tsp parsley flakes
½ tsp salt
¼ tsp pepper
¼ cup hot water
1 tbsp butter

Wash fish and pat dry, especially inside cavity. Rub inside with 1-2 tsp salt. Fish is now ready for stuffing. Combine butter, celery, onion, cracker crumbs, lemon juice, parsley, salt and pepper and toss to mix thoroughly. Add ¼ cup hot water and mix. Lightly pile stuffing into fish but do not pack tightly. Skewer the opening and fasten with string. (These fish used to be cooked in long specially designed fish cookers which few homemakers own today—we do however, have foil wrap). Place fish on greased foil wrap; baste with butter. Completely seal fish in foil and place on a cookie sheet. Bake at 400°F for 10 minutes per inch thickness, plus five minutes to allow for penetration of heat through the foil.

Baked Haddock with Cheese

2 cups milk
3 tbsp butter
2 or 3 haddock fillets
2 tbsp flour
½ tsp salt
⅛ tsp pepper
2 cups grated cheese

Melt the fat in a saucepan. Add the flour and when smooth add the milk, salt and pepper. When thickened, add the grated cheese and stir constantly over a low heat until the cheese is melted and the sauce is smooth. Meanwhile, arrange the haddock fillets in a baking pan and pour the cheese sauce over all. Bake in a moderate oven of 350°F for 30 minutes or until the fish is tender. Serves 6.

Finnan Haddie

The fishermen call the delicious smoked haddock by the name Finnan Haddie, and the name caught on. It originated at Findon, Scotland, where it used to be cured in peat smoke.

I remember eating the fish as a child, simmered in water and when removed, dredged with butter. I loved it with new potatoes and fresh green peas.

Creamed Finnan Haddie

2 lbs finnan haddie
2 tbsp butter
½ cup cream or top milk

Cover fish with cold water and simmer 10 minutes. Drain. Place on a hot platter, dot with butter and add the hot milk or cream just before serving. Garnish with parsley.

Finnan Haddie Savory

1 finnan haddie
1 large onion
1 chopped seeded green pepper
2 tbsp chopped parsley
1½ cups milk
¼ tsp paprika
4 tbsp butter
¾ tsp salt

Clean the finnan haddie carefully. Arrange in a large baking pan and dot over with the fat. Then sprinkle with the chopped onion, green pepper and parsley and the paprika and salt. Cover with the milk and bake in the oven at 375°F for one hour, basting frequently as the milk evaporates. Serves 6.

Island-Style Casserole

Nothing could be more typically "Island" than a combination of potatoes and fish.

1 12-oz can chicken haddie, flaked
1 19-oz can diced potatoes, drained
1 10-oz can mixed vegetables, drained
¼ cup onion, finely chopped
1 10-oz can cream of celery soup
1 tsp seafood seasoning
1 cup milk
1 cup cheddar cheese, grated

Combine all ingredients except the grated cheese in a greased casserole. Sprinkle with grated cheese and bake in a 350°F oven 35-40 minutes. Serves 4.

Mainlanders have an image of P.E.I. which includes the availability of year-round supplies of fresh seafood, readily available at low prices. According to the newspaper, Prince Edward Island Register of January 8, 1825, it was "astonishing in 1825 that there was no regular supply of fresh fish in town and no proper fish market either." We hear the same cry echoed today by consumers who, during the winter months, shop in just about the same manner as the folk in Upper Canada for seafood.

Cod

Although widely eaten and enjoyed, the cod is not recognized as a favourite fish and ranks low in people's esteem. Perhaps the reason lies with its availability—it's just too common to be appreciated.

There is good cause for believing that the cod was at least partly responsible for the discovery and settlement of North America. Certainly, if we look back, the first Europeans to come to Prince Edward Island's shores came to fish—and it is often noted that the fish most often caught, and most easily handled, was the cod.

Cod and similar species can be dried and salted for easy storage and transport. In that manner they have, at times, been the staple food for Maritimers.

To Prepare Salt Cod

Soak salt cod in cold water at least overnight, changing the water at least three times. Drain and place in a large skillet or pot; cover with fresh water and bring to boil. Immediately reduce heat and simmer without boiling until you are ready to use it.

Salt Cod Dinner

One of the most popular ways to serve salt cod is with egg sauce and potatoes.

Prepare the cod as above and either add potatoes to it to cook, or cook them in a separate pot. Prepare a white sauce and add to it chopped hard boiled eggs. Serve by placing cod on a platter, surround with potatoes and pour over egg sauce (or serve sauce in a separate bowl). Traditionally accompanied by cooked peas, carrots, boiled onions or turnip.

Baked Cod and Cheese

Again a white sauce is the basis for this dish, which can be made with salt cod, prepared as above or any fresh, boned fish.

1-2 lbs white fish
Salt and pepper
1 cup medium white sauce
1 cup cheddar cheese, grated
½ tsp mustard (prepared)

Prepare the white sauce, and stir in the cheese and mustard until melted. Place the fish in a baking dish; sprinkle with salt and pepper and cover with the cheese sauce. Bake at 350°F for about half an hour.

For over 300 years, inshore fishermen have been catching codfish off the banks of Prince Edward Island. In the census of 1728, there are recorded 127 fishermen. They had eight schooners and nineteen shallops engaged in the fishing industry. Their total catch for the year was 487,400 pounds of cod.

Codfish in a Nest

1 cup shredded salt cod
1 cup white sauce
3 cups mashed potatoes
½ cup fine dry crumbs
½ cup grated cheese
1 tbsp melted butter

Scald the codfish and drain as dry as possible. Combine with the sauce. Rub a shallow baking dish with butter; line with the potatoes; put the codfish mixture in the center; spread a little potato over the top; cover with the crumbs, cheese and butter, mixed, and brown in a hot oven (375°F), about 30 minutes.

Codfish Cakes as served in Maine

1 lb salt codfish, soaked
overnight in water to cover
4-5 medium potatoes, sliced
about ½-inch thick
¼ tsp pepper
1 egg

Drain fish. To the same pot add potatoes, 1 cup cold water and bring to a boil, cooking until potatoes are done. Drain and return again to same pot. Mash the fish and potatoes together, adding the whole egg and the pepper. Beat "with a silver fork". Scoop out by the spoonful and shape into cakes with the fork. Slide onto a platter and keep in a cool spot until ready to fry in ¼-inch dripping. They will be crusty gold on each side and delicious.

Note: In Maine—and thus on the Island—salt cod and potato boil was often served with beets and Johnny cake.

Salt Codfish Pie

½ lb boneless salt cod
4 slices bacon, diced
⅔ cup chopped onion
1 tbsp flour
1¼ cups milk
¼ tsp dried thyme (optional)
¼ tsp pepper
2 eggs separated
1 cooked pie shell (9 inch)

Prepare the cod by soaking in cold water overnight. Drain; cover with fresh water and bring to the boil. Drain; flake the fish.Fry bacon until crisp; remove and save the scraps. Add the onion and cook until tender. Sprinkle with flour and add 1 cup milk, stirring until thickened and smooth. Add flaked fish, bacon, thyme and pepper. Beat egg yolks with remaining milk; add to fish mixture and cook three minutes longer. Beat egg whites until stiff, but not dry, and fold in the fish mixture. Fill the pie shell and bake in a moderate oven (350°F) for 20 minutes or until lightly browned. Serves 4.

Tomcod

You will occasionally see reference to Tomcod, a small edition of cod. It can be treated in a manner similar to cod and fried, poached or baked. Tomcod is most frequently caught through the ice where it joins the more common smelt in seeking food in the bays and rivers.

Mackerel

"Mr. Rob Angus, manager of the Telephone Company, Summerside, had on exhibition at the Hotel Russ the largest

mackerel ever caught here. It measured 23½ inches in length, about 5½ inches in width and weights 3 lbs. 6 oz. It was hooked at Tignish, by Capt. Frank Gallant. Mr. Angus intends to have it stuffed and sent to Washington, to show the Americans what kind of mackerel we get inside the three mile limit."

The P.E.I. Agriculturist
1888

Mackerel is without doubt my favourite fish. One of the 'fatty' fish, it has a fine strong flavour which must be fresh or smoked for me to truly enjoy it. Of course, mackerel is also salted, pickled, canned (its delicious too) and even frozen. Try barbecuing it, or fry up in a cast-iron pan over a camp fire—delicious.

Baked Spanish Mackerel

1 medium-sized mackerel
2 cups bread crumbs, medium stale
½ small onion, minced
1 tbsp bacon, minced
½ tsp minced green pepper
¼ tsp summer savory
3 slices bacon
⅓ tsp salt
few grains pepper

Mix together the bread crumbs, onion, chopped bacon, green pepper and seasonings and spread on the fish, which should be dressed for broiling. Place a slice of bacon on this and fold over the fish so that the dressing shows. Place on a trivet in a baking pan; lay the remaining bacon on top of the fish, and bake 30 minutes in a hot oven of 425°F, basting frequently with the fat in the pan. Serve on a platter decorated with alternating rings of green pepper and sliced lemon. Accompany with the following sauce: Mix together 2 tsp chopped green pepper, 4 tbsp mayonnaise, 3 tbsp chili sauce and use at once. Serves 6.

Good Housekeeping's
Book of Meals, Favorite Recipes
and Menus, 1930

Mackerel Fillets and Cheese

6 mackerel fillets
salt and pepper to taste
1 tbsp onion, chopped fine
½ cup milk
1 cup grated cheddar cheese
½ cup bread crumbs

Grease baking dish and lay fillets side by side. Sprinkle with salt, pepper and onion. Pour milk over all then top with the cheese and then bread crumbs. Bake in hot (450°F) oven for 10-12 minutes.

Millie's Soused Mackerel

2 lbs mackerel or herring,
  skinned and filleted
1 cup vinegar
2 thin slices onion
1 tbsp mixed pickling spice
1 tsp salt
½ cup water

Cut fish into six pieces. Put into a baking dish, adding vinegar, onion, spices, salt and water. Cover dish. Bake at 350°F for 20-30 minutes. Serve hot or cold.

Broiled Salt Mackerel with Parsley Butter

1 salt mackerel
lemon
melted butter
paprika
squares of toast
Parsley Butter Balls (see index)

Cut the mackerel in three-inch squares, and scald, allowing fish to stand in the water a few minutes; turn and dry thoroughly. Rub with the cut surface of a lemon, then with melted butter. Dust with a little paprika and broil seven minutes. Serve on squares of toast, with a small parsley butter ball on each piece.

Brook Trout in Clam Juice

Place cleaned trout in a shallow pan. Cover with clam juice (broth or buy in bottles) or water mixed with juice. Add a piece of onion and a pinch of celery seed. Bring to a boil then cover, reducing heat and simmer 5 minutes per pound of fish. Drain and serve with a side bowl of melted parsley butter and lemon.

Fried Trout Â La Quebec

Clean trout and dip each one in corn meal. Fry sliced salt pork until brown; remove and then fry corn-mealed fish in the fat remaining in the pan. Garnish with the pork slices and lemon to serve.

Marinated Trout

10-12 small trout
½ cup cider vinegar
2 cups white wine
1 large onion, sliced thin
1 carrot, sliced thin
1 tbsp salt
3 whole cloves
¼ tsp thyme
6 peppercorns
½ tsp celery salt

Place in a saucepan: vinegar, wine, onion, carrot, salt, cloves, thyme, peppercorns, celery salt. Bring to a boil and simmer 20 minutes. Meanwhile, clean trout, leaving whole (remove heads if you wish). Place in the hot liquid and simmer 20 minutes. Remove fish to a dish and pour the liquid over them. Cover and refrigerate in juice. Will keep 15-20 days in refrigerator.

Pâté

(Mackerel or Trout)

In days past there were many individuals scattered around the province who smoked fish of all kinds. A few of the old-style smokehouses still remain, however, it wasn't until Atlantic Fish Industries opened that smoked fish again became readily available. Their products are fast gaining world-wide recognition, particularly the smoked trout, mackerel and salmon. It is gratifying to see a traditional food resurrected so successfully. All smoked fish is delicious served simply—on a plate with crackers and toast rounds nearby. It is also wonderful made into a pâté such as this.

8 oz smoked trout or mackerel
4 tbsp butter, melted
⅓ cup bread crumbs
1 lemon
pinch nutmeg
salt and pepper to taste
½ cup cream
½ cup aspic jelly (buy commercial or prepare as below)
1 tsp parsley, finely chopped

Remove skin and bones; then flake the flesh of the fish until it is fine (chop if desired). Combine butter, bread crumbs, parsley, the juice and finely grated rind from the lemon, salt, pepper and nutmeg. Add the fish, then the cream. Spoon into a crock and seal with aspic jelly or gelatine which is gelling and almost set. Chill and serve with toast rounds or crackers.

Aspic Jelly

This is an English version of homemade Aspic Jelly from Royce Publications *The Complete Cookery Encyclopedia.* Amber colored savoury jelly, deriving its name from a herb called 'spike which was at one time used to flavour it', aspic jelly can be used to set meat, game, fish and vegetables in a mould and as an exterior coating for decorating cold game, hams, tongues, raised pies, galantines, poultry, fish and so on. Chopped aspic jelly is used for garnish. This is the best recipe for it which I have ever found.

rind of 1 lemon
1 carrot
1 turnip
1 onion
a little celery
2-3 tbsp lemon juice
2-3 tbsp tarragon or chili vinegar
2-3 tbsp sherry
6 peppercorns
½ tsp salt
1½ oz gelatine
1½ pts good stock
shells and whites of 2 eggs

Wipe the lemon and peel or grate the rind. Prepare the vegetables, cutting each into about 4 pieces, and place them in a large saucepan with the lemon rind and juice, the vinegar, sherry, peppercorns, salt, gelatine and stock. Wash and crush the egg shells and add them, with the egg whites. Put over a low heat; begin to whisk vigorously and bring nearly to boiling point whisking meanwhile. Stop whisking and allow the froth to rise to the top of the pan, then draw it aside and leave in a warm place for 5 minutes. Strain the liquid through a clean scalded cloth or jelly bag, passing it a second time through the cloth if not absolutely clear.

Salmon

Just imagine the delight of the first settlers when they discovered salmon in Island streams. It was a fish familiar to all Europeans and had been highly valued in their homelands. The first mention of salmon in North America was reportedly when Eric the Red recorded that the Vikings had spotted "larger salmon than they had ever seen before". In fact, so plentiful was the fish that in colonial America of the 19th century, indentured servants had a clause in their contract limiting the amount of salmon they were to be fed.

Today, of course, salmon is considered a luxury, particularly whole fresh salmon. How lucky we Islanders are to still be able to catch them in season. And, of course, we have ready access to canned and frozen salmon.

The following recipes call for canned salmon. Don't forget, however, that you can also use any left-over salmon, by measuring out the same quantity.

Salmon Croquettes

One can of salmon with liquor drained off, 2 cups mashed potatoes (use while warm), 2 eggs, mustard, celery seed, nutmeg, ground cloves and allspice; 1 tablespoonful vinegar, 2 tablespoonfuls catsup, a little red pepper and salt. Form into any desired shape; roll in cracker crumbs and fry in hot lard. Try these; they are very nice.

H.F.

Salmon Chowder

2 slices salt pork (or margarine)
3 or 4 slices onion, diced
3 cups diced potatoes
Salt and pepper to taste
1 cup water
1 tall can salmon (pink is most economical)
1 qt milk
1 tbsp butter or margarine

Cook salt pork until fat is "tried out"; remove, then cook onion in this fat. Put water, potatoes, salt and pepper in a chowder kettle. Cover and bring to steaming, then cook on low heat about 15 minutes, until potatoes are tender. Break up canned salmon, removing skin and bones. Leave salmon in as large chunks as possible and add it and liquor to kettle. Stir gently, adding milk and a piece of butter or margarine. You may want to season. The longer this chowder ages, the better. Serve with common crackers.

West River Salmon Pâté

If you should happen to be cooking a whole salmon, chances are that you will have bits and pieces left over. Don't throw them away, instead take a few minutes to create this pâté to enjoy with toast or crackers.

The salmon should be cooked, so if you have leftovers from cutting off steaks, put the backbone and any scraps into a pot, and boil them until the flesh is opaque. Drain. Pick off all flesh from bones and skin and let cool. Mash the cooked fish with a fork and moisten with a little mayonnaise, about a half teaspoon of horseradish and chopped parsley.

Salmon Macaroni Salad

2 cups raw macaroni
2 cans (7¾-oz) salmon
1 tbsp minced onion
½ cup chopped green pepper
1 cup chopped celery
¼ tsp seasoned pepper
1 cup diced firm cheese
½ cup mayonnaise

Cook macaroni according to package directions; rinse, drain and cool. Break salmon into chunks and combine with remaining ingredients, except macaroni and mayonnaise; toss lightly to mix. Add macaroni and mayonnaise; blend in gently. Chill thoroughly before serving in a pretty bowl or on a bed of lettuce. Serves 4-6.

Salmon Spoonbread

1 can (7¾-oz) salmon
2 cups milk
2 tbsp butter
1 tsp sugar
1 tsp salt
¾ cup corn meal
¼ cup onion, finely minced
4 egg yolks
4 egg whites, stiffly beaten

Drain salmon juices into heavy saucepan. Add milk, butter, sugar and salt; bring to a boil. Add corn meal slowly, stirring constantly. Continue stirring over low heat 3-5 minutes until thickened. Stir in flaked salmon, onion and egg yolks. Fold in beaten egg whites. Turn batter into greased 1½-quart casserole. Bake at 375°F for 30-35 minutes, or until a toothpick comes out clean. Serve immediately. Serves 4.

Smelt

Smelt, said by many early homemakers to smell like violets (although it seems more like cucumber to me), have an unusual taste like no other fish. They are a great favourite with Islanders perhaps because there is a special magic to building a smelt shack, dragging it out onto the ice and then sitting in one's own private world waiting to spear the silvery fish lured to a hole in the ice. Even today smelt shacks mark estuaries where the small fish can be found.

Traditionally, a man's domain, the smelt shack, can be a home away from home with comfortable chairs, a heater of sorts and even a supply of beer to enjoy while patiently waiting for the fish to come along. One cannot consume too much though for a sure eye and swift hand are needed to spear the swift fish.

To Prepare: Smelt being a small delicate fleshed fish, cannot be cleaned in the same manner as other fish. The practice is cut off the head, just behind the gills, and pull the insides through the gills as they do so. Those with less dexterity can use a teaspoon to scoop the insides out after slitting the underside with a sharp knife. Some people like to cut the tail and fins off with scissors.

Every time we serve smelt I think of my father, who fastidiously removes the bones from smelt before eating them. We, on the other hand, just eat the bones as they are soft. Now I have been told by a wonderful cook whose husband and sons fish the West River that smelt can be boned by slitting them down the underside, spreading out on a chopping board, skin side up, butterfly fashion. Hit them with a flat, heavy mallet (any flat, heavy object will do it; she uses the smooth side of a mallet which is for pounding meat) along the spine, several times. The tail and backbone should easily pull away, leaving a fish which can be gently folded back into its original shape.

Camp Fire Smelt

3 lbs dressed smelt, fresh or frozen
2 tsp salt
3 strips bacon, cut in half
dash pepper
⅓ cup chopped onion
⅓ cup chopped parsley

Thaw frozen fish. Clean, wash and dry fish. Cut 6 pieces of heavy-duty aluminum foil, 12 × 12 inches each and grease lightly. Divide fish into 6 portions, place on foil. Sprinkle fish with salt and pepper. Place onion and parsley on fish. Top with bacon. Bring the foil up over the food and close edges with tight double folds. Make 6 packages. Place them on grill about 4 inches from hot coals. Cook for 10-15 minutes or until fish flakes easily when tested with a fork. Serves 6.

Outdoor Grill Smelt

These can be cooked on the grill or broiled. These days the best way to cook them outdoors is to use a sandwich grill; spray it with oil and cook fish in that. The sandwich grills are especially good for fish as they prevent it from all falling apart.

2 lbs dressed smelt
¼ cup chopped onion
2½ tbsp chopped green pepper
1 clove finely chopped garlic
2½ tbsp butter
1 tbsp tomato sauce
1 tbsp sugar
¼ tsp pepper

Combine all but first ingredient and simmer for 5 minutes. Cool. Marinate fish in sauce for 45 minutes, turning once. Place on grill or broiling rack; broil for 5-10 minutes, basting with sauce. Turn and repeat, until they flake easily.

Creamed Smelt and Onion

2-3 lbs dressed smelt
3 medium onions, chopped or sliced
2 tbsp dripping or butter
¼ tsp pepper
1 cup milk or cream
salt

Fry onions in dripping or butter (or use vegetable oil); when brown push to one side of skillet. Fry the seasoned fish until brown on both sides. Remove fish to hot platter. Add cream or milk to onions and simmer 5-10 minutes. Pour over fish and serve. Enough for four.

Variations: use tomato juice instead of milk.

Smelt Du Chef

1 lb smelt, dressed
3 eggs, beaten
1 tsp tarragon
salt and pepper
bread crumbs
fat or oil for frying

Dry smelt. Combine eggs, tarragon, salt and pepper. Add smelt and leave overnight. Heat oil to 375°F. Roll smelt in bread crumbs; deep fry until golden.

Broiled Stuffed Smelts

12 large smelts
¼ cup soft bread crumbs
few drops onion juice
2 tbsp lemon juice
½ tsp minced parsley
2 tbsp melted butter
salt and pepper
sliced cucumber and/or Lemon
  Horseradish Butter (see
  index)

Clean and split the smelts; make a dressing of the crumbs, onion, lemon juice, parsley and one tablespoon butter. Stuff the smelts with this; place on an oiled broiler; brush with remaining melted butter and broil about seven minutes. Season with salt and pepper and serve with sliced cucumbers and/or Lemon Horseradish Butter.

Eels

"The Ramsays and McIntoshes who were the first immigrants to Malpeque, settled there in 1770. What is now Malpeque was then a dense unbroken forest of immense hardwood chiefly, and some softwood. Huge trees extended even to the banks on the seashore, river edges and Richmond Bay beaches. For several years provisions were very scarce. The landlord's at 'home' in Britain, to encourage people to emigrate, told them that sugar was growing on the trees (maple sugar), that all kinds of fruits were plentiful, that fish was abundant, and that provisions were in profusion. Hence nearly all the first settlers brought no food with them, and they were exposed to many privations. A few French inhabitants sparingly supplied them. This humane people would go to the North Cape, catch sea-cows, preserve the flippers, carry home, and also haul on dog sleighs, and give a considerable portion of this, their own chief food, to the newcomers.

Two poor men of the British were early one spring short of all kinds of provisions except potatoes. They launched their canoe to search for eels. They spent two days paddling away up along the shores to the Barbara West River, and were returning nearly starved and melancholy because their cruise was thus far fruitless, when they noticed shallow grounds covered with eel grass out in the Malpeque Bay, and they thought that for the curiosity of the thing they would try. No sooner had they poked their spears into the mud, than they caught them full of the long-looked for and much desired fish.

They soon loaded the canoe, landed, dug a hole on the snow covered shore or bank, returned to the eel ground, re-loaded, and again emptied their craft, and the third time filled the canoe, when they joyfully paddled home. Usually in winter eels were found to be very numerous when speared through holes cut in the ice, half barrel of them being frequently got from a single hole."

The Presbyterian
Jan. 3, 1878

Even today hardy individuals fish eels through the ice each spring.

The liking for them has never died and, in recent times, they have been making a comeback of sorts and are again available in some grocery stores. Usually they are skinned when purchased and can even be found smoked.

Fried Eels

Clean and cut the eels into pieces three inches in length; cover them in a saucepan with cold water, in which salt, pepper, thyme, onions and carrots sliced thin, and one-half of a glass of vinegar have been put. As soon as they boil, take from the fire, and let them become cool. Then drain them and dry. Mix egg and bread crumbs, beating the egg first, and dip each piece in. Fry them brown in drippings (see index). Place them on a dish, and have a tartar sauce ready to serve with them.

Bessie's Broiled Eel

Skin and clean a good-sized eel; remove the backbone and cut the eel into five or six pieces. Dip each piece into egg and then into bread crumbs which have been salted and peppered. Put on a greased gridiron (grill) with the skin side downward, over a clear fire, and broil, turning over when done on one side. Put on a hot dish with parsley and serve.

Boiled Eels

I have been told of small eels, cleaned and with the head removed (I think) being simply boiled in water and served whole with melted butter.

Eel Pie

1 lb eels
chopped parsley
1 shallot
grated nutmeg
pepper and salt to taste
the juice of ½ a lemon
small quantity of forcemeat
 stuffing (see index)
¼ pt Bechamel sauce (see index)
puff pastry

Skin and wash the eels; cut them into pieces 2 inches long, and line the bottom of the pie dish with forcemeat. Put in the eels, and sprinkle them with the parsley, shallots, nutmeg, seasoning and lemon juice, and cover with puff pastry. Bake for 1 hour, or rather more; make the bechamel hot, and put it into the pie. Reserve left-over sauce to serve with the meal.

Mrs. Beeton's Book
of Household Management
1861

Shellfish

Lobster

The lobster has done a complete reversal in importance in this province. Once so plentiful and 'common' that it was used to fertilize fields and only eaten by the poor, it now ranks among our most important foods. Every Islander longs for the lobster season to begin. The few who don't crave this delicious crustacean associate fishing season with spring and warm weather, so anticipate its arrival just as strongly as the rest of us.

Aside from the Islanders' love of lobster is its important role in the economy of the province. In the late 1800s, early 1900s, lobster fishing and canning provided employment for men and women in communities all around the province. Most of the factories are gone now, but a new "industry" has replaced them—the lobster supper. Commercially run suppers attract thousands of tourists each year—not to mention local folk. As well, church suppers, restaurants, wharf-side shacks, offer lobster from its most simple to its most elegant.

About Lobster

- When buying lobsters live, look for the lively ones—don't buy one which isn't moving.
- Many Islanders prefer the smaller canners to large lobsters believing they have better flavour.
- When taking live lobster home keep them in the refrigerator. Do not put them in fresh water—ever; they will die. If you keep a lobster in a cool, damp environment, it should survive up to 36 hours. But don't keep them any longer.
- Lobsters are usually dark green or mottled when live. They turn bright red when cooked.
- If having a feed at home cover the table with newspaper and place a chopping block, an old, sharp knife (it may chip so don't use a new one) and a hammer in the middle. Have a pot for shells.

Joan's Lobster Casserole

This is one of those "throw it all in a pot and cook it" recipes. It's delicious!

Sauté green pepper, onion and celery, chopped, in butter. Open two cans cold pack lobster and drain. Using part of the liquid, make a white sauce. In a casserole mix together the above; add a "good shot" of very dry (Cold Sac) Sherry, and mushrooms. Top with buttered bread crumbs and bake until done.

You can use half scallops and half lobster—but be warned, it's very rich!

If you have teetotallers in your midst, just add the sherry and don't tell anyone!

Hot Lobster Sandwiches

1 lb can lobster
2 tbsp butter
2 tbsp cooking sherry
paprika
toast
mayonnaise

Flake lobster and heat in butter. Add sherry. Spread on buttered toast with lettuce and little mayonnaise. Sprinkle with paprika; serve immediately.

Lobster Sausages

Use a blender to replace the mortar and canned or frozen lobster!

Pick the flesh from a medium-sized freshly boiled lobster (or use canned or frozen). Mince fine and pound it in a mortar with two ounces of fresh butter, a little salt, cayenne, and pounded (ground) mace, and half of the coral, which has been pounded separately, and press through a hair sieve with the back of a spoon. Shape the mixture into rolls like sausages; sprinkle the rest of the coral over them, and place them in oven with a moderate fire (350°F) until they are quite hot. Serve them on a folded napkin, and garnish with lettuce leaves.

Freda's Lobster Farcie

(Farcie meant to stuff)

Remove the lobster from the shell, and cut the fish into small pieces. Stir in the meat a thick cream sauce (see index). Season with salt, red pepper, Worcestershire Sauce, and a small quantity of onion juice. Put into shells again; sprinkle with bread crumbs, and brown in the oven very slowly.

We prefer this poured over toast and browned or in a scallop shell rather than trying to keep lobster shells presentable.

Forcemeat

Quite often in older cookbooks and handwritten records a reference is made to forcemeat. Generally this is simply another term for stuffing (a preparation that is put inside something, such as a fish or a turkey). Forcemeats are occasionally rolled into balls or cooked alongside the main ingredients (as is dressing or stuffing).

Forcemeat Balls for Fish Soups

1 middling-sized lobster
½ an anchovy
1 head of boiled celery
the yolk of a hard-boiled egg
salt
cayenne and mace to taste
4 tbsp bread crumbs
2 oz butter
2 eggs

Note: The original recipe follows with reference to using a mortar and pedestal, very necessary tools in early kitchens. In this particular recipe a blender can do the same job. Pick the meat from the shell of the lobster, and pound it, with the soft parts, in a mortar; add the celery, the yolk of the hard-boiled egg, seasoning and bread crumbs. Continue pounding till the whole is nicely amalgamated. Warm the butter until it is in a liquid state; well whisk the eggs, and work these up with the pounded lobster meat. Make into balls of about an inch in diameter, and fry to a nice pale brown. Sufficient, from 18 to 20 balls, for 1 tureen of soup.

Mrs. Beeton's
Book of Household Management 1861

Crab

Rock Crab is abundant in most fishing areas of P.E.I. The crustaceans are commonly found on a sand or sandy mud bottom. They are fished by using a baited trap; but as every beachcomber knows, they can be seen scuttling back and forth in shallow waters. Crab can most easily be purchased today removed from the shell in fresh, frozen or canned form. It is possible to purchase live crabs should you wish to cook them yourself.

Crab Tips

— Cooked crab should smell fresh and joints should not be flaccid or floppy. Be sure you are buying crab, not imitation.

— A crab of decent size will yield just under half its weight in meat.

Crab Chowder

2 tbsp butter
1 onion, finely chopped
1 tsp flour
6 oz fresh crab meat (pick out any shell or cartilage)
¼ cup chopped celery
salt and pepper to taste
3 cups scalded milk
1 10-oz can cream of mushroom soup
1 12-oz can corn kernels
6 slices of bacon (cooked and crumbled)

Melt butter in large saucepan. Add onion and celery; sauté until soft. Stir in flour. Add milk and soup and simmer; add corn, bacon and crab meat. Simmer until heated thoroughly. Serves 6.

Crab Au Gratin

This dish is customarily served on the shell, but if you choose to buy the crab removed from the shell, you can use scallop shells, small oven-proof bowls or even a shallow baking dish to broil the crab.

crab meat
1 oz bread crumbs
½-to-1 oz butter

These amounts are sufficient for one large crab. Arrange the crab meat in shell or dish and cover with bread crumbs, then melted butter. Heat under the broiler until it just starts to brown, then add a layer of finely grated cheese and brown.

Vary with the addition of thinly sliced onion, fried; a dash of Worcestershire Sauce and a little curry powder, and thinly sliced tomato is good.

Devilled Crab from Stanley Bridge

The abundance of crabs on the north shore promoted this family recipe to a place of honour on cool summer days when the oven could be used. Use scallop shells or individual baking dishes rubbed with butter, for four.

1½ cups fresh crab meat
1 lemon, juice one half and cut the other into wedges for garnish
¼ tsp dry mustard
⅛ tsp pepper
4 tsp Worcestershire Sauce
½ tsp Tabasco Sauce
4 tbsp butter
½ cup mayonnaise
¼ cup heavy cream (optional)
seasoned bread crumbs

Toss crab meat and lemon juice gently together. Sprinkle on the mustard, pepper, Worcestershire and Tabasco. Melt the butter, then toss the crab gently into it, trying not to break up the chunks of meat. Add the cream if desired (I did not use it and like the dish without). Mound one-quarter of mixture into each shell that has been greased, handling the meat lightly. Apply a thin coating of mayonnaise; sprinkle with the crumbs and bake at 250°F until heated thoroughly and crumbs are a bit crunchy.

Oysters

"John McGregor, who was Sheriff for the Island during thirty years after Holland's Survey (1765), writes of the oysters: 'they are considered the finest in America and equally

Grappling for oysters on the Mill River. The old, and slow method of fishing the prizes shellfish.

(Public Archives of PEI, B.H. "Jack" Turner Collection, accession 2767)

delicious as those taken on the English shores', and adds: 'there are two or three varieties, the largest of which are from six to twelve inches long.' What a meal one of those oysters would have made! John Stewart writing at the beginning of the Nineteenth Century, says 'The oysters are in great plenty in all the harbours of the Island; in some places beds of them of several acres extent may be found; most of the lime hitherto used here has been burnt from their shells, and it is commonly the practice to burn the live oysters for that purpose, putting many hundred barrels of them in a kiln together.' The late Mr. Lawrence Burpee in the Canadian Geographic Journal for November 1946 says: 'What makes the practice all the more reprehensible is that, even in Stewart's day, the oysters of the Island were preferred to any other American oyster by Europeans who have eaten them.' Burpee continues, 'It is enough to make all living epicures to grind their teeth, and all dead epicures to turn restlessly in their graves. Need one add that eminent statesmen in Ottawa prize their membership in the Rideau Club, not because it is exclusive, but because it happens to be one of the few places where a man may still be served with Malpeque oysters.'

Carrie Ellen Holman
Our Island Story (Broadcasts given over CFCY Radio Charlottetown in the winter of 1948)

In light of early practices, and Mr. Burpee's report on the short supply of Malpeque oysters, we are indeed fortunate today to have a ready supply of one of the finest shellfish in the world.

Oyster lovers all over the world savour the Malpeque oyster from P.E.I. as the most prized. On the outside, it looks pretty much like any other oyster—rock-like, wrinkled and squat. But once you open it up and plop that first juicy Malpeque oyster into your mouth, the clean, sharp flavour tells you why it ranks so highly with the experts.

They get their name from a deep inlet on the north shore where they originated and where they are cultivated today. So well are the cultivation techniques that oysters are farmed all around the Island.

Because oysters were so readily available, they were often eaten by Islanders as snacks. Stories of men sitting out back of the barn with a pail of oysters between their knees, just gossiping, shucking and slurping back oysters abound. From the way some of the old timers talk, it seems that it was common practice to down a pail full each. Since they are said to be an aphrodisiac, I wondered if they were the indirect cause of so many large Island families.

While the men rhapsodize about oysters on the half shell—raw, the women and children seemed to prefer them deep fried. Whichever way they were served, oysters have long been a much enjoyed part of the Islander's diet.

About Oysters

— Always look for a closed shell when buying them.

- To open, put on a pair of work gloves; wash well but do not let stand in water. Hold the oyster with the cup half of the shell down (flat side up); insert a strong, blunt knife between the shells near the hinge and twist until the shells come apart. You may have to take a hammer and chip the edge of the shell enough to allow the knife in. Cut the muscles holding the shell together and holding the oyster to the shell. Remove any particles of shell. They are now ready to serve on the half shell or set aside to cook. If you are going to prepare a dish full, strain the liquor through a shell to catch any pieces of shell.
- Shucked oysters and juice can be stored in the refrigerator in a tightly covered container for several days.
- Live oysters in the shell can be kept up to 10 weeks in proper conditions. Old timers say they used to keep them in the cold cellar. Fisheries recommend no more than a month in the refrigerator.
- If cooking in the shell, discard any that do not open. Cook only until the shells open. Do not overcook; they will go tough.
- Oysters can be cooked in the oven at 450°F, in their shell, until they open (20-25 minutes). I was also told of placing them in a fire until the shell opened, but this was not the usual. Anyone eating them outside usually doesn't bother with cooking.

Escalloped Oysters with Tomatoes Au Gratin

1 pt oysters, shucked and picked clean of shell
2 cups soft bread crumbs
½ tsp salt
⅛ tsp pepper
3 tbsp melted butter
2 large tomatoes, sliced thin
⅓ cup fine dry bread crumbs
½ cup grated cheddar or Parmesan cheese
1 tbsp butter

Oil a shallow quart-size baking dish. Mix the soft bread crumbs with the salt and pepper and the three tablespoons melted butter and arrange a layer in the bottom of the dish. Cover with a layer of crumbs and more oysters and sprinkle a few crumbs over the top.

Over this place the tomatoes, sprinkle lightly with a little salt and cover with the fine dry crumbs, mixed with the grated cheese and the remaining tablespoon butter. Bake 30-35 minutes at 350°F, or until the tomatoes are tender and the crumbs browned.

Little Oyster Pies

2 tbsp butter
3 tbsp flour
few grains mace
few drops onion juice
¼ tsp salt
⅛ tsp pepper
1 cup milk
1 pt small oysters
Rich pie crust

Melt the butter; stir in the flour and seasonings and gradually add the milk, cooking and stirring until sauce reaches the boiling point. Then add the oysters. Transfer to four greased, small baking dishes. Cover with the pie crust, slashed, to allow steam to escape, and bake 20-25 minutes at 375°F.

Oyster Casserole from "Up West"

Potato stuffing (see index)
½ tsp thyme
24 oysters, shucked, with liquor saved
clam juice (bottle)
6 tbsp flour
salt and pepper
⅓ cup coarse dry bread crumbs
2½ tbsp butter

When preparing the stuffing, substitute thyme for poultry seasoning. Place the oysters in a large saucepan with enough juice to just cover and simmer gently until edges curl. Don't overcook. Remove from the heat and take out the oysters, leaving all the juice behind. Measure these juices and add enough clam juice to make two cups; blend in the flour and mix thoroughly. In a deep, well-buttered casserole layer stuffing, oysters, 1 cup liquid, salt and pepper, stuffing, oysters, the remaining liquid, stuffing and top with bread crumbs dotted with butter. Bake 30-40 minutes in a preheated 350°F oven until golden brown. Serve immediately.

Oyster Rarebit

Make the sauce as for Scallops Mornay and add precooked oysters. Cook the same as for Scallops Mornay, or use the old recipe below.

Clean and remove the hard muscle from one-half or a pint of oysters; parboil them in their own liquor until their edges curl, then remove to a hot bowl. Put one tablespoonful of butter and one-half a pound of grated cheese, one saltspoonful of salt and a few grains of cayenne into a dish; while the butter is melting beat two eggs slightly and add to them the oyster liquor; mix this gradually into the melted cheese; add the oysters and turn at once over hot toast.

Scallops

Scallops have always been highly valued as a shellfish. In the past they were not as easy to obtain as clams, mussels or lobster because they are found in deeper water. Today they are rather expensive when you look at the cost per pound. However, remember that scallops are very rich, especially when cooked with a sauce, so that they go further.

Should you be fortunate enough to obtain your scallops in the shell, be careful opening them and save the shells. They wash beautifully and are grand for cooking individual servings of many seafood delicacies. To open the scallop, place it in your left hand with the dark side of the shell down and insert the blade of a knife into the hinge. Do be careful! Scoop the knife down into the bottom and cut the muscle, then do the same for the top. Open the shell and pull the little white muscle from the rest of the scallop. You are ready for cooking, just check for small hard pieces on the sides of the scallop and cut them away if necessary. Once you've done a couple, it becomes a simple trick and like shucking oysters will surely impress visitors "from away".

About Scallops

— Delicious pan fried in butter
— Try deep frying. Roll in egg and bread crumbs or use a Beer Batter.
— Poached scallops can be sliced and used to make a delicious, cool summer salad when combined with quartered tomatoes, hard—cooked eggs, green onions and cucumber, all presented

on lettuce leaves.

— Combine scallops and mushrooms with a white or cheese sauce; place in cleaned shells and broil.
— Scallops wrapped in a half slice of streaky bacon are wonderful when barbecued or broiled.

Julie's Scallops Mornay

This is my favourite dish, always a hit and a never-fail treat. I particularly like cooking it for company because it is so easily stretched, can be made ahead and refrigerated until cooked; and it also can be warmed up again in the oven. This is so much my favourite recipe that it is repeated from my previous cookbook, Seafood Cookery of Prince Edward Island.

1 lb scallops, cut any large ones in half
2-3 tbsp butter
1 medium onion, roughly chopped
½ lb mushrooms, cut any large ones in half
⅓ lb old cheddar cheese, grated (we like strong cheese so use old; vary for your taste)
2 tbsp flour
2 tbsp butter
1 cup milk
pepper
½ cup grated cheese for topping
2 slices bread, toasted dark brown and rubbed together to make brown bread crumbs

In a large cast-iron casserole or frying pan sauté scallops in butter. Remove when brown, then sauté onion and mushrooms lightly in same butter and also set aside. Make a cheese sauce in the same pan by first melting the butter, then stirring in flour. Wait 2-3 minutes; add milk and cook until thickened. Add cheese, a sprinkle of pepper if desired, and stir until melted.

Stir in the scallops, mushrooms and onions into the sauce. Sprinkle toast crumbs, then grated cheese over the top. Cook in 375°F oven for 20 minutes.

To stretch, double the cheese sauce and add more whole mushrooms. If serving on a buffet, put in a fondue pot to keep warm and serve over vegetables, toast rounds or rice.

Old Settlers Scallops

This method was found handwritten, very faded, with no clue as to the source other than the faint ink and brittle paper. It is still one of the favoured ways to quickly cook up a batch of scallops and, as one fisherman's wife told me, "Can be ready at the side of the stove and cooked up while the old fellow washes his hands and takes off his boots." Presumably the fat was kept hot, and ready for having your fat hot enough is the secret to success as in all deep fried dishes.

"This fish much resembles an oyster, though it is larger, and tastes like a crab. Dry them after washing, and trimming away the beard and black parts, then roll in cracker dust, afterward in egg and crumbs, and drop them into boiling fat for a minute, so they will take on a light brown. The crumbs must have salt and pepper mixed with them."

Clams

Clam digging is great fun. I often envision a mother in those early days on the Island, sending her children out to get supper. No chore I'm sure, the finding and digging of clams is as much fun as just about anything a youngster can do and is the best excuse in the world to get out and dig in the mud and sand. Then, of course, one must swim to get clean—right!

About Clams

— Dug clams will be sandy inside. Fill your bucket with fresh, clean salt water and throw in a handful of oatmeal or corn meal. Leave the clams for a few hours, and they will digest the cereal and pass through much of the sand.

— Soft-shell clams will be much more tender that the large quahogs. Both can be used in the following recipes, but quahogs are best steamed, minced and then used in cakes, chowders, etc.

— If you want to dig clams, check with Fisheries or the Visitors Information Bureau—they will tell you the places to dig!

- To steam clams, place in a large kettle with salted water, or in white wine; cover tightly; bring to a boil and steam 8-10 minutes until the shells open. Discard any that do not open. If saving the liquor, strain it.
- Clams can be served on the half shell; be careful to save liquor and serve with a squeeze of lemon or lime and black pepper.

Mosser's Clam Chowder

One of the most enjoyable sights to come across in P.E.I. today is the harvesting of Irish Moss. After a storm from the north, all hands will turn to the beaches where men riding heavy horses bareback direct their steeds into the surf, draggin' rakes behind them. Gathering moss is hard work, wet and often cold. It means hours of backbreaking shovelling, first on the beaches loading the moss onto wagons or trucks, then later spreading it to dry. Because it is a fleeting source of income, they do not stop work until the job is done or darkness falls. Even then, upon arriving home, the mosser's work is not done, horses have to be tended before anyone can sit down to a meal.

A mosser's wife told me that this gives her just enough time to prepare this warming, nourishing chowder for the men folk, as the clams and potatoes are precooked.

1½ cups clams (drained with liquor reserved) poached or steamed, bottled or canned)
3-4 slices salt pork or bacon, cut into small bits
1 medium onion, finely chopped
2 medium potatoes, diced and parboiled until just tender. RESERVE WATER
2 cups light cream
thyme
(If you wish, garnish with paprika and parsley.)

Fry out the salt pork until crisp; remove, then brown the onion. Allow potato water to cool a little, then add bacon, onion, potato and clam liquor. Bring to a boil, then simmer 5 minutes. Season with salt and pepper to taste. Add cream gradually until it comes just to boiling point, then add clams. Just heat them through; sprinkle with a very tiny pinch of thyme and serve with biscuits.

Note: You can use milk, milk and half and half, or more clam liquor but this gives the best chowder.

Rappie Pie made with Clams

Englishman, Alan Davidson, one of the world's most authorative and knowledgeable writers on seafood included this recipe in his book, North Atlantic Seafood. His research led him to this Acadian dish which "survives strongly in Prince Edward Island." He noted that Island students would take some along when going to off-Island universities for a new term and share it with favoured professors and lecturers.

Never one to accept things without delving into them, Mr. Davidson relates that Rappie pies can be made with meat or chicken, but "there are grounds for thinking that the version with clams may be the earliest."

The secret of the dish is to extract all the liquid from the potatoes and replace it by another liquid.

18-24 soft-shelled clams
3 pounds potatoes
½ lb salt pork
pepper to taste

Peel and grate the potatoes. Take a cup at a time and place it in a cheesecloth, which must then be twisted so as to wring out as much liquid as possible. Collect the liquid in a bowl, so that you can measure it; for you will later need the same quantity of clam juices and water. Put the wrung-out potato, which will seem like snow, into another bowl.

Steam the clams open. Reserve the juices and mince the meat.

Dice the salt pork finely and try it out in the bottom of an oven pan, until this is coated with melted fat. Then remove the pieces of salt pork. Meanwhile, add to the clam juices enough water to bring the volume up to that of the liquid extracted from the potatoes. Bring this mixture to the boil, then add the wrung-out potato to it, little by little. The potato will swell up as it absorbs its new liquid. When this operation is completed, place a layer of the potato in the bottom of the oven pan; cover this with minced clams, then another layer of clams, then another layer of potatoes and so on—the pie can have three layers or five. Season with pepper to taste, and sprinkle the little bits of salt pork over the top. Bake in a moderately hot (400°F) for 20 minutes, then reduce the heat to moderate (350°F) and continue to bake for another hour or so, when the top of the pie will be brown and crusty.

Deep Fried Clams

There seems to be three basic ways the old timer likes to eat clams—steamed, in chowder and deep fried. Depending on whose kitchen you are in, the deep fried ones are in a batter or bread crumbs. Either way they are good and an easy meal. When you consider that clams have always been there for the digging, it's easy to understand why some families fry up a batch for a late night snack. I wonder what they dream about though!

The following quantity is from a large family who served them with ketchup, tea for the grown ups and milk for the youngsters for as long as they can remember.

Clams in Batter

4 dozen clams, cleaned in corn
  meal and shucked
2 egg yolks
2 egg whites
1 cup milk
"spoonful of marg" (I used
  2 tbsp butter) melted
salt and pepper to taste
1 cup flour
fat (or oil) for deep frying

Beat the egg yolks into half a cup of milk and then drizzle in the melted butter. Combine the flour and salt (sift) and add. Beat with a fork until it's smooth. Beat the egg whites until stiff, then add the rest of the milk to the batter and follow by folding in the egg whites.

Drain the clams and dump them onto a cloth to absorb excess moisture. Dip one at a time into batter, taking care that they are all evenly coated and separate in the fat. Fry in hot fat until nicely browned. Drain to serve.

If you are feeding a crowd, keep them warm in the oven by placing in a basket lined with towels (use paper towels), and place a cloth over them while you cook the next batch.

Clams in Bread Crumbs

Follow the usual method of drying clams well. Combine an egg and a tablespoon of water, beating well. Dip clams in dry bread crumbs, then egg, then bread crumbs. You can add salt and pepper to your bread crumbs if desired. We prefer to just place the salt and pepper shaker on the table.

Jellied Clam Soup

"With the approach of spring the thoughtful housewife prepares her menus accordingly, and naturally one of the lists contains iced soup. Here, then, is a recipe for an iced jellied clam soup:

2 cans of clam nectar (small)
1½ tsp gelatine dissolved in
quarter cup cold water
⅛ tsp celery salt
⅛ tsp salt
⅛ tsp pepper and paprika
1 tsp lemon juice

Soak the gelatine in cold water 10 minutes. Heat the clam nectar to boiling point; add the seasonings and the lemon juice, then add the gelatine and stir well to dissolve. Strain into a bowl and put into the icebox to set. Serve in soup cups topped with a teaspoonful of whipped cream and paprika. Serve with salted wafers for supper or luncheon."

The Charlottetown Guardian
April 5, 1932

Clam and Corn Casserole

1 cup left-over clams, minced or
1 8-oz can (at least) with
liquid
2 tbsp butter
2 tbsp flour
¾ cup milk, plus clam liquid
1 whole egg
1 egg yolk
1 cup corn niblets
1 tbsp pimiento (optional)
2 tbsp onion, finely chopped

1 tbsp parsley, finely chopped
½ tsp salt
1 tsp lemon juice

Melt butter in saucepan. Blend in flour. Add milk and clam liquid. Simmer, stirring until thick and smooth. Beat eggs; add clams, corn, pimiento, onion, parsley, mustard, salt and lemon juice. Stir in white sauce. Turn into buttered casserole. Bake in moderate 350°F oven 45 minutes. Serves 2.

Island Clams First to Go Another Shipment

"Following the announcement in the Guardian last week of the arrival in good condition of the first carload of fresh clams ever shipped from the Maritime Provinces to Central Canada, word was received yesterday of the arrival in Toronto of another car from Summerside. This is an excellent beginning in the Provinces on a profitable basis, and proves beyond doubt that fresh shipments can be made to the Central Provinces.

Incidentally, it may be mentioned that the canning company which is purchasing this product of Island fishery formerly operated in the United States and was established in Canada following the inauguration of the Bennett Government's protective tariff policy."

The Charlottetown Guardian
June 29, 1932

Clam and Bacon Pie

1 quart soft shelled clams
flour
pepper
1 medium onion
3 slices bacon, diced
Rich baking powder biscuit dough (see index)

Wash the clams. Steam over a cup of hot water; drain and reserve the liquid. Cut the necks from the clams, then dip the clams in flour mixed with a little pepper. Use enough flour to coat the clams. Place the onion in a good-size frying pan with the bacon and sauté slowly until the onion is yellowed and the bacon browned. Rub a shallow baking dish or deep pie plate with bacon fat and put in a layer of the clams. Cover with half of the onion and bacon mixture, then put in the rest of the clams and sprinkle with the remaining onion and bacon. Pour in the reserved clam liquid (through a strainer).

Roll the biscuit dough to a half-inch thick and shape it into small rounds. Cut a small piece out of the center of each biscuit so the steam can escape, and place the biscuits scarcely touching, on top of the pie. Bake twenty minutes in a hot oven, 375 to 400°F.

Mussels

There is no question that the earliest inhabitants of the Island recognized the mussel as a source of food. The Scots, after all, were familiar with the bluish-black shellfish. In fact a burgh in Scotland Musselbrough is said to owe its name to the shellfish. It was originally a Roman station and apparently named for the shellfish. Although considered the poor man's shellfish, there is no question that it was eaten and enjoyed by many a newcomer to our land.

It was not until the 1970s, however, that the mussel took its rightful place, for until then it simply could not compete with the other shellfish. The change which gave us the affordable shellfish felt by many to be superior to clams and even equal to the highly prized oyster, occurred when off-bottom rearing techniques were introduced. Cultivated mussels are commercially farmed on specially designed collectors suspended in a mesh column, entirely free from the ocean floor. The method of "farming" produces a cleaner, more meaty mussel, completely free of pearls.

The taste of mussels is a mix between the subtle blend of clams and oysters, although many find the cooked meat much sweeter. They are versatile and can be steamed, fried, baked, breaded, stewed or prepared in many other ways. They make an economical and excellent substitute in most recipes calling for clams or oysters.

Mussel Chowder

4-5 lbs mussels, cleaned and steamed
1 tbsp butter
1 cup diced onion
2 cups diced potatoes
2 tbsp flour
4 cups milk

2 cups light cream
salt
pepper
4 strips bacon, fried crisp

Remove the meat from the steamed mussels, retaining the broth (strain). Add enough water to the broth to make 4 cups. Melt butter in a large pot; add onion, and sauté until transparent. Add flour and stir to blend thoroughly with fat; gradually add broth mixture; bring to a boil. Add potatoes; simmer until nearly done; add mussels and gently stir in hot milk and cream. Season lightly with salt and pepper. Garnish with bacon strips.

Mussel Brose

We spoke about the mussel being a shellfish common to the Scots. This recipe is said by the gentleman who gave it to me to be the old traditional way of eating mussels which, you will note, were not cultivated but wild and sandy.

mussels
oatmeal
stock (or use milk and water
mixed)

Wash the shells in several waters, scraping them well, then put them into a colander and run cold water on them until it runs away quite clear and free of sand, after which put them to steep for two hours. Drain them, put them on the fire in an iron stew-pan, closely covered, shake them occasionally until the shells open, and remove immediately from the fire. Strain the liquor into a basin; take the mussels out of the shells, and remove the beards and black parts. Put the liquor on with some fresh fish stock or some milk and water. Bring to the boil; add the mussels, and make hot, but do not cook. Have some oatmeal toasting before the fire. Put a handful or so in a bowl and dash a cupful of the mussel bree over it. Stir up quickly so as to form knots; return to the pan for a minute or two; serve very hot.

Mussel Stew

Mussels, cleaned, steamed, meat removed to make 2 cups and set aside.
¼ cup butter
¼ cup onion, chopped fine

1 tbsp green pepper, chopped
  fine
$\frac{1}{2}$ cup mushrooms
$\frac{1}{4}$ cup flour
1 tbsp cornstarch
3 cups milk
1 cup light cream, or blend
$\frac{1}{2}$ tsp salt
$\frac{1}{4}$ tsp pepper
2 tbsp lemon juice
parsley

Melt butter; add onion, green pepper and mushrooms. Sauté until tender. Combine flour and cornstarch. Stir into butter mixture until well blended. Add milk and cream all at once. Cook, stirring constantly until smooth and slightly thickened. Season with salt, pepper and lemon juice. Add mussel meat and allow to simmer for about 30 minutes. Garnish with chopped parsley. Serves 4.

Cheesy Baked Mussels

4 pounds mussels, cleaned and
  steamed.
6 slices bacon, chopped
2 tbsp lemon juice
$\frac{1}{2}$ cup finely chopped onion
1 cup grated cheddar cheese
salt and pepper, to taste

Remove the meat from the shells and place in a buttered baking dish. Add the rest of the ingredients and bake at 375°F 15-20 minutes, until bacon is cooked. Serves 4-6.

Irish Moss

Irish Moss, a green or purple seaweed, parsley-like in appearance litters the beaches of P.E.I. after a storm. Who would dream that this seaweed is one of our important exports. It seems to fall neatly between the best known exported commodities—seafood and agricultural products.

If you drink chocolate milk or beer, eat ice cream or salad dressing, wash your hair or clean your teeth, chances are you're making use of the starch-like, non-caloric substance that comes from Irish Moss, carrageenan. Today used as a stabilizer in food

Irish Moss drying on raised beds. For many years salt cod was dried outdoors on flakes as shown here.

(Public Archives of Prince Edward Island photo accession no 2320, item 23-5)

processing, cosmetics, etc. Irish Moss used to be used to make pudding-like blanc mange, which was considered particularly beneficial to the invalid.

The harvesting of Irish Moss is a special time for visitors to the province who love to see the heavy horses ridden into the surf of the north shore, dragging rakes to capture the precious "crop" from the sea.

To Dry

Anyone can pick and dry Irish Moss. After a storm it is easily found along the north shore. Take clean moss; wash and remove any debris and sun dry. When you wish to use it soak, drain and clean if necessary, then boil in water or milk for 15 minutes or so. Strain off the liquid; discard the moss, and sweeten liquid or add flavourings to taste. Stir in cream, milk or beaten egg white when it begins to set. Similar to a Blanc Mange.

After drying, Irish Moss had to be picked clean, a job that often fell to youngsters.

(Public Archives of the Prince Edward Island photo accession no. 2320 item 23-2.)

Irish Moss Jelly

Recommended for invalids. "Should be perfectly cooked, attractively served, suited to the digestive powers of the patient."

1 ounce Irish Moss
2 cups water
1 cup milk
sweetener to taste

Blend moss and water and cook mixture. Cool; stir in milk. Sweeten to taste.

From the Green Grocer and the Garden

Vegetables

"All kinds of garden vegetables that are common in England grow here with very slight cultivation, but from the length of the winter, are of course later in their season: asparagus from the middle of May to the middle of June according to the age of the beds, green peas are not in plenty until the middle of July, cabbages and savoys about the middle of August, and new potatoes about the same time.

English gooseberries, black, red, and white currants, grow remarkably well, are large and well flavored, and the bushes produce in greater abundance than I ever saw anywhere else.

Apples, cherries, and plums also grow well, it is probable that the winter is too severe for the finer kinds of stone fruit, but as yet no trials have been made, on which a judgement can be formed. A great many old apple trees left by the French are still alive and bearing, and though it might be seen by them what the climate was capable of producing, it was long after the commencement of the settlement, before any attention was paid to this branch of husbandry: it is chiefly to our late worthy Lt. Gov. General Fanning, that we are indebted for spreading, by his example, a taste for fruit trees, which though not so general as could be wished, is increasing, and enough has been done to shew, that perfect reliance can be placed on our climate, for producing abundance of valuable fruit, when I state that some of our fruit, the natural produce of ungrafted trees is superior to the produce of any trees we have yet imported; fruit gardeners will be able to judge what may be expected from our climate,

As part of the MacDonald Consolidated School program (c. 1908) gardening, household science, and manual training were added to school curiculum in a program sponsored by native Islander Sir William MacDonald, founder of the MacDonald Tobacco Company. Prizes were given for the best school plot and the best home gardens.

(Public Archives of PEI Accession 2755)

under a well-directed system of management. (A Mr. Beers of Cherry Valley, is said to have already five hundred bearing trees.)"

John Stewart 1806

Storing Vegetables

The best vegetables for storing are carrots, parsnips, beets, turnips, potatoes, onion and cabbage.

All bruised and broken vegetables should be rejected. At least an inch and a half of the tops should be left on beets, carrots and turnips. They should be stored in bins or boxes of sand or garden soil and buried on their sides in rows and surrounded with enough sand or soil between, on top, and below, so they will not touch each other, and the soil should be kept slightly moist. Too much moisture causes the vegetables to rot.

Just before the frost comes, tomato vines which contain a good many green tomatoes may be pulled up, roots and all, and hung stem downward in the cellar where they will ripen gradually.

Onions require thoroughly curing and drying, and they must be kept in a cool, dry place.

Potatoes must be picked over and those that are injured, scabby, or touched with rot or frost set aside to use at once. If you have a cement floor, lay a few planks over it and put the potatoes on the planks. Do not pile them too deep. Remember to keep the storage cellar dark; don't let the room get below 32 degrees. Too dry air shrivels the potatoes; too wet air causes them to rot.

The homes of early Canadians had one distinct advantage over the modern ones of today. Basements were cool and most homes had a storage cellar. There is nothing today that can compare to the cool air of the clay cellar which so many Islanders made good use of to store the produce of their labours.

Dried Peas and Beans

Allow the peas or beans to mature on the vines. Be sure they are dry before storing. Spread on plates or pans in the attic or in a sunny room to dry. Stir frequently to prevent molding.

Green peas may be shelled and dried in the same way.

Dried Celery Leaves, Parsley and Other Herbs

Celery tops, parsley, mint, sage, onion tops, pepper and cress are easily dried. Wash them well; drain and wipe off the water; place them on racks and dry very slowly in an oven.

Many other fruits and vegetables can easily be dried; and, of course, today we are able to purchase a great variety in health food stores, natural food and grocery stores.

We have, unfortunately, forgotten the many delicious dishes using these products which used to grace the table.

To Glaze Vegetables

2 tbsp butter
¼ cup brown sugar, packed

1 tbsp liquid, vegetable stock or water
cooked vegetables (to be glazed such as carrots, parsnips or sweet potatoes)

Drain vegetables; blend butter, sugar and water in a heavy frying pan over low heat until the sugar melts. Add the cooked vegetables and cook over low heat, turning several times to coat. Keep the heat low to prevent scorching. Enough for about 3 cups cooked vegetables.

Artichoke

More than three centuries ago, French explorers saw North American Indians eating what resembled a large reddish root. They took some of these roots back to Europe and, with skill and knowledge, it was bred and refined into what we know today as the Jerusalem (or American) artichoke. According to Katherine Tapley in an article which appeared in the Atlantic Advocate, they are easier to grow than potatoes; and Maritime gardeners would find them so hardy that they would grow in almost any kind of soil, and "pieces will sprout even if they are cut up by a tiller or plow."

They should be left in the ground until you wish to cook them. Like parsnips they can be left in the ground all winter and harvested as needed (a thick layer of mulch should be laid on top of them). To prepare for a meal, toss into a bucket full of water, then scrub with a brush. Peeling is unnecessary but can be done if you prefer. Artichoke can be pickled, baked, mashed, juiced, sautéd, boiled, or eaten raw in salads. When ground they can be added to meat loaves or vegetable casseroles.

About Artichoke

— Can be eaten raw—they have a sweet nutty taste and crisp texture but are more usually boiled.
— They are cooked when they can easily be pierced with a knife.
— Store in wet sand in a damp cellar with a temperature around 34°F.
— Do not freeze or they can turn black. They do pickle well.
— Never cook in an iron pan; they will turn black.
— Bake unpeeled, in the drippings of a roast.

Country-Style Artichokes

1 lb Jerusalem artichokes,
washed thoroughly
2 tbsp butter
2 tbsp parsley, chopped
3 green onions, sliced
thyme and rosemary to taste

Boil artichokes for 10 minutes until almost tender. Drain and slice. Fry slices in butter mixed with seasonings. When cooked, top with green onions and parsley.

The above goes very nicely with roast chicken.

Pickled Artichokes

2 qts apple cider vinegar
¼ cup honey
2 tbsp fresh dill
¼ cup white mustard seed
2 tbsp dry mustard
¼ cup salt
2 whole peppercorns
4-6 pieces ginger root (to taste)
4 lbs Jerusalem artichokes

Boil vinegar; remove from heat; add other ingredients except artichokes. Scrub artichokes and slice thin. Pack into sterilized jars and pour cooled pickling mixture over. Seal bottle. Allow it blend its flavour for three weeks before eating.

Asparagus

Asparagus, a member of the lily family has been cultivated for at least 2500 years and been considered as a luxury food for most of that time. What excitement it must have generated among early settlers to find it growing wild on the Island! It has to be one of the most popular harvests, for asparagus is one of the first edibles to be found in spring. Even today it is not any unusual occurrence to see people out walking near roadside fences and wooded areas seeking this wonderful addition to the table.

About Asparagus

— The experts tell us that the size of the stalk has no relationship to tenderness, so whether thick or thin, select firm straight stalks which are fresh looking with closed, compact tips and the greenest color. For easiest cooking select stalks of a uniform size.

— In Europe and some of the "upper crusty" restaurants, one most often sees white asparagus. This is not peeled, but is grown in mounds of mulch, and never exposed to sunlight. Personally, I prefer our home-grown variety.
— Wash and then snap or cut off the white stem end (these can be peeled and sliced into a salad, or used in a soup). You can peel up almost to the tip but it isn't necessary.
— We prefer to lay asparagus spears in a large bamboo steamer. More traditional method is to lay flat in a wide pan and cover with boiling water (only about an inch), a sprinkle of salt and cook covered for 15-20 minutes.
— They may be cooked standing upright by tying with string (or use foil) and standing in a deep pot (a glass coffee percolator works great) with an inch or so of boiling water. Cook them 15-20 minutes, watching that your water doesn't get too low. Do not overcook. Like most vegetables, asparagus is best when crisp and tender. Don't overlook other cooking methods for asparagus; it can be baked, fried, used in soup and sauces and even raw.

Freda's Deep Fried Spears

Prepare this at least one hour before cooking.

Asparagus spears, precooked
Bread crumbs
Parmesan cheese
1 egg, beaten

Roll asparagus spears in dry crumbs which have been mixed with parmesan cheese. Dip in beaten egg, then roll in crumb mixture again. Chill at least one hour then, just before serving, fry in hot fat until golden brown. Drain on paper towels to serve.

Cream of Asparagus Soup

1 lb fresh asparagus, cut into
 one-inch pieces
3½ cups water
3 chicken bouillon cubes
¼ cup butter

¼ cup light cream
¼ cup flour
½ tsp salt
⅛ tsp pepper

Cook asparagus in one cup water mixed with one bouillon cube to make a broth, until tender (12-15 minutes). Melt butter in a deep saucepan. Remove from heat and stir in flour. Add 2 cups broth made with rest of water and bouillon cubes. Cook, stirring until slightly thickened. Stir in cream, seasonings and cooked asparagus with liquid. Heat through and serve. Enough for 6.

Asparagus Marinade

A modern version of an old additional to a cold supper.

½ cup salad oil
1 clove garlic, crushed
½ tsp salt
½ tsp dried leaf tarragon
¼ tsp sugar
¼ tsp minced fresh onion
1/16 tsp pepper
3 tbsp fresh lemon juice
1 tbsp minced cucumber
2 lbs fresh asparagus, cooked
until crisp and chilled

Combine first seven ingredients and let stand at least one hour. Add lemon juice and cucumber. Mix thoroughly. Pour over asparagus and marinate at least one hour. Serve as a vegetable or with salad greens. Serves 6.

Beans

While we often credit Indians with giving us corn, we tend to forget that they gave us another vegetable that is even more widely used today and was a staple of the early settler's diet. That vegetable is, of course, the bean. Not only are beans a native of North America but, by the time the white settler arrived, Indians had developed many varieties and learned how to dry them for long storage. Today we have thousands of varieties of beans, originating in Asia, North and South America.

You will see beans called Haricot, which is a French term, and usually applies to oval white beans from a bush or tall climbing plant.

The most common bean here in early days was the Navy Bean, so named because sailors used to get them from Indians and take them to sea. Filling, easily transported, nourishing and easy to cook, they became almost indispensable to sea goers in the days before refrigeration. These small white round beans are most often found in Boston Baked Beans.

About Beans

— To prepare remove ends of snap beans. According to preference, they can be left whole, cut or snapped into one-inch pieces or "French" cut by cutting into strips lengthwise. Cook in a small amount of water.
— Top hot beans with butter, salt and pepper or with basil, dill or chopped mint.
— Green Bean Amandine can be made by sprinkling slivered toasted almonds over cooked and buttered French cut beans.
— Good raw, chilled in salads or marinated
— Broad beans should be shelled like peas and washed. They are particularly good with ham.

Cooking Dried Beans

The best thing to do here is to follow the directions on the package. If it says soak, then soak for some preservatives should be washed away.

One way to do them is in a pressure cooker. After washing, put beans in pressure cooker and cover them with cold water. Seal; bring to the boil and cook for five minutes. Cool the cooker under the tap; open and drain the beans. Return to cooker with flavouring such as onion, bouquet garni, garlic, etc., and salt. Cover with boiling water; seal and bring up to pressure. Cook 40 minutes.

Fresh Beans

While beans were and are important in their dried form, they are also a very popular fresh vegetable. Green and Yellow "snap" beans, lima beans, broad beans can be eaten fresh, in pickles, etc.

Snap beans are a favourite with gardeners, because they can be harvested for so long from one plant.

Baked Beans from Maine

The lady who gave me this recipe told me it came straight from Maine some 15-20 years ago and was, as far as her daddy knew, as authentic as could be got. He remembered bean pots in the oven and the wonderful aroma that would be released when the lady they stayed with lifted the cover to add more water. To a hungry lad from P.E.I. who had just come in from a hard day in the lumber woods, it was a treat indeed to enjoy Baked Beans with lots of Brown Bread to "sup" up the gravy.

1 lb dry beans (about 2 cups)
2 tbsp granulated sugar
1 tsp salt
sprinkle of black pepper
½ tsp dry mustard
2 tbsp molasses
½ lb salt pork
2½ cups boiling water with
 more on the simmer

Wash the beans and remove any debris or bad ones. Cover with cold water and soak all night. Be sure dish is large as they swell. In the morning drain; place in a bean pot. Mix seasonings together, then pour over beans and stir until coated well. Don't add more molasses for the beans will harden. Add boiling water to cover. Score salt pork by making gashes in it.

Wash pork in hot water, then place on top of the beans. Cover the bean pot and place in the oven set at 250°F where they should cook eight hours. Do not stir, but do check every so often to be sure that they are kept covered with boiling water at all times. The bean pot should be kept covered until the last hour of baking, then remove cover so the beans will brown on top.

Serve with Boston Brown Bread, and for a truly authentic and satisfying Maine meal, Codfish Cakes.

String Bean Pickles

"Wax beans are best for these pickles. Cut off the ends, string and steam over boiling salt water until they are easily pierced with a fork; drain on a cloth and when cold pack in a jar, putting a little red pepper between the layers. Make a spiced vinegar by adding 1 cup of sugar and a teaspoonful each of

white mustard and celery seed to each pint of vinegar. When hot pour this over the beans, weight and let stand for 3 or 4 days in a cool place. Then drain, reheat the vinegar, cover the beans with horseradish leaves, pour on the hot vinegar or syrup, and let stand a week before using. These are fine."

The People's Home Recipe Book
Toronto, 1919

Dilled Beans

1 lb green beans, trimmed
1 cup onion, finely chopped
¾ cup oil
½ cup vinegar
3 tbsp lemon juice
1½ cups liquid from beans
1 tsp salt
1 tbsp dill weed
½ tsp dried mint (or 3 leaves fresh mint)
1 garlic clove

Cook beans until just tender. Drain, reserving 1½ cups liquid. Cool beans thoroughly and add onion. Combine oil, vinegar, lemon juice and the juice from the beans. Pour over beans. Sprinkle with salt, dill and mint and add the whole garlic clove. Toss; cover and let stand 24 hours at room temperature. Place beans in a one-quart mason jar; pour liquid over top and seal. May be stored in refrigerator up to one month.

Broad Beans

3 lbs broad beans, unshelled
¼ cup butter
1 onion, chopped
1 tsp marjoram, crumbled
salt and pepper to taste

Shell the beans. Melt butter in saucepan; add the onion; stir until transparent. Add the beans, marjoram and just enough water to cover. Cook for about 20 minutes until beans are tender. Drain, saving the liquid, and put the beans in a warm oven. Return the liquid to the pan; reduce to about ½ cup and season to taste. Pour over the beans and serve. Serves 4.

Beets

One of nature's most efficient vegetables. It is easy to grow and the whole thing is edible. In our family Jack, my husband, eats the tops, steamed or boiled with a pat of butter, while I boil up the bottoms for a hot vegetable with dinner or to slice into cider or malt vinegar to eat cold. Done this way they will keep for months in the refrigerator. Each fall I usually do up a couple of large jars to enjoy during the winter. The usual way to pickle beets is with a recipe like the one following. I, however, prefer them without the sugar or spices.

About Beets

- Hot—top with butter and lemon juice, or cook very small beets with tops on for an early "beet and green" vegetable.
- Cold—dice cooked beets and stir in your favourite mayonnaise or salad dressing to serve with cold meats; pickle in a mild or spicy vinegar solution.
- When cooking beet roots, do everything you can to stop them bleeding (see cooking directions below).
- The red juice can be used as dye and, before food coloring was even used, to color icing. For that purpose, grate beets raw; soak in lemon juice, and squeeze the juice out in a cloth. If the juice is extracted in this way, then concentrated by boiling (not too long or it will turn brown), its earthy taste is not noticed.
- Raw beets have a pleasant nutty taste.
- Beets go well with allspice, cloves, caraway, mustard, horseradish, celery, onion, chives, garlic and capers.
- For a simple salad toss them with an olive oil and vinegar dressing.
- To store beet root, put them in a box, right way up, and cover them with dry sand, soil or peat. They must be kept dry or they will sprout or become mildewed.

Spiced Beets as Nanny did Them

3 qts small beets
1 pt vinegar (cider preferred)
2 cups granulated sugar
3 tsp ground allspice
12 whole cloves

Boil beets until tender and then peel in cold water. As fast as beets are peeled, drop them into hot sterilized jars. Combine vinegar and sugar and boil three minutes. Into each pint jar of beets put ½ teaspoon allspice and 4 whole cloves. Pour in boiling vinegar and seal. Store in a cool place.

Note: When preparing beet roots to boil leave about two inches of stem and the root intact. Wash, but do not scrub to puncture the skin. This will stop your beets from bleeding all of their rich red color into the boiling water. When they are done (test with a sharp knife) drain and cover with cold water. When cool enough to handle, just push your thumb against the stem and the stalks and skin will just come away. Trim off the thin root.

Beet 'N Cheddar

A favourite sandwich — Toast dark bread, butter and place cheddar cheese and sliced beets on. You can eat as an open-faced sandwich and broil the cheese or have two slices of bread.

Harvard Beets

2 tbsp sugar
1 tbsp cornstarch
½ tsp salt
2 cups cooked beets, diced
(canned or fresh)
3 tbsp cider vinegar
2 tbsp butter
¾ cup liquid from cooking
beets or drained from canned
(add water to bring up to
¾ cup)

Mix sugar, cornstarch and salt in saucepan, then stir in liquid and vinegar. Bring to boil, stirring constantly. Add beets and butter; bring to boiling, stirring gently. Simmer 8 to 10 minutes and serve in a hot dish.

Beet Greens

Tender young beet greens can be boiled or steamed in the same manner as spinach or swiss chard.

Beet Salad

Since beets bleed, you must consider what you mix them with in a salad—for appearance sake.

2 lbs beets, cooked and sliced
1 large onion, cut in rings
½ cup vinegar
1 tbsp granulated sugar
1 bay leaf
4 peppercorns
2 whole cloves
½ tsp salt
½ tsp caraway seeds (optional)

Place beets and onion rings in a deep salad bowl. In a saucepan, bring the vinegar, water, sugar, bay leaf, peppercorns, cloves, salt and caraway seeds to a boil. When just to boiling, pour this marinade over the beets and onions. Let cool and refrigerate until ready to use. Serves 4.

Broccoli

Although broccoli is one of the oldest known vegetables and is known to have been eaten by Greeks and Romans more than 2000 years ago, it seems to be a relatively newcomer to the Island. Since it is my own favourite vegetable and held in such high esteem for its benefits to one's health, we have included broccoli as an important addition to the vegetable section.

Broccoli, unfortunately, is often looked at with a negative eye, because it used to be a favourite hiding place for a "worm" which was large (up to an inch and a half in my own experience) and almost perfectly hidden in the flowerettes. When cooked they turn white but cling to the vegetable and would often get as far as someone's plate without detection. Today we seldom find such unwanted guests in broccoli purchased from a super market, but they do occasionally crop up in vegetables purchased from farmers' markets, roadside stands or that from your own garden.

The solution to these little critters is to soak your broccoli for several hours in heavily salted cold water. They will usually float to the top. If you have any concern at all, simply check your flowerettes as you remove them from the water and remove any you find.

About Broccoli

— Broccoli should have compact, firm and dark green or purplish heads with tightly closed buds. If the buds are yellow, if flowers are present or if the stem is limp or hard, select another bunch. The best way to tell good broccoli is by smell, it should be fresh, earthy and distinctive, no strong pungent odor.
— To prepare broccoli for cooking, cut heads into evenly sliced flowerettes, checking for insect pests. Stems can be sliced and cooked along with heads. If they seem tough, peel them and use just the inside either sliced across or lengthwise. Soak in salted water for at least an hour if desired.
— Broccoli can be steamed, boiled, added to soups and stews, eaten raw or added to a quiche or casserole. I often drop large spears over the top of a roasting chicken for the last half hour, and it steams quite nicely for a one-pot meal.
— Left-over cooked broccoli is nice used as a bed for creamed poultry or fish dishes, served chilled with oil and vinegar or pureed and stirred into sour cream and chopped chives to serve as a topping over baked potatoes or cooked fresh vegetables.
— We particularly enjoy steamed broccoli with Hollandaise or cheese sauce.

Broccoli and Ham Strata

1 lb cooked ham, chop fine
1 bunch fresh broccoli, chopped
 to make four cups
½ cup onion, chopped
3 cups, cheddar cheese,
 shredded
6 slices bread, crusts removed
6 eggs
½ tsp dry mustard
1 tsp Worcestershire sauce
3 cups milk

Mix together ham, broccoli, onion and two cups shredded cheese. Butter a 3-quart baking dish. Place trimmed bread on bottom, then spoon the preceding mixture over. Beat eggs with the mustard, Worcestershire sauce and milk; pour over all and sprinkle with the remaining cup of cheese. Let stand 10 minutes before baking. Place baking dish in a pan of hot water, and bake at 375°F for 50 minutes or until a knife inserted in center comes out clean. Let stand 5 minutes before serving. Serves 6-8.

Piquant Broccoli

1½ lb broccoli, cooked
3 bacon slices, diced
1 clove garlic, crushed
¼ cup vinegar

While broccoli is cooking, pan fry bacon with garlic until crisp. Drain off excess fat; add vinegar and heat. Pour over cooked broccoli just before serving. Serves 6.

Broccoli on Toast

1 bunch broccoli
6 slices toast
1 tsp onion, finely chopped
2 hard-cooked eggs, minced
2 cups white sauce

Wash broccoli and scrape the stems lightly if they are not young and tender. Then cook until tender. Cut into individual portions and arrange on toast. Meanwhile, add the chopped onion and minced eggs to the white sauce and pour over the broccoli. Serve as a main dish. Serves 6.

dated 1930

Brussel Sprouts

This member of the cabbage family which gives us perfect miniature cabbages has long been a favourite with gardeners and cooks alike, because it matures late in the year and is actually better if it gets a few frosts before it is harvested. Many of the modern varieties do not need frost to sweeten the sprouts as used to be believed.

About Brussel Sprouts

— To prepare, trim stems and outer leaves. Cut a cross in the bottom to facilitate quicker cooking inside.
— Because of the possibility of insects lurking in the tight leaves,

soak sprouts for at least 15 minutes covered in water to which you have added at least 2 tbsp salt.

— Top with butter and one of the following: dill seed, thyme, crushed garlic, caraway seed.
— Brussels are nice added to a stew as long as your family likes their fairly strong flavour.
— In our family, left-over brussels were added to Bubble and Squeak or warmed in gravy, along with roast beef and other vegetables.
— If your brussels taste too strong, try adding a few sprigs of parsley to the cooking water; it is said to mellow their taste, as well as cooking odours.

Tangy Brussel Sprouts

2 cups brussels of uniform size
¼ cup butter, melted
2 tbsp lemon juice

Boil sprouts in one inch of water or steam until tender crisp, about 10 minutes. Combine butter and lemon juice; pour over drained sprouts. Serves 4.

Sprout Fritters

Brussel sprouts are delicious when made into fritters, served either with meat and potatoes or by themselves, well seasoned. The batter should be made of three and a half tablespoons of flour, a dessertspoonful of salad oil, quarter-pint of warm water, and an egg white (the latter should be stirred into the mixture after it has stood for an hour). The sprouts should be cooked in boiling water for 15 minutes before dipping in the batter and dropped in boiling fat.

Oct. 23, 1937
A clipping from the
Liverpool Weekly Post

Marinated Brussels

3 cups cooked sprouts
2 tbsp thinly sliced green onion
tops

½ cup vinegar
½ cup oil
1 small garlic clove, minced
1 tsp salt
dash Tabasco sauce

Combine last five ingredients well, then pour over brussels and onion. Mix all well together; cover; chill overnight and serve the next day.

Cabbage

Probably the most frequently used method of eating cabbage is in boiled dinners and cole slaw. Cabbage Rolls, a favourite today, were never found in early writings, however, the following methods of cooking cabbage were.

About Cabbage

- Stuff cabbage leaves with meat and/or vegetable fillings and cook in tomato sauce. Choose a loose-leaf cabbage.
- Solid core cabbage will keep 4-5 months stored in a humid basement at a temperature just above freezing, however, a strong odour can come from cabbage as they get older. Layer in wet sand to prevent.
- Overcooking causes the strong cooking odours associated with cabbage. And, turns cabbage mushy. Do not overcook.

Bubble and Squeak

In my early days Bubble and Squeak was the name given to left-over potatoes and vegetables that were browned in butter. In our house that usually meant potatoes and brussel sprouts along with other vegetables. We usually ate it with cold slices of the roast from the day before. The following recipe is a little more fancy—and delicious.

1 head of cabbage, shredded
2 large potatoes, boiled and cubed
2 cups grated sharp cheddar cheese
¼ tsp ground marjoram

½ tsp minced chives
2 tbsp butter or margarine
salt and pepper to taste

Melt the butter in a large cast-iron skillet over a medium-high heat; add the vegetables and spices. Stir until it squeaks; add the cheese and stir until it bubbles. Serves four.

Sauerkraut by the Jar

The old way of making sauerkraut was in crocks, a method which is not usually practical for today's homemaker. This recipe is more modern but gives the same tasty 'kraut'.

5 lbs green cabbage (about 2
medium heads—choose firm
mature heads)
3 tbsp coarse salt

Remove the outer leaves and any undesirable portions from the cabbage; wash and drain. Shred the cabbage (use a shredder or sharp knife) into thin shreds about as thick as a dime. In a large bowl thoroughly mix salt and cabbage. Allow to stand for several minutes to wilt slightly. This allows packing without excessive breaking or bruising of the shreds.

Pack salted cabbage firmly and evenly into clean quart mason jars, using a wooden spoon or hands. Press down firmly until the juice comes to the surface. Place cabbage to just below shoulders of the jar. Cover with a pad of cheesecloth, and to hold the cabbage under the brine during fermentation, cut wooden stir sticks into 2-inch pieces to fit crisscrossed under the shoulders of the jar.

Cover the jar with the metal lid and screw band and place jars on a tray and leave at a temperature of 68°-72°F to ferment. Fermentation is usually completed from 2-6 weeks. Formation of gas bubbles indicates fermentation is taking place. When fermentation is complete, store jars of sauerkraut in refrigerator until ready to use.

Fermentation may cause brine to overflow jar—keep jar and tray clean by wiping if necessary. Makes 2-3 quarts.

Cooking Sauerkraut

Simply heat in a saucepan. Good served with sausage, corned beef, etc. To eliminate the odour, try adding a celery stalk cut into pieces. Also nice if you drain well and fry up in a little butter.

Carrots

The garden carrot is said to be one of the most important root vegetables in the world and has been cultivated for several thousand years. With its tremendous adaptability to all manner of cooking methods and its easy storage, it is no wonder it is so loved by cooks.

There is nothing as nice as those tender young baby carrots which can be harvested over several weeks from the garden. Whether raw or cooked they are superb.

Carrots contain more sugar than any other vegetable except beets and can be made into jam, used in desserts or to make those delicious carrot cakes which have become so popular.

In days past homemakers used root vegetables such as carrots, potatoes and turnip to stretch meat loaves, meat pies and such. Cooked mashed carrots will naturally thicken a sauce or left-over gravy.

About Carrots

- Top cooked carrots with parsley or chives and butter.
- To make carrot curl garnishes cut long, paper thin slices of carrot, using a vegetable peeler. Roll each slice around your finger and fasten with a toothpick. Remove toothpick just before serving.
- Place carrots around a roast to cook, and use to garnish the platter when serving. Delicious. Also add carrots to stew for colour and flavour.
- Carrot can be used half and half with cabbage when making slaw. Or for a carrot and raisin slaw, mix 6 cups grated carrot, 1 cup raisins, ⅔ cup mayonnaise, 1½ tbsp white vinegar, 1½ tsp sugar and a sprinkling of pepper. Combine well together in a glass bowl. Refrigerate for several hours. You can adjust the sugar and vinegar to taste.
- Mash carrots with a little butter and pepper. Add cream if you like and keep hot in oven to serve. Combine mashed carrots with mashed potatoes and garnish with chives for a traditional look for your table.
- Steam carrots over water to which you have added a little rosemary or cinnamon.
- Julienne and blanch carrots for a garnish in soups, etc.
- Briefly blanch carrots, then marinate for a quick pickle or appetizer dish.

— Finely grate carrots; marinate in lemon juice with lots of black pepper sprinkled over.

Carrots à la Hollandaise

2 carrots
4 white turnips (These are smaller than the usual turnip we find in stores—ask for them as they are not as common as they used to be.)
parsley
Hollandaise Sauce (see index)

Clean; scrape the carrots and cut in dice. Throw them into boiling water and cook slowly until tender. Pare the turnips; cut a slice from the stem; scoop out the center, leaving a cup. Put into plenty of unsalted boiling water and simmer until tender. When tender lift the turnips from the water and drain. Drain the carrots; mix with the Hollandaise Sauce. Fill these in the turnip cups; garnish with parsley and serve.

Carrots are very nice cooked with peas; or cook plain and season with one tablespoon of butter, one of flour and a teaspoon of Kitchen Bouquet.

Honey'd Carrots

8 medium carrots, peeled and sliced
3 tbsp butter
2 tbsp honey
¼ tsp salt
pinch cinnamon
pinch nutmeg

Cook carrots in a small amount of boiling water until tender crisp. Drain. Add butter, honey, salt, cinnamon and nutmeg. Cook over low heat, stirring until sauce thickens and carrots are coated. Serves 6.

Carrot Jam to imitate Apricot Preserve

A very old recipe—showing the adaptability of the 1800's homemaker.

Carrots: to every pound of carrot pulp allow 1 pound of pounded sugar, the grated rind of 1 lemon, the strained juice of 2 (lemons), 6 chopped bitter almonds, 2 tablespoonfuls brandy.

Mode: Select young carrots; wash and scrape them clean; cut them into round pieces; put them into a saucepan with sufficient water to cover the, and let them simmer until perfectly soft, then beat them through a sieve. Weigh the pulp, and to every pound allow the above ingredients. Put the pulp into a preserving pan with the sugar, and let this boil for 5 minutes, stirring and skimming all the time. When cold, add the lemon rind and juice, almonds and brandy; mix these well with the jam, then put it into pots, which must be well covered and kept in a dry place. The brandy may be omitted, but the preserve will then not keep; with the brandy it will remain good for months.

Candied Carrot

Carrot cakes, breads and other desserts can be topped with candied carrot made by heating together ⅓ cup sugar, 1 cup apple cider and 1 cup shredded carrot. Cook over low heat until liquid is reduced and barely covers the carrots. Cool in the liquid; drain and use as a decoration.

Cauliflower

No one seems to know when cauliflower arrived in P.E.I., although as it has been cultivated in Britain since the 18th century, it seems certain that people knew of it even if they found it difficult to grow. Similar to broccoli, except in color, the cauliflower can have a snowy white head. (By tying the long outer leaves up over the head, it can be blanched to a pure white favoured by many cooks for its lovely presentation at the table); or be a cream color. There is also a purple variety; those goes pale green when cooked.

About Cauliflower

— Cook until just barely tender for best flavour and nutrition.

— Excellent served with sauces, hot or cold, especially cheese or Hollandaise.

— In days gone by, people who could not drink milk were often given pureed cauliflower. Today we know that the wise folk were doing the right thing (as they so often did without the benefits of our new technology) for cauliflower contains calcium and iron!

- Cook in a small amount of water or steam. Serve with butter and basil, parsley, rosemary or thyme.
- Superb raw with a dip or in a salad.
- To keep cauliflower white while cooking, try adding a little milk to the cooking liquid.
- Choose heads that look and feel fresh and firm. Avoid those with brown spots or wilted leaves. They will store about two weeks if wrapper leaves are left off. To prepare for cooking, leave whole, cutting out the core, or cut into florets. To remove any insects that may be present, soak for 15 minutes in a quart of water with two tablespoons salt. Rinse.
- Do be careful not to overcook—it can go mushy, become dark and strong flavoured.

Cauliflower and Tomato Casserole

1 cauliflower, about 1½ pounds
6 slices bacon
¼ cup bacon drippings
1½ cups soft bread crumbs
3 medium tomatoes, cut in eighths
2 tbsp green onion, chopped
¼ tsp oregano
¼ tsp salt
dash pepper

Separate cauliflower into florets. Cook until just tender and drain. Pan fry bacon until crisp; drain reserving ¼ cup drippings. Crumble bacon. Toss bacon, bread crumbs and drippings together. Combine tomatoes, onion, seasonings and cauliflower in a greased 6-cup baking dish. Top with crumb mixture. Cover and bake 10 minutes at 400°F. Uncover and continue baking until cauliflower is tender and topping is lightly browned, about 5 minutes more. Serves 6.

Celeriac

Celeriac used to be a fairly common vegetable. Also known as turnip-root celery, celery root or celery knob it has a concentrated celery flavour that some find bitter. It is frankly quite ugly, with a hairy root. On the plus side it is much easier to grow than celery.

In England during World War II, celeriac was widely cultivated because it was less trouble than regular celery, would grow in shallow or stubborn soil, and could be stored for winter use. During the past winter I actually saw celeriac in the stores, proving that it is indeed still with us.

- The most common way to serve celeriac was to peel the root, slice into strips, boil it up and serve with a white or cream sauce.
- Cut into small cubes and sauté.
- Wash small roots; drop in a saucepan of boiling water and boil gently until tender. It will take an hour or more depending on size. Cool and peel. This cooked celeriac can then be sliced, layered in a buttered dish with tomato sauce and parmesan cheese, ending with a cheese layer and baked in a preheated 350°F oven for half an hour.

Celeriac Hot Pot

1 pound stewing steak, cubed
1 oz seasoned flour
3-4 tbsp dripping
1 medium onion, sliced
¾ pt beef stock
2 sticks celery, chopped
2 potatoes, peeled and cut into chunks
salt and pepper to taste
7 oz can sweet corn
¼ lb mushrooms, chopped
1 medium celeriac, peeled and sliced thinly
good pinch mixed dried herbs
1 oz butter

Toss the steak in the flour. Heat fat and fry meat a little at a time to brown. Remove with draining spoon and transfer to casserole. Add onion to pan and cook until softened. Add stock and stir well to loosen sediment at bottom of pan. Pour over meat in casserole and add celery, potatoes and seasoning. Cover with lid and cook 1½ hours at 350°F. Remove from oven and stir in sweet corn and mushrooms. Top with celeriac (lay thin slices on top in a petal pattern), sprinkle with herbs and dot with the butter. Return to oven to cook for a further 45 minutes or until celeriac is cooked through and golden.

Celery

"With a good heart, and nicely blanched, this vegetable is generally eaten raw and is usually served with the cheese. Let the roots be washed free from dirt, all the decayed and outside leaves being cut off, preserving as much of the stalk as possible and all specks or blemishes being carefully removed. Should the celery be large, divide it lengthwise into quarters, and place it root downwards in a celery glass, which should be rather more than half filled with water. The top leaves may be curled, by shredding them in narrow strips with the point of a clean skewer, at a distance of about 4 inches from the top.

This vegetable is exceedingly useful for flavoring soups, sauces, &c., and makes a very nice addition to winter salad."

Isabella Beeton

Today, with improved cultivation techniques we do not need to blanch celery to enjoy it; in fact, we tend to overlook celery as a cooked vegetable as it is so enjoyed raw.

Celery Meat Loaf

1 cup soft bread crumbs
⅔ cup milk
2 tbsp butter
¼ cup chopped fresh onion
1 cup finely chopped celery
1 ½ lbs ground beef
1 tbsp Worcestershire sauce
2 tbsp prepared mustard
1 tsp prepared horseradish
½ tsp salt
½ tsp dried leaf thyme
2 tbsp chopped celery leaves
1 egg

Soak crumbs in milk in large bowl. Melt butter in large skillet; add onion and celery; cook until tender. Add to bread crumbs. Add remaining ingredients and mix well. Pack in a loaf pan. Bake at 350°F for one hour. Let stand 5-10 minutes. Turn out on platter and garnish with Sautéed Celery (see following). Serves 6.

Sautéed celery

Melt 3 tbsp butter in skillet; add 2 cups sliced celery; sprinkle with salt and cook about 5 minutes, until tender crisp.

Braised Celery

4 cups celery, diagonally sliced
1 tbsp butter
½ tsp salt
1 cup beef bouillon
1 tbsp cornstarch
1 tbsp water

Sauté celery in butter 1 to 2 minutes. Sprinkle with salt and add bouillon. Cover and cook gently until just tender, about 10 minutes. Remove celery from pan. Combine cornstarch and water; add to pan. Stir and cook until thick and clear. Return celery to pan and heat through. Serves 6.

Carrot and Celery Casserole

3 cups carrots, diagonally sliced
2 cups celery, diagonally sliced
¼ cup butter, melted
1 tsp sugar
1 tsp salt
pinch pepper
¼ cup water
1 tbsp chopped parsley

Combine carrots and celery in lightly greased 6-cup casserole. Add half the butter, the sugar, salt, pepper and water; mix well. Cover and bake in 350°F oven for 45 minutes, or until vegetables are tender. Drain off any liquid. Add rest of butter; toss. Sprinkle with parsley. Serves 4-6.

Corn

According to radio-carbon dating of remains found in caves, corn has been cultivated in North and South America for 3,000 years. It was often called maize, or mais by the French. In some European countries the name corn applies to other grains. The Scots for instance called oats corn, while the English referred to wheat. Because of this confusion, it is hard to know whether some early Island accounts are referring to sweet corn or a grain.

We do know that many of the early dwellers ate hominy. Made from hulled corn, it was one of the staples of the Indian diet and was adopted by pioneers. Taking its name from the Algonquin language (rockahominy), it was originally made by soaking and boiling corn in wood lye (ashes and water) until the outer skin of the grain could be rubbed off. It was used as a starchy food instead of potatoes. Today, in the form of grits it is most common in the southern states; however, hominy can still be purchased in cans in Charlottetown shops.

About Corn

- Look for creamy, plump, not firm kernels; dry silks, still attached.
- Removed from the cob, it is excellent in casseroles, soups, chowders or scrambled eggs.
- Serve corn niblets with butter, cream and seasoning. It can also be mixed with a good white sauce, set in buttered scallop shells and lightly browned in the oven.
- to make creamed corn scrap kernels from cob, sauté, then add cream and reduce to a thick creamy mixture.
- When removing corn from the cob, you must cut with a sharp knife if you want whole kernels (or niblets). When scraping, you will get the juices and the inner flesh with much of the skin left on the cob. If putting into a chowder, this "scraped" corn is good because the milky flesh acts to thicken it.

Hominy

How to make lye hominy: Dissolve 2 to 3 ounces or tablespoonfuls of concentrated lye or caustic soda in each gallon hot water used. Soak hard, white corn in lukewarm water for 30 minutes, then drain. Boil in lye solution long enough to loosen hulls, about 30 minutes and drain. Wash thoroughly in fresh cold water. Rub to loosen hull and dark portion of the kernel near germ. Let stand in fresh water for 3 hours, changing water occasionally. At this stage it was canned.

Those who do not wish to make hominy may purchase it from the grocer. Wash and soak overnight in cold water. Several things could then be done with hominy such as the following:

Cracked Hominy

2 cupfuls cracked hominy
6 cupfuls boiling water
2 teaspoonfuls salt
1 tbsp lemon juice or vinegar

Wash and soak hominy overnight in 1 quart warm water. Drain. Put in pan, with boiling water, salt and lemon juice. Cook 60 minutes at 15 pounds pressure in a pressure cooker. Drain; blanch and serve hot.

Hominy with Carrots

3 cupfuls cooked hominy
1 cupful cooked diced carrots
½ cupful grated cheese
½ teaspoon salt

Mix hominy and carrots in a baking pan; add salt. Cover with cheese; place on rack in pressure cooker and steam 15 minutes at 10 pounds pressure. Serves 6.

Hominy with Cheese

3 cupfuls cooked hominy
1 cupful grated cheese
½ cupful cream or top milk
½ teaspoonful salt
⅛ teaspoonful pepper
⅛ teaspoonful paprika

Put hominy in buttered baking dish with seasoning and cream. Cover with cheese and steam in pressure cooker 30 minutes at 10 pounds pressure. Serves 6.

Cream Corn Chowder

In my search for recipes for this book, I heard often that pea soup and corn chowder were favourites during the winter. A friend found this recipe which substitutes cream-style corn for a corn pulp originally used. She said this is from Ontario but tasted much like what her mother used to make. If you wish to be more authentic, try blending corn in a blender to make the required amount.

2 large potatoes peeled and cubed (you should have about 2-2½ cups cubed)
1 onion, chopped
2 cups water
2½ cups corn (creamed or blended)
1 cup milk
1 tbsp butter
salt and pepper to taste

Cook the potatoes in boiling water five minutes; add onion and cook another five minutes, then add milk, corn and seasonings and heat through. When potato is tender, serve.

Clam 'n Corn Chowder

A variation of an early chowder which was traditionally served with hot Johnny Cake.

2 medium, or one large onion, chopped
2 tbsp butter
1¼ cups chicken broth
2 cups potatoes, diced
1 bay leaf
¼ tsp celery salt
2 cans (approx. 7 oz) minced clams
1 can (16-oz) creamed corn
2 cups milk
salt and pepper to taste

Using a large chowder pot which will hold at least 3 quarts, sauté onions in butter until soft, but not brown. Add broth, potatoes, seasonings and clams. Cook covered about 15 minutes, until potatoes are cooked. Add corn and milk and heat. A richer soup can be made by using a mixture of cream and milk. Enough for about 8.

Note: If using fresh clams, steam, then chop or mince enough for two cups.

Creamed Corn Sausage Hot Pot

I have no idea when canned creamed corn became available in shops but, whenever it did, it seems it became an instant hit, especially when used in dishes like these casseroles.

1½ lbs sausages, browned and drained
2 onions, sliced in rings
2½ cups creamed corn
1 tbsp flour
½ cup milk
1 cup bread crumbs

Fry the onion rings in sausage fat until lightly browned. Layer sausage then onion in an oven-proof dish. Measure out 2 tbsp sausage drippings and set aside the rest. Add flour to measured drippings and cook briefly over medium heat (not more than a minute). Add the milk, stirring until thick and smooth. Combine with the corn, then pour all over the sausages. The original recipe calls for mixing the bread crumbs lightly with some of the remaining dripping, however, I find it too fatty and prefer butter. Sprinkle over top of mixture in dish and bake at 350°F for half an hour.

Carol's Corn Casserole

So often the simplest of dishes are the ones the family loves best. This easy-to-make casserole is even better the next day.

potatoes, enough for family
1 lb ground beef
2 large cans cream corn
milk
onions to taste
salt and pepper

Peel potatoes and slice as for scalloped potatoes then precook by boiling for 10 minutes. Cook the hamburger and drain fat off. In a large pan or dutch oven layer ingredients starting with potato in bottom, then hamburger, onion, salt, pepper and creamed corn. Repeat. Pack around the edges and then add milk till it comes just to the top (no more than one cup). Bake at 350°F one to one and a half hours. Leftovers can be warmed the next day and will be even better. Serves 6.

Skillet Corn

3 cups corn kernels
6 slices of bacon
1/3 cup chopped green peppers
1/3 cup chopped onion
1 tsp salt
dash pepper
green pepper

Cut raw kernels from cob. Pan fry bacon until crisp. Remove from pan; drain and crumble. Add corn, green pepper rings and onion to drippings. Cover and cool gently until tender (no more than 10 minutes). Season with salt and pepper. Garnish with crumbled bacon and green pepper rings. Serves 6.

Cucumbers

Cucumbers, or cukes, have been around for 4,000 years. They were transported to the Americans in 1494 when Columbus called on Haiti and soon spread to the mainland. They were so liked by the Indians that they were soon being grown all over North America.

About Cucumber

— When buying cucumbers always look for young firm ones. Older ones will have big seeds and tend to be more watery.
— Older cucumbers can be stuffed. Cut in half lengthwise and scrape the seeds out with a spoon. The 'boat' you have left is excellent for filling with such things as chicken salad, pureed or mashed vegetables, any colourful salad, meat, fish or creamed item. They are best peeled because skins on older, larger cukes can be tough.
— Today's cucumber is rarely bitter, but if you think it may be, score the peel with a fork or follow the old method and salt sliced cucumber by sprinkling generously with salt, let them sit a minute, then tip onto a cloth (or paper towel) and squeeze the moisture out. This also gives a drier vegetable for salad.
— Cucumber is too often forgotten when it comes to sandwiches. Sliced thin, on thin homemade or specialty bread, it is delicious. Try it with cheese, mayonnaise, onion, watercress, etc.

— Because cucumber is so good in salads, pickles and such, we forget that it is an excellent cooked vegetable. Sauté slices or grated (and drained) cucumber in butter; parboil, then sprinkle with sugar and chopped chives as they sauté; blanch in boiling water 3-5 minutes for quarters or 7-8 minutes for halves; steam. They cook rather quickly. Serve with a white (or other sauce); toss with dill, chives or salt and pepper.
— Cooked cucumber is excellent with fish.

Boiled Cucumbers

Select good-sized cucumbers and pare them; cut in halves; scoop out the seeds, then cut each in two crosswise. Throw these into boiling salted water until tender, about thirty minutes; drain. Lift into a hot serving dish and pour over a white sauce, seasoned with grated onion and chopped parsley. Hollandaise Sauce is also good with these cucumbers.

Braised Cukes with Onion

2 large cucumbers, sliced thick
3 tbsp green onion, sliced
¼ cup butter
1 tsp salt
pinch black pepper

In skillet sauté green onion in butter. Add cucumbers and seasonings. Cover and heat quickly to form steam, then reduce heat and cook gently until cucumbers are tender crisp (about 3 minutes). Stir frequently to prevent sticking. Serve immediately. Serves 6.

Cucumber Vinegar

Very useful for salads, especially when cucumbers are out of season, or not to be had when wanted.

Take as many cucumbers as required, and to each one allow one shallot. Wipe the cucumbers; slice them up, but do not peel, then put them into wide-mouthed bottles, adding the shallot to each in proportion, also a teaspoon of white pepper, one of salt and a clove of garlic (allow these quantities to every quart of vinegar used). Let the whole be covered with cold vinegar, and leave for a fortnight (2 weeks). Strain into bottles and cork tightly.

Grandmother's recipe

No-fail Mustard Relish

Sauce:
1 cup flour
6 cups white sugar
5 cups white vinegar
4 tbsp turmeric
2 tbsp mustard (powder)
2 tsp ginger
3½ cups water

Vegetables:
2 large celery stalks, chopped fine
16 cucumbers, chopped fine
2 red peppers, chopped fine
2 green peppers, chopped fine

Put vinegar in large-size pot and heat until it steams. Thoroughly mix all other ingredients in sauce and gradually add to vinegar, stirring well; cook 20-25 minutes until thickened.

Add vegetables and cook over low heat about 1 hour. Cut vegetables up previous night and sprinkle with salt (scant cup). Squeeze vegetables well before putting in sauce.

Bottle in prepared jars, by approved methods.

Helen's Sweet Sliced Pickles

Bread and butter pickles — very crisp.

2 gallons cukes
14 small white onions
5 large onions
4 large red peppers (optional)
half head cauliflower, in small flowerets (optional)
¾ cup coarse salt

Slice cukes in ⅛-inch slices without paring. Slice onions likewise, but peppers and cauliflower in fine bits. Mix salt and all vegetables. Let stand three hours. Drain and add:

10 cups white sugar
1 tbsp turmeric
1 tsp celery seed

¼ cup mustard seed
2½ qts vinegar (buy strong
pickling vinegar)

Combine above and place over low heat. Heat thoroughly, but do not boil; stir often. Pack into sterilized jars and seal. Store in a cool place.

India Relish

This is a good way to use up green tomatoes—but be warned its a long job! You can make it easier with a food processor.

3 lbs green tomatoes
3 lbs cucumbers
3 tbsp salt
3 cups cabbage, finely chopped
2-3 medium onions
3-4 large green peppers
3 hot red peppers
2½ cups sugar
3 cups cider vinegar
⅓ cup white mustard seed
1 tbsp celery seed
½ tsp turmeric
¼ tsp ground mace
½ tsp ground cinnamon

Wash tomatoes and cucumbers thoroughly. Stem and remove blossom ends. Cut into quarters. Put cucumbers through food chopper, using the coarse knife. Then put tomatoes through food chopper, but let them drop into a separate bowl. Stir half the salt into each bowl of vegetables. Invert a small plate on top of each; press down firmly. Weight plate to hold it down. A small jar filled with water makes a good weight. Let stand overnight. Next morning, turn each vegetable separately into a colander. Press down firmly with hand to force out brine.

Combine drained vegetables. Shred cabbage very fine, then cut across the shreds. Peel onions and quarter. Wash peppers; remove stems and seeds. Divide membranes from green peppers. Put onions and peppers through a food chopper separately. Measure each; there should be 1½ cups chopped onion and 2 cups chopped green pepper. Mix all vegetables. Place over low heat and slowly bring to simmering point. Stir gently from time to time. When vegetables are tender, add sugar, vinegar and spices. Reheat just to boiling point. Pack into hot, sterile jars. Leave one-half inch head space. Clean jar rims. Seal immediately.

Fiddleheads

Both Micmac Indians and early settlers refer to eating young ferns, often calling them the first greens of spring. Today we know them as fiddleheads, so named for their resemblance to a part of the fiddle. The early growth of the Ostrich Fern, Fiddleheads grow abundantly along many North American rivers and now are harvested and available in grocery stores.

About Fiddleheads

- To pick them you must get out in early spring and look for the fronds poking through the earth. The season is short, and they very quickly uncurl and grown into tall, graceful ferns.
- Fiddleheads can be treated as any vegetable and served with meat, fish or poultry. Try them with a cheese or Hollandaise sauce.
- First trim the brownish ends with a sharp knife; wash in cold water several times briskly swishing them around to loosen any loose particles. Drop into briskly boiling water (about three cups per pound) and simmer until cooked. The amount of cooking times depends on how you like vegetables. In our family we prefer them still crunchy so 5-10 minutes is plenty. You may prefer to leave them for 12-15 minutes—try one. Drain and serve with butter, salt and pepper or a few drops of vinegar, or a sauce.

A Taste of Spring

Should you really want to experience life as early Island dwellers would have, take time off on a spring day to head out to your favourite spot in the woods (with a fishing license in hand of course). Hopefully, you will be lucky enough to catch a trout or two and collect a bag of fiddleheads as you walk along the banks of your favourite stream. The two were often enjoyed together—a true sign of springs arrival. Pan fry the trout; drop the fiddleheads into boiling water for three minutes only. Drain. They will be crunchy, but cooked. Dot all with butter and a sprinkle of pepper. To be really authentic—do it all over a campfire.

Horseradish

A peppery taproot which originated in Europe and now grows wild in North America cultivated for its flavour.

About Horseradish

- Scrub root clean and cut off any discoloured parts, then grate fine, or scrape, discarding root.
- Mix with mayonnaise to go with fish or salad.
- Grated horseradish does not retain its pungency for long, however, commercially dried fares better than bottled sauces.
- Sliced horseradish can be dried in the oven at a very low temperature.
- Goes well with chicken and eggs as well as the traditional beef and fish.

Horseradish Sauce (serve cold)

a root of horseradish
1 gill of cream
1 tbsp vinegar
seasonings

Grate finely a small root of horseradish and mix with it well, off the fire, a gill of cream slightly whisked, a pinch of sugar, a little salt and the vinegar. Stir till the sauce is quite smooth and keep in a cold place till wanted.

Suitable to serve with cold roast beef, rump steak, ham, tongue, salads or boiled codfish.

Horseradish Sauce

Wash 1 pound horseradish root; cut or scrape off thick peel and grate. Mix well with strong white vinegar to cover. Add three tablespoons and bottle.

For a variation mix in three grated sour apples and, if desired, a few chopped almonds, or mix ¼ cup of above with 1 cup mayonnaise and serve.

Lettuce

Grace MacPhail, in her nineties, remembers fresh lettuce being washed and dried and then eaten with sugar and vinegar when she was a child. There was no such thing in her home as mayonnaise, when she was age 10, but remembers they always had lettuce.

Her family was well educated and fairly well to do. "Mother always had a maid and the dining room table was always set—with real silver." She particularly remembers the Scots as having good gardens with tomatoes, cucumbers, corn but no peppers. Her family had water piped into big puncheons (molasses came in them) from a spring.

Mushrooms

When people are poor and hungry, they start gathering everything available to eat. Such was the case with mushrooms. I'm sure that early residents had a very good knowledge about mushrooms (but wonder if they enjoyed the effects of "magic" mushrooms as some folk have in the 1980s). I know several country dwellers, who will pick up a mushroom or puff ball as they walk the fields with complete security that it is safe to eat.

For amateurs though, I would urge you don't try and gather your own without the assistance of an expert. There is no simple rule or test to distinguish edible and poisonous mushrooms according to Tom Stobart's Cook's Encyclopedia. I believe him and buy mine in a store.

About Mushrooms

- For a more concentrated mushroom flavour, use dried mushrooms. To dry: trim and slice unpeeled mushrooms that have just been picked. Cut the stems crosswise. They should be dried quickly. Spread on a board or paper and set in a sunny place or in an oven, not too hot, lest they steam and spoil. A place near the furnace or in the furnace encasement is best. Rinse well in cold water before cooking.
- Morrels will dry easily without slicing by putting a string through them and hanging them up in the kitchen or any dry place. Settlement Cookbook, 1928.
- Serve fried with scrambled eggs, raw in salads, or stuffed with a mussel or oyster and broiled. Broil caps alone, top down for a snack.

Nanny's Stewed Mushrooms

1 lb mushrooms

2 oz butter
1 gill brown stock
1 tsp corn-flour
lemon juice
pepper and salt to taste
parsley

Wipe and peel mushrooms and take off the stalks. If large, cut into pieces. Put the butter into a casserole and fry the mushrooms in it for a few minutes, then season, and add a few drops of lemon juice. Put the lid on and simmer very slowly for about 10 minutes or till tender, stirring now and again. Make the corn-flour into a smooth paste with the stock and add, stirring gently. Bring to the boil and cook very slowly for a few minutes. Sprinkle with chopped parsley when about to serve.

Oven Stewed Mushrooms

1 lb mushrooms
1 oz butter
1 teacupful milk
pepper and salt
garnish

Put the mushrooms into a casserole with the milk, pepper and salt and put a piece of butter on each. Cook in a moderate oven till tender, allowing about half an hour for forced mushrooms, and about 20 minutes for the natural ones.

Home Management
1934

Mushroom Croquettes

1 cup mushrooms, sliced and cooked—canned is fine
3 tbsp butter
4 tbsp flour
1 cup milk
½ tsp salt
pepper to taste
1 tsp Worcestershire sauce
2 strips bacon, crisp and crumbled

flour
1 egg beaten with 1 tbsp water
bread crumbs
deep fat for frying

Melt butter; stir in flour. Blend well. Add milk gradually, stirring until thick and smooth. Do not boil. Add salt, pepper, mushrooms, Worcestershire and crumbled bacon. Cool until easy to handle. Shape into patties, cones or what pleases you. Dip in flour, then in egg mixture and finally in bread crumbs. Fry in hot fat, 375°F (test by dropping in a cube of bread—it should brown in one minute). Drain on paper before serving.

Dried Mushrooms

Wash mushrooms and gently wipe dry. String with a needle and heavy thread, with the needle going through the center from top to bottom. Hang horizontally until dry, about 3 days. These are delicious when added to soups, stews, etc. Terrific to take camping.

Mushroom Caps with Chicken Liver

Large mushroom caps are delicious stuffed with everything from cheese to mussels. This chopped chicken liver was originally broiled on toast rounds and is delicious in mushroom caps. This makes enough for about 36 medium mushroom caps. Great at parties.

4 tbsp butter
1 small onion, chopped very fine
½ lb chicken livers
pinch nutmeg
2-3 strips streaky bacon, chopped and partially cooked

Sauté onion until transparent in the butter; add chicken livers and cook until they are browned outside but slightly pink inside. Remove and mash with a fork, removing any tough or stringy portions. Most cooks precook the mushrooms by placing upside down under a broiler and brushing with butter; I prefer not to precook as the juices are lost, and we like mushrooms raw as well as cooked. Fill each cap with liver paste and pop under the broiler 2-3 minutes. Top with a piece of bacon and brown.

Onions

Onions come in more distinctive types or forms than any other Island vegetable. Over the years Island gardeners have discovered different varieties serve different needs. From talking with people it seems that Multipliers (they divide in the soil) were the most common and cooking onion, which stored well, were the most frequently grown. With so many to choose from on today's markets, we have briefly described each below:

About Onions

— Place whole onions around a roast; use to garnish when serving. Delicious.
— Sauté, then sprinkle with nutmeg, thyme or chopped parsley.
— Top boiled onions with buttered bread crumbs and grated cheese.
— Bake small to medium whole onions in a casserole with a small amount of water if you are using oven for other things. Season with salt, pepper, etc. and spread with butter.
— Don't cry—peel onions under running water, or slice all but the root part (it is where the irritating fumes come from).

Yellow or Cooking — Highly valued because they store well (choose clean, firm onions with skins that are dry, smooth and crackly). A multi-purpose onion with full pungent flavour. Good chopped, sliced, diced or fried.
Silverskins — Small white onions best in stews, soups or creamed for side dishes. Both these and small yellows are best used in pickles.
Spring or Green Onions — Actually used before the bulbs form, they are eaten raw with meat, cheese or fish. Green tops can be sliced into salads, egg dishes, soups, and simply added to cottage cheese. Colourful garnish for anything, green onions are easily grown. They can even be boiled and served like asparagus. Store them in a plastic bag in the refrigerator.
Spanish — Sweet and juicy, these jumbo fawn coloured onions are excellent raw, in sandwiches, french fried, stuffed or baked. They do not keep well and should be used while fresh. Try in cider vinegar with a sprinkle of pepper.
Bermuda — Mild and sweet tasting, they are large, flatly shaped and usually golden in colour. Tasty raw or cooked whole.
Leeks — A mild tasting member of the onion family, cylindrically

shaped with a large white base and wide green leaves. With the exception of the roots, the whole leek can be used for cooking. They add a unique flavour to soups and stews or can be served as a different side dish. Slice and eat them raw as a relish. Choose small or medium leeks for the most tender eating. They do not keep long, even refrigerated, so use within 3-5 days of purchase.

Shallots — A delicate tasting cousin of onion and garlic. Reddish brown skinned bulb is divided into cloves like garlic. Use as a subtle, yet tangy flavouring agent. Buy firm, dry and well-rounded bulbs. Store in a cool, dry, well-ventilated place up to two months.

Onions and Apples

Try this with roast pork.

1½ cups sliced onions
2 tbsp butter
2½ cups apple wedges
2 tbsp brown sugar
salt and pepper to taste

Sauté onion in butter until transparent, about 3 minutes. Add apples. Cover and simmer until apples are tender, about 6 minutes. Stir in brown sugar and seasonings. Serves 6

Braised Onions

2 lbs onions, thickly sliced
(about 12)
2 tbsp tomato sauce (ketchup)
2 tbsp water
1 tbsp honey
1 tbsp butter
½ tsp dry mustard
salt and pepper (a pinch)

In slightly salted boiling water, cook onions for 10 minutes. Drain and put in a 6-cup casserole. Mix together ketchup, water, honey, butter, mustard, salt and pepper. Pour over onions. Bake in 350°F oven for 1 hour or until onions are tender and glazed. Serves 6.

Molasses Glazed Onions

Perfect with roasts and easy to fix.

Place boiled, small white onions in a skillet with butter and molasses, turning until they glaze.

Velvet Onions

Boil small, sweet onions and cover with a smooth white sauce. Sprinkle with black pepper for a perfect partner for poultry. These are also nice served over toast and covered with grated cheese.

Pickled Onion Rings

1 cup water
1 cup vinegar
¼ cup sugar
6 inches stick cinnamon, broken into pieces
½ tsp salt
½ tsp whole cloves
1 small sweet onion, thinly sliced
1 small red onion, thinly sliced

In saucepan, combine water, vinegar, sugar, cinnamon, salt and cloves. Simmer, covered 10 minutes. Strain. Separate onions into rings and pour the hot mixture over them. Chill all afternoon (about 4 hours), turning from time to time. Drain and serve.

Jean-Marie's Onion Pie

1½ cups onion, chopped very fine
⅓ cup butter
3 tbsp all-purpose flour
1 cup cream
¾ tsp salt
⅛ tsp black pepper
2 eggs, well beaten
8-inch unbaked pie crust.

Sauté the onions in butter until a light brown. Sprinkle with flour. Add the cream slowly. Season with salt and pepper.

Continue cooking and stir until the mixture has thickened; add the beaten eggs and stir. Pour into the pie crust and bake at 400°F for 30 minutes. Serves 6.

Cold Cure

I will always remember my father, the few times he had a bad cold, boiling up a pot full of onions. He devoured them with relish, claiming they were to treat his cold, but I think he liked boiled onions. In my research I heard of others doing this on the Island. Try adding a beef bouillion cube. Serve as is or with butter and black pepper.

French Canadian Onion Soup

3 tbsp butter of flavourful drippings
2 qts good beef stock
1½-2 cups cheese (the type depends on personal taste; Gruyére is nice; I like a sharp cheddar and some like mozzarella)
6-7 medium onions or 5 large, sliced
French Bread, sliced into at least 12 slices
1 tsp sugar

Sauté onions in butter, sprinkling with a tsp of sugar (this will caramelize them), till they are golden but not brown. Add the stock a sprinkle of pepper and simmer for half an hour. Toast 12 slices of the bread then place half of them in an over-proof tureen or individual soup pots. Cover with half the grated cheese. Pour in the hot soup, then put the rest of the toasted bread over and top with the remaining cheese. Lightly brown under the broiler. Serves 6.

Onion Ragout

1½ cups coarsely chopped onion
3 tbsp bacon, ham or meat drippings

2 chopped green peppers
1½ cups tomato (optional)
¼ cup bouillon
1 bay leaf
½ tsp chopped parsley
¼ tsp thyme
salt and pepper to taste

Sauté onions with green peppers in drippings until soft; stir in tomatoes, bouillon, bay leaf, parsley, thyme, salt and pepper. Bring slowly to a boil. Simmer very gently about 15 minutes, stirring occasionally. Good sprinkled with grated cheese. You can also add diced potatoes, before the tomato.

Stuffed Onions

Hollow, large, boiled, Spanish onions and filled with chopped cooked mushrooms, and seasoned bread crumbs, pureed spinach or flavoured rice. They are best when topped with a white or cheese sauce and broiled until it browns.

Warehouse Wine

The story is that a fellow who married into an Island farm family, and into the family business of farming as well, was rather dismayed to find his new in-laws were staunch teetotalers. Missing his normal daily nip he quickly learned that news of any visits to the bootlegger got back home before he did, so the inventive fellow decided to tackle his problem at home. Before long he had a brew cooking in the back of the potato warehouse that turned out to be a surprisingly good wine; which in the following years as family temperance eased, found its way to the dining table. His formula, which was given to me by a son who swore me to secrecy was for double this quantity, but we felt this a good amount for readers to try. I haven't made it myself but did enjoy a "wee nip".

½ lb good potatoes, peeled and diced
½ lb yellow onions, sliced as thin as a dime
1 lb raisins, seedless, chopped
3 lbs sugar
1 cake dry yeast (or an envelope)
1 gallon of lukewarm water

Add the sugar to the water in a stone crock. Stir until sugar is gone then add the onions, spuds (potato) and raisins. Add the yeast which had been prepared as directed on the package, then cover and leave for a week. Strain through cheesecloth, but don't squeeze. Put into bottle and cap loosely. When fermentation (bubbling) stops and sediment has settled, siphon off into bottles and cork tightly.

Note: Visit a wine supplies outlet for the bottle and please use corks, not metal bottle caps.

Parsnips

Parsnips, the experts tell us, reached Virginia in 1609. A century later, they were being grown by the North American Indians. It seems a certainty that Islanders brought them along from the old country. They are a winter vegetable and, at one time, it was believed they had to be frosted to be edible. The later they are harvested the sweeter they are. However, left too long, they can grow to a huge size and develop a wooden core. I know some gardeners still leave a few parsnips in the gardens over the winter, especially the rural old timers following the traditional ways. They used to fill the gap between winter and the growth of new spring crops.

About Parsnips

— Young parsnips can just be washed and cooked, or scraped; old ones should be peeled and cut in pieces.

— They are often boiled before they are dressed in a variety of ways.

— Good flavouring for stews, around roasts and soups.

— They cook quicker than carrots.

— Try julienne, cutting equal amounts of parsnips and carrots. Boil together until just tender; drain and add to a clear chicken consomme for an elegant first course.

— Shape left-over mashed parsnips into croquettes and deep fry or patties and pan fry in butter.

— Parsnips are sweet—some like to sprinkle them with sugar to serve.

— Grate and use in salads.

Parsnip and Onion Loaf

Root vegetables have often been used as substitutes for meat in days gone by—a habit we would be wise to imitate, especially when this good.

1 lb parsnips, cooked and mashed
1 large onion, chopped
1 oz dripping (or butter)
1 oz parsley and thyme stuffing mix (save a little from when you stuff a bird, or use packaged)
salt and pepper to taste
2 tbsp chopped parsley
2 eggs, beaten
shredded lettuce and parsley for garnish

Fry the onion in fat until golden. Blend with stuffing, parsnips, seasoning, parsley and eggs. Turn into a well-greased two-pound loaf tin, cover with greased paper (or foil) and bake for one hour at 350°F. Turn out onto a serving dish and garnish. Serve hot or cold.

Murray Harbour Parsnip Casserole

2 tbsp butter
1 tbsp brown sugar
1 tsp dry mustard
½ tsp salt
⅓ cup water
4 cups parsnip (peel and coarsely grate to four cups)

Preheat oven to 350°F. Melt fat in 1½-quart casserole in oven. Stir in brown sugar, mustard, salt and water. Add parsnips, stirring to combine ingredients. Cover; bake in moderate (350°F) oven 35-40 minutes or until parsnips are tender. Serves 6.

Parsnip Fritters

4-5 parsnips, whole and boiled
Fritter batter (see index)
Maple syrup, other syrup or honey

Prepare fritter batter. Put the fritters on pan and slice parsnips lengthwise. Lay 2 or 3 slices on top of each fritter. The number of slices to use on each fritter will depend on size of the fritters. Brown nicely, and serve with any good syrup or honey.

Parsnip Faggots

4 medium parsnips
½ pt stock
¼ pt water
2 oz shelled nuts (ground)
1 egg, beaten
½ oz butter
3 tbsp fine bread crumbs
salt and pepper
1 tbsp flour

If nuts are not ground put them through a nut mill or mincer. Prepare the parsnips and cut them in quarters. Put them in a stew pan with the stock and water and cook until they are quite tender, and the liquid is almost absorbed. Season with salt and pepper, and mash them until smooth. Form them into balls with floured fingers and leave until quite cold. Then dip them into the beaten egg; coat them with nuts, then with fine bread crumbs. Pack them into a greased tin and brown in a hot oven. Serve very hot. Lemon or tomato sauce can be served with them if liked.

Peas

Peas have been cultivated since at least the bronze age. An important food source because they are a good source of protein, grow easily and store well. There are two types of peas and have been for as long as Islanders have been gardening. The Garden Peas are the sweet varieties which we grow in the garden and eat when green and tender. Then there are the field peas which are grown to be dried, sometimes split, and kept for winter. These were very necessary too before the days of modern storage. After soaking they were cooked for a long time to make soups and puddings. Today we have to add pea pods to our varieties; they are eaten whole when young and still flat. This isn't totally a new idea for I can remember, as a child sitting at the back of my grandmother's house, shelling peas and with my cousins, eating the tender pods.

About Garden Peas

- Don't shell peas until you plan to use them; store in pods in refrigerator.
- Cook in boiling salted water 8-12 minutes (or steam)
- Season when cooking with marjoram, basil, savoury, nutmeg, dill or green onion.
- Tender first-picked peas are delicious if a few springs of mint are added to cooking water.
- Add a few to any soup, stew or chowder for appearance.
- Peas and minted, new potatoes were traditionally served with roasted spring lamb in many Island homes.

Creamed Peas

My husband recalls his grandmother making a white sauce, adding cooked peas (or canned) and serving them over toast for lunch or as a vegetable for dinner.

French Style Peas and Onions

12 small cooking onions
½ cup boiling water
3 cups shelled peas
1 tsp salt
2 tsp sugar
2 tbsp butter
2 tsp flour
¼ tsp rosemary or chervil (or
 1 tbsp chopped fresh mint)

Cook onions covered, in boiling water for 5 minutes. Add peas, salt and sugar. Cover and cook gently until vegetables are just tender, 8-12 minutes. Drain; reserving liquid. Melt butter; blend in flour and herbs. Gradually stir in liquid, then add vegetables. Stir and cook over low heat until sauce thickens.

Acadian Pea Soup

2 onions, chopped
2 stalks celery, chopped
2 carrots, chopped
1 lb split peas
Meaty soup bones (ham bones
 were often used)
1-2 small potatoes, diced

Soak peas a few hours in enough water to cover. Add enough stock to make three quarts. Add bones; bring to a boil; skim the surface. Simmer slowly for two hours. Add vegetables and cook 20 minutes (they may be pureed or left). Season with salt, pepper or your choice. Serve with croutons or crackers.

Soup aux Pois (French Canadian Pea Soup)

A different version of pea soup which came from a neighbour of the woman who gave me the preceding recipe. A friendly argument developed of which was the true "French" version. Through sheer doggedness, the gentleman who presented the following won. It makes a thick, yellow "stick-to-the-ribs" soup.

2 cups dried peas
water
¼ lb side bacon
1 large onion, minced or
 chopped very fine
½ tsp savory
1 Bouquet Garni

Wash the peas and soak overnight in a quart of cold water. When you are ready to start cooking, add four cups of water (check the package directions for correct soaking). Add onion, bacon, savory and Bouquet Garni, then simmer over low heat for three hours. Serve with fresh rolls or biscuits and butter. Serves 4.

Peppers

Peppers, to me, have always been associated with Italy; however, they were mentioned in cooking, usually stuffed or in pickles in the early 1900s. Early cookbooks of that era which originated in England usually have them "parboiled, drained, then the pulpy contents extracted with a spoon." Those books which originated on this side of the Atlantic used green and red peppers in pickles, and they seemed to have been popular stuffed.

Some people, it seemed, used to go to great lengths to peel both red and green peppers. They would be charred, then steamed so that the skin would be easily peeled off. I can only assume that we have improved the produce so much now that we don't need to skin them.

About Peppers

— Peppers and tomatoes complement each other, so add to

tomato sauce, sauté them with onions or use in salads.

- Don't rub your eyes with your hands after cutting hot peppers; like onions they will irritate.
- To stuff peppers cut around the stem at the top, gently tug to release the seeds and then scrap membrane out carefully with a spoon, then stuff.
- Cut into chunks, rub with oil and bake at 425°F until tender.
- Cut smaller and sauté.
- When choosing peppers to stuff and bake, stand them on their ends to be sure they will sit level.
- If your filling doesn't need a long cooking time, blanch peppers first.

Stuffed Sweet Peppers

6 sweet peppers
2 cups cooked meat
1 onion
1 tbsp butter
1 tbsp parsley
1 tsp salt
½ cup mushrooms
¼ cup bread crumbs
1 cup water or stock

Cut the peppers crosswise in half, remove the seeds and cut off the stem, or leave them whole, saving cuttings off a cap. Chop the meat (this may be veal, chicken or lamb) fine, also the onion and mushrooms. Mix all the ingredients together except the stock or water; fill the peppers and stand in a pan and pour the hot stock or water around them, basting often. Bake slowly three-quarters of an hour. A nice luncheon dish.

Pepper Sandwiches

Always a favourite with those who prefer dainties that are rather pungent.

Chop a pepper fine, removing all the seeds. Place in a saucepan with a tablespoon of butter and allow it to heat without browning. Stir briskly. Add a little salt and remove from the fire. When quite cold, spread between thin slices of bread adding a little grated cheese before putting the slices together.

Popcorn

Stored where the outside atmosphere may have free access to the corn will maintain a fairly uniform moisture content of about 13 per cent, which is about ideal for best popping results. Popcorn should not be stored where it will be subjected to dry air.

Farmer's Magazine, September 1939

Today, wise gourmands of popcorn store it in the refrigerator.

Pumpkin

The pumpkin, related to summer, acorn and pattypan squashes, has been cultivated in North America since long before the white man arrived. I have read as early as 2000 B.C. but often wonder just how anyone who hasn't been there can know that. The most well-known use of the pumpkin is to carve them into Jack-o'-lanterns for Halloween. When people were more careful of their pennies, they would be displayed outside October 31st, to let youngsters know that treats were to be had inside, then on November 1st would be rescued and used by the cook of the household.

Today we are not as thrifty and indeed tend to overlook the variety of uses for the pumpkin. It can be used as a vegetable or sweet dish (it is a vegetable). It can be put in stews and soups, served with rice and cheese sauce, mashed and fried after being dipped in eggs and crumbs, or you can fill the shell with other ingredients and bake it.

About Pumpkin

- Pumpkin can be preserved in a variety of ways including canning, preserving, pickling and drying.
- Leave about two or three inches of stem on the pumpkin when harvested. Dry in the sun for a week or two, then place in an attic, spare bedroom or root cellar where the temperature can be maintained at around 55 degrees Fahrenheit. Do not let it get much lower or your pumpkin will deteriorate.
- Slice in two, remove the seeds and strings and bake at about 350°F cut side down, until the rind can be pierced by a fork. This should take just over an hour, depending on the size of the pumpkin. After the halves have cooled, remove the rind and puree (push through a sieve or use a blender or food processor).
- Cut pumpkin into small chunks and place in a basket or steamer and steam for several minutes until tender. Cool, peel and puree as with baking.

— Serve in the same manner as squash or use in recipes such as bread, pie, muffins, cakes, soup or as a vegetable stuffing.

Pumpkin Pecan Loaf

Excellent warm or cool. Try it with honey and butter, or cheese.

⅔ cup solid vegetable shortening
2⅔ cups sugar
2 cups cooked pumpkin
4 large eggs
⅔ cup water
3⅓ cups flour
2 tsp soda
½ tsp baking powder
1½ tsp salt
2 tsp cinnamon
½ tsp nutmeg
1 cup chopped pecans

Cream shortening and sugar in a large bowl. Add pumpkin, eggs and water, and stir with a wire whisk until thoroughly blended. In a separate bowl, combine the dry ingredients and add them to the pumpkin mixture. Stir to moisten and then fold in the nuts. Divide batter into two greased loaf pans (9 × 5 × 3 inches). Bake in moderate oven 350°F for one hour.

Pumpkin Baked in the Shell

A New England supper dish that found its way to the Island.

Take a small, very ripe pumpkin which has a hard shell; slice off the stem end so that you have a cover with a handle. Scoop out seeds and pith so that only the "meat" remains. Fill with milk (half and half or blend, the best replacement for the 'new milk' that was used before pasteurization). Set the cover on and place in tin or roaster to cook in the oven for 6 to 7 hours. When ready to serve, milk was added to the brim, and the pumpkin eaten straight from the shell.

Roasted Pumpkin Seeds

A fall treat which not only offers a good snack, but can involve the family after the Halloween Jack-o'-lantern has been carved.

Rub butter and salt on a tray; add a single layer of pumpkin seeds which have been washed clean and dried. Roast in the oven. It only takes a few minutes.

Pumpkin Spread for Bread

one pound pumpkin flesh (pare and remove seeds from pumpkin before measuring)
one pound sugar
one small orange or lemon

Grate the pumpkin coarse. Put it—the sugar, the grated skin of the fruit and the juice (strained)—in a preserving kettle. Bring to a slow boil, stirring often. Skim well, till all is smooth, thick (like marmalade); put into sterilized glass jars that are still warm and seal.

Pumpkin Fritters

Boil the pumpkin, then pour off the water. Let it get quite cold. Take a plate and press the pumpkin down, so as to squeeze out all the watery particles still left. Stir in 2 eggs and some flour (well dried) to make a batter. From a spoonful of the batter you will have a fritter which must be baked in a pan with boiling fat. Set the pot not to be too sparing, the deeper the pot you fry them in the less you use and the nicer the cake. Mix pounded cinnamon and sugar and serve with the cakes.

Pickled Pumpkin

1 pumpkin (seed, and cut out 4 cups of flesh)
¾ cup white vinegar
1 cup sugar
¼ cup corn syrup
1½ tsp cinnamon
10 cloves
1 tsp salt

Place all in a saucepan and boil. Cook over low heat until pumpkin becomes transparent and a fork can easily be inserted. Pack into sterile jars and seal.

Spinach

Trends in food and its preparation change, just as trends do in clothing. Having had a long and passionate dislike for spinach, it was quite a surprise to me to discover that it is a very likable vegetable. I had just always been served it cooked in the old way "immersed deeply in salt water, boiled hard for 45 minutes to an hour"; or at least it seemed that way, for it was always a tasteless ball of green mush. Now I know better and steam it lightly or add it to salads.

About Spinach

- Don't use aluminum pots or utensils with spinach; it will discolour and taste metallic.
- Buy spinach with dark green leaves that are undamaged, and as little stem as possible.
- The stems can be left with young spinach; but when it is older, remove stems and even tear them back on the leaf.
- When washing leaf vegetables such as spinach and swiss chard, immerse in a sink full of water then remove the leaves from the water; this way you leave any grit at the bottom.
- Since spinach looses so much weight in cooking, allow about a half pound per person.
- Delicious in salads; always choose small tender leaves.
- Cook spinach in butter over a high heat if you have some left over.
- Add onion, celery or shallots if desired.
- Spinach with cheese makes a nice stuffing for chicken or turkey breasts.
- When the spinach is chopped fine, it can be pressed through a pastry bag and tube, or if you have any left it can be moulded in small cups and served as a salad with mayonnaise or French dressing.

Creamed Spinach

½ peck (4 qts) spinach
2 tbsp butter
¼ cup cream
1 tsp salt
2 hard-boiled eggs
pepper
4 triangles of toast

Cook spinach, drain and press out the water. Chop fine, return it to the saucepan, add all the seasonings and stir over the fire until hot. Have the eggs quartered and toast ready. Press the spinach into a mould or dish, then turn out onto a serving dish. Garnish with the toast and eggs and serve.

French Spinach

Cook, strain and chop very fine, or put through a sieve. Place in a pan with butter, turn about rapidly with a wooden spoon. Add salt, pepper and a pinch of sugar. Sometimes a little cream is added to the cooked spinach instead of butter, and a creamy puree is made when the beaten yolks of one or more eggs are added. Served on toast, with Mornay Sauce, it makes a change.

Squash

This vegetable particularly valued even today for its easy storage is not an European import. In fact, the earliest explorers recorded it as being cultivated by North American Indians.

What we know as squash, pumpkin, gourds and marrows are all members of the same family. More distant relatives include cucumbers, gherkins, melons and even zucchini. Since squash, as we are talking about here, come in so many shapes, sizes, colours and mature at different times of the year, they have often been named for things they resemble such as acorn, butternut, turban and even pattypan. Winter squashes (hubbard, turban, butternut and mammoth) take longer to mature than the summer (including pumpkins, marrows, scalloped summer squashes, pattypans and ornamental gourds) thus the distinction. One of the more modern variations of a summer squash is now being touted as a low calorie substitute for pasta. The spaghetti squash is boiled till the skin is tender, then cup open, the "spaghetti" fibre forked out until it is fluffy and served with the usual spaghetti sauces.

The vegetable referred to by the British as a marrow is in fact a member of the squash family.

Nutmeg Squash

3 lbs Hubbard squash
2 tbsp butter
2 tbsp brown sugar
½ tsp salt
½ tsp ground nutmeg

Cut up squash. Cook, covered, in boiling salted water till tender (about 25 minutes). Drain. Scoop out pulp, mash. Place in saucepan; cook, uncovered, till desired consistency, then stir in the remaining ingredients. Serves 6.

We've all heard of zucchini bread and carrot pudding, so why not:

Squash Muffins

1 egg
¼ cup sugar
½ cup cooked mashed squash
1¾ cup flour
½ cup milk
2 tsp cream of tartar
1 tsp soda
½ tsp salt
4 tbsp melted shortening (or oil)

Beat egg and sugar; add milk and squash. Sift flour; measure and sift with dry ingredients. Combine lightly with beaten egg mixture. Add shortening. Turn into greased muffin tins. Bake at 375°F for about 20 minutes.

Baked Winter Squash

Any variety can be simply baked and served with butter, salt and pepper. Or, for a change try this:

Winter squash, sufficient when
mashed to serve 4-6
4 tbsp butter
½ tsp salt
¼ tsp pepper
2 eggs, well beaten
½ cup bread crumbs
¼ lb grated cheddar cheese

Cut the squash and boil it. Drain, remove the skin and mash with the butter, salt and pepper. Stir in the eggs. Butter a baking dish; put squash mixture in; sprinkle with bread crumbs and then the grated cheese. Bake uncovered at 350°F for about 30 minutes.

Maple Acorn Squash Bake

— Squash it seems can be cooked right side up or upside down.

The squash should be washed, cut in half and have the seeds removed with a spoon. Rinse, turn upside down in a baking pan and pour ¼ inch cold water in the pan. Bake at 400°F for ½ hour.

Remove and turn right side up. Salt and pepper and sprinkle over with maple syrup (or brown sugar). Place a piece of butter in each half. Return to the oven; bake 30 minutes longer.

Nanny's Marrow and Apple Chutney

One of my earliest remembered food associations is of my mother enjoying one of her favourite meals, pork pie, which she and my father had made; and marrow and apple chutney, which my grandmother had made; with a piece of sharp cheddar cheese. Both my parents and my grandparents grew marrows, a long rounded, pale yellow variety which became quite large. I spent some of my high school years living with my grandparents and will always remember Nanny, cutting up a marrow for chutney, when she suddenly sliced off the end of her thumb. I panicked at the sight of so much blood, but she calmly searched among the vegetable for the piece of her thumb, stuck it back where it was supposed to be, put sticky tape over it and (after rinsing the blood off the marrow) calmly went back to her chopping. I was traumatized for a week expecting some awful infection to set in, but all she had to show for it was a thin scar around one thumb.

2 lbs marrow
1 lb apples
½ lb onions
1 pt vinegar
½ lb lump sugar (lump sugar is cubed and I have no idea why it is specified over granulated white sugar)
A few chili and peppercorns
2 oz whole ginger (bruised)
½ oz turmeric
1 tbsp cornflour

Cut up marrow into small chunks; sprinkle with salt; let it stand for 12 hours; strain and add chopped apples and onions, sugar and vinegar. Put spices into muslin bag, then boil altogether for one hour. Moisten turmeric and cornflour with a little vinegar; pour into the mixture and boil quickly for 5 minutes, stirring all the time. Bottle in sterilized jars.

Swiss Chard

A member of the beet family, swiss chard is grown both for its leaves, which can be treated like spinach, and its thick stalks and ribs. The stalks can be treated like asparagus. Many people favour chard over spinach as having a better taste and texture. It certainly grows well in P.E.I. and seems to be an ongoing plant which can be harvested continually.

About Swiss Chard

- When the plant is young and leaves and stems tender, cook together.
- As harvesting continues and stems require more cooking than leaves, separate them for cooking, treating leaves like spinach and stems as substitute for celery or asparagus.
- Left-over ribs can be added to stews, soups and salads.
- Chard likes to grow in salty soil near the sea, according to legend.
- Chard or spinach that is left over is nice spread on toast, covered with cheese, or cheese sauce and broiled.
- Large leaves can be stuffed in the same way as cabbage leaves.

Tomatoes

We find tomatoes referred to in very early accountings of life on the Island; however, since the growing season was short, and as we have said before, many of the early settlers—not particularly skilled gardeners or farmers—they often did not have time to ripen and thus large numbers were eaten green. In the fall, as the danger of frost increased, the tomatoes would be taken in and many of them made into pickles and relishes to enjoy all winter long when fresh produce was not available. Green tomatoes were also fried.

About Tomatoes

- Cook only in stainless steel, enamel or the new coated pans or you may have an undesired taste.
- Tomatoes can be added in layers to casseroles for excellent flavour and appearance. For example macaroni and cheese, or a layer of apples, then green tomatoes topped with sliced apples in a pie.
- Make tomato scallop by starting with a layer of bread crumbs in the bottom of a dish, then tomatoes, salt and pepper, a little sugar and butter. Repeat until dish is full. Bake covered until cooked, then brown quickly. This is best done with bottled or

canned tomatoes.

- Tomatoes are also nice broiled or fried, either green or ripe. They must be cut rather thick, rolled in egg and bread crumbs, and then fried, browning on both sides.
- Tomatoes should be purchased semi-ripened and instead of storing them in the refrigerator, you should leave them at room temperature on a window sill or, to ripen quickly, wrap them in newspaper or brown paper. They will lose flavour if you keep them in the refrigerator.

Genuine Longfellow Pickles

1 peck green tomatoes
1 doz onions
4 green peppers
2 cups sugar
1 tbsp ground cloves
1 tbsp ginger
1 tbsp cinnamon
1 tbsp allspice
1 tbsp mustard seed
1 tbsp celery seed
cider vinegar
¾ cup salt

Wash and slice the tomatoes, onions and peppers into a large bowl and sprinkle with salt. Stand overnight; the next morning drain, and put into a preserving kettle with the spices and cover with good vinegar; cook until tender. Put away in jars being careful not to break the slices of tomatoes.

Green Tomato Pickles

Chop fine 8 pounds green tomatoes; add 4 pounds of brown sugar and boil 3 hours; add 1 quart vinegar (use strong pickling vinegar), 1 teaspoonful each mace, cinnamon and cloves, and boil 15 minutes. Bottle.

Piccalilli

One gallon green tomatoes sliced, 6 good-sized onions sliced, 1 pint granulated sugar, 1 quart pure cider vinegar, 1 tablespoonful salt, 2 tablespoonsful mixed spices. Mix all together and stew until tender, stirring continually; put in fruit jars and seal.

Tomato Higdom

Mix 1½ cups of salt with 1 bushel of green tomatoes chopped fine and let them stand overnight. In the morning, after pressing hard to extract all juice, add 1 cup mustard, 3 pounds sugar, 12 red peppers chopped fine, ½ cup celery seed. Mix thoroughly and pack in jars. Over this pour half a gallon of hot vinegar.

Green Tomato Sandwich Spread

1 qt chopped green tomatoes
1 cup chopped onions
3 green peppers
3 red peppers
½ cup salt
1 cup water
1 cup chopped sweet pickles
7 tbsp flour
1½ cups sugar
2 tsp mustard
1 cup vinegar
2 cups sour cream
3 eggs

Wash and core tomatoes; put them through a food chopper and measure out one quart. Peel onions and put through food chopper. Wash peppers, quarter, remove seeds and put through chopper. Mix tomatoes, onions and peppers and sprinkle with one-half cup of salt. Allow to stand for an hour or more and then drain. Add 1 cup of water to drained vegetables and cook until tender. Add chopped sweet pickles and keep mixture hot while preparing dressing. Mix and sift flour, sugar and mustard. Mix to a paste with cold vinegar. Add sour cream gradually and then well beaten eggs. Cook in a double boiler until thick, stirring constantly.

Pour hot dressing over hot vegetable mixture and stir until well mixed. Pour into hot sterilized jars and seal at once. If melted paraffin is used, pour a layer over the hot mixture and then, when the contents are cold, apply another layer of melted paraffin.

Escalloped Tomatoes

6 or 8 tomatoes
1 tbsp butter
2 tbsp grated onion
bread or croutons

salt and pepper

Scald and peel the tomatoes and cut in slices, or if canned ones are used, one-half can will be necessary. Make croutons of the bread by buttering, cutting half-inch squares and toasting. Butter the baking dish and put a layer of the croutons in the bottom, then a layer of tomatoes and a little of all the seasonings, then another layer of bread, tomatoes and so continue, having bread last on top, with bits of butter, and bake in a quick oven about half an hour.

Tomatoes du Barry

4 tomatoes
1 large tbsp butter
1 tsp salt
4 drops onion extract
pepper
parsley

Select smooth, small tomatoes; wash; put into a stew pan and cover with rapidly boiling water; add salt and keep boiling at a gallop for about ten minutes or until the tomatoes are tender, when pierced with a fork. Remove carefully with a skimmer to a hot platter. With a sharp pointed knife cut out the little hard stem and cut a horizontal and vertical gash across the top of each. Turn or roll back for a little ways the outside skin and pour over and around the tomatoes, the butter and seasonings carefully melted by standing in hot water. Chop parsley very fine and sprinkle over the top of each tomato, and garnish the dish with nice bunches of parsley at each end.

Cheesy Tomato Fries

Slice the tomatoes, pepper then dredge in flour. Fry in butter and sprinkle with grated cheddar or parmesan cheese and serve hot.

Tomatoes on Toast

Wash and cut the tomatoes in halves crosswise; set in a buttered baking pan, sprinkle with salt, pepper and a little finely chopped parsley; put a little piece of butter on the top of each and bake in a moderate oven about half an hour. Do not bake too long or they will fall to pieces. Have the toast ready, carefully lift one-half tomato on each piece. Meanwhile, have made a sauce with the following:

1 tbsp butter
½ cup cream
½ cup milk
1 tsp finely grated onion
1 tbsp flour
salt and pepper

Make sauce in the baking pan from the tomatoes, rub together butter and flour, then add the other ingredients and stir until thickened. Pour this over the tomatoes and toast. This is nice for breakfast, luncheon or supper.

Turnips and Rutabagas

We had an agreement in our household. I would, on occasion, cook turnip for my husband as long as I didn't have to eat it. Like many others, I intensely disliked the strong taste of this root vegetable which seemed to be one of many perils I had to face after we emigrated to Canada. I could not look with a kindly eye on this vegetable until we moved to our Island home and I was invited to a meeting of the local Women's Institute. Program for the night was . . . the Rutabaga! When I heard that I wondered what on earth I had gotten myself into. As a working mother, I could not envision myself wasting a whole evening discussing the turnips which I so disliked. It is still a mystery to me how I came to enjoy that evening so much or how the topic could prove to be so funny. After learning that the two are in fact different, with turnips being members of the mustard family who have been around since ancient times and rutabagas a more modern (1700's) creation; I decided the darn things couldn't be all bad and started adding them to stews and such. There I quite like them. Some day perhaps I will graduate to the most common way Islanders enjoy them, mashed, with a sprinkle of sugar.

While they are different, turnips and rutabagas are often cooked the same way and can be substituted for one another.

Turnip was to the early Acadian, what the potato was to the Irish. A stable food, that sometimes appeared on the table by itself. It was the turnip upon which these early settlers relied as it stored well and grew better in the rich Island soil.

Turnip is even today, most often served boiled, mashed and flavoured with just a little sugar. The following certainly adds a new image to the common root vegetable.

About Turnip

- Turnip, carrot and winter squash can be interchanged in most recipes as long as you remember the carrot is sweeter.
- If turnips are old or large, blanch them in boiling water for 5 minutes before using in recipes to remove the strong bitter flavour.
- Raw turnip can be cut small and used like radishes.
- If you are slow cooking a roast, stew or ragout add very small turnips halved, or slices of larger ones. Like carrots they will absorb juices and be delicious to eat while adding flavour to the meat.
- Left-over mashed turnip fried in butter and onions is a family favourite.
- If you are using your oven, try baking small turnips whole (peeling is optional). Just brush with butter and bake at 350°F for 45 minutes. Test with a fork.
- If you grow your own turnips you can enjoy the freshly picked, young, green leaves much as you would Swiss chard or spinach. If thinning your garden, sauté the small young turnip; cut into slices and when it is done, cook the leaves in the same manner.

Turnip Supreme

2 tbsp butter
1 tbsp chopped onion
3 cups mashed yellow turnip
1 tsp salt
1 tbsp sugar
dash black pepper
2 egg yolks
2 egg whites

Melt the butter and cook the onion until a golden brown. Add turnips and seasonings. Add the beaten egg yolks. Fold in the egg whites, which have been stiffly beaten. Turn into a greased baking dish. Bake uncovered at 375°F for 1 hour. Serves 6.

Scalloped Turnip

As we mentioned, the early French settlers relied on turnip as a stable food and used them in much the same manner as the English were using the potato. Scalloped turnips were made by layering with butter, flour and milk. Onions are optional and should be used in a quantity you like.

4 cups turnips, sliced quite thin
4 tbsp butter
2 tbsp flour
½ tsp salt
pepper to taste
1½ cups milk or 1 cup milk and
 ½ cup light cream
½ cup onions, sliced thin

Butter well a baking dish. Lightly fry onions in 1 tablespoon of the butter; do not brown. Begin layering turnip, onion, flour, a sprinkle of salt and pepper, and a tablespoon of butter. Repeat three times. Pour the milk and cream over all then cover and bake at 350°F for half an hour. Remove the cover and continue baking until tender and bubbly. Cheese can be added to the top for a nice crusty scallop.

Turnip and Potato Puff

4 cups mashed potato
1 cup mashed turnip
¼ cup milk
1 tbsp butter
½ tsp salt
⅛ tsp pepper
2 eggs

Combine potato and turnip and mash until quite smooth. Add milk, butter and seasonings. Mix well. Add well beaten eggs. Pile in mounds on a greased baking sheet and brown in moderate oven (350°F).

Grandmother's old Purity Cookbook

Turnip Toss Up

2 cups diced cooked turnip
1 cup sliced cooked celery
1 cup boiled green beans
butter
pinch ground allspice
powdered dill

Toss with butter and sprinkle of seasonings and serve hot.

Watercress

Found in shallow pockets beside streams, this bright green plant was valued in the spring and early summer. Later on it becomes very peppery. It can be eaten in a sandwich with a sprinkle of salt and good homemade bread and butter. The leaves and fine stems are delicious chopped in salads. Chopped even finer they can be added to creamed butter for a nice herbed butter to put out on the table. They can be lightly fried and for a more modern variation, try sprinkling with a little soy sauce.

Watercress Soup

4 onions, thinly sliced
4 tbsp butter
6 large potatoes, peeled and diced
5 cups chicken stock
2 cups watercress, chopped
1 pt heavy cream
½ cup sour cream
grated nutmeg

Fry the onions in butter until just softened. Add potatoes and stock. Bring to a boil and simmer until potatoes are cooked then add all but 1 tbsp of watercress. Simmer 3-4 minutes more and rub through a sieve (today this is best done by putting in a blender to puree). Reheat; add cream. Do not boil. Serve with a spoonful of sour cream, sprinkled with a few pieces of chopped watercress and nutmeg.

Note: I recently read a suggestion that if a watercress soup is not tangy enough, adding ½ to 1 tsp of horseradish will perk it up.

Wild Rice

The earliest inhabitants of the Island were reported to have harvested wild rice in several areas. Canoes were paddled into the rice and a stick used to bend the stalks over the boat where the seeds were knocked from the stalks and allowed to fall into the bottom of the canoe. When the weight made the boat hard to handle, they would return to shore and spread the rice out to dry.

Small amounts of wild rice are still harvested on the Island; and as far as I can determine, methods have not changed noticeably. Today it is considered a delicacy and is very costly to buy.

About Wild Rice

Wild rice should be well washed in cold water. It can then be cooked by slowly adding a cup of rice to 1½ cups rapidly boiling water with a little salt added. Cook 30-40 minutes at a boil. Test by sampling—you should be able to easily bite a grain. Drain and let stand in cooking pot close to the heat until the steam evaporates and the rice dries.

For fried wild rice follow the above procedure. Then peel and finely chop an onion and sauté it in butter until golden brown. If you have bacon or ham, or other vegetables, all finely chopped, they can be added with the rice stirred in last. Fry lightly for 10 minutes and serve.

Mrs. Doucette's Wild Rice Stuffing

This is particularly nice with duck but can be used in any fowl.

1 cup wild rice, washed several times in cold water
4 cups cold water
1½ tsp salt
½ cup chopped shallots
10 mushrooms, chopped
1 large onion, chopped
Liver from the bird, chopped
1 tsp poultry seasoning
4 tbsp butter
1 cup coarsely chopped toasted nuts (we prefer almonds)

Put rice, cold water and salt to boil, and continue boiling 35-40 minutes, until tender. Drain and return to element that has been turned to "off". This will dry some of the moisture out of the rice. In the meantime, fry the shallots, mushrooms, onion, liver and seasonings in the butter until onion is transparent, then stir in the rice and nuts. If your bird is not going straight into the oven, cool before stuffing.

Plain Wild Rice

1 cup wild rice
3 cups water
1 tsp salt

Wash wild rice well in cold water, drain and stir slowly into the boiling water which has been salted. Cook without stirring until tender, about 40 minutes. Alternatively, the rice can be parboiled about 5 minutes, then removed from the heat and left to soak, covered, for about 1 hour. Other wild grains can be cooked in the same way, but the ration of water to grain will vary. Serves 3-4.

For an interesting variation of this basic recipe, substitute deer (or pork) broth for the water, and sprinkle with maple sugar before serving. This recipe was adapted from a description of the indian way of life.

Blue Potatoes

Many a Maritimer associates home with Blue Potatoes and will go into almost the same state of ecstasy as that produced by hand delivering fresh lobster to a good old Island boy land locked in Upper Canada, if given a few in the fall of the year.

Before the era of the white potato Early Roses, Dakota Red and, of course, Blues were popular. (After the turn of the century the whites were introduced: the Irish Cobbler, Green Mountains, Sebagoes, Netted Gems, etc.)

Today most Blues are offered at farmers markets or obtained from a traditional gardener. They are cooked in their skins and have a very distinctive taste.

The Blues were used with salt fish and one recipe for cooking them was: "Fill a large pot with potatoes in their jackets, add a handful of coarse salt and boil (after adding water we suppose). When they can be pierced with a fork take them to the back door and drain off water. Lift cover and give them 3 shakes in the wind."

FOLKLORE,
James & Gertrude Pendergast

Potatoes

Prince Edward didn't earn its nickname, "Spud Island," without good reason. Islanders like to think of our million acres farm as being the potato capital of the world and you won't find many folk who would dispute it.

Potatoes have played an important role since the first settlers stepped onto the shore; for many it was the first crop they planted in their new home. Their success or failure could mean the difference between starvation and survival, particularly in the early years before they learned how to cope with what nature had to offer. There is a story about an immigrant farmer in Stanhope who in the spring planted his seed potatoes but could not wait for them to grow. His family were starving, and he had to go back to his field and dig the potatoes back up. The descendants of this man are still living in Stanhope area today, so obviously he was able to overcome those early hardships.

About Potatoes

- Occasionally potatoes discolour while cooking. This can be a sign of improper storage. Remember they should be stored properly. Discoloration can also be caused by iron in the potato. Try adding ¼ tsp cream of tartar to the cooking water during the last 10 minutes of cooking.
- Do not eat green portions of potatoes. It can be bitter and should be well removed.

Baking Potatoes

Choose a Russet, Netted Gem, Kennebec or Sebago for best baking. Look for a long (vs round) potato that is clean and free from blemishes and green areas. Prick the skin of a scrubbed potato with a fork. Rub well with butter if a soft skin is desired. Bake at oven temperature between 325°F and 425°F, depending on what else is in the oven. At 350°F allow 55-65 minutes. At 425°F, 40-50 minutes.

When the potatoes are cooked make a crosswise cut in the center and press to let the steam escape.

Note: Potatoes baked in foil will have a soft skin, but they tend to steam rather than bake.

Potato Salad Ring

An attractive way to serve potato salad is to press it into a ring mould, chill and carefully invert to serve. Potato salad, a mixture of cubed, cooled potatoes, mayonnaise and other vegetables, even egg, to taste; can be mixed to the taste of your family. Many Maritimers make it with drained, canned peas, yellow beans and onion added to the potatoes with prepared mustard mixed into the mayonnaise.

For a fancy molded ring, sprinkle the inside of the damp mold with chopped parsley and unmold onto lettuce. Garnish with tomato and radish.

Potato Pastry

1½ cups all-purpose flour
½ cup lard
½ tsp salt
¼ cup mashed potatoes
1 egg yolk

Combine flour and salt and cut in fat using 2 knives or a pastry cutter until mixture is crumbly. Add mashed potatoes and egg yolk and toss with a fork (do not add water) until a ball is formed. Divide into two balls. Roll out pastry from center outward, with a light even pressure to form a circle larger than your inverted pie plate. Place in the pie plate. Prick with a fork and bake at 350°F for 12-15 minutes for 2 nine-inch pie shells.

Potato Bread

6 potatoes, cooked and diced to
  make 4 cups
½ cup butter
1 cup hot milk
1 tbsp salt

Mash together potatoes, butter and a small portion of the hot milk. Mash vigorously until smooth, then stir in the remaining milk and salt.

1 cup lukewarm water
2 tsp granulated sugar
2 pkgs yeast
9-10 cups all-purpose flour

Pour the cup of lukewarm water into a small bowl and stir in sugar, mixing until it's dissolved. Sprinkle the yeast over this water, but do not stir. Let sit for 10 minutes and it will be foamy. Stir down the yeast with a fork and stir this into the potato mixture (this should be cool). Measure out two cups of flour and beat in vigorously until well mixed. Continue adding flour and stirring in until it becomes too stiff to stir. Turn onto a floured board and knead for 15-18 minutes, working in more flour as the dough becomes sticky. When the dough becomes smooth and satiny, form into a ball. Lightly coat the dough with grease (this is easiest if you grease a large bowl, then turn the dough in it until it's coated all over). Cover the bowl with wax paper (grease it first) and a damp cloth and set in a warm place. When the dough has almost doubled (in just over an hour) return the dough to the floured board and knead again for about 5 minutes, adding more flour if needed.

Divide the dough in two and shape to fit in generously greased loaf pans (they should be 9 × 5 × 3 in size). Cover again with greased wax paper and your damp cloth, and again set aside. In about an hour they will rise to double and should be baked in a 375°F oven for 45-60 minutes. Test by tapping; if it sounds hollow it is done. Remove to a rack and after about 5 minutes turn out of pans.

The lady who gave me this recipe read it over the phone, then the next day her son appeared in the office with a loaf of potato bread, still warm and a pat of butter. It was delicious.

Scalloped Potatoes

A much favoured way of serving potatoes, especially with ham.

Melt 2 tbsp butter, stir in 1 tbsp flour. Add slowly 1½ cup milk stirring constantly. Cook and stir over low heat until thickened. Add ¾ tsp salt and a dash of pepper. Remove from heat. In a buttered baking dish place 4 potatoes which have been peeled and sliced and one onion, chopped fine. Pour the sauce over the top and bake in a 350°F oven for 1¼ hours or until potatoes are tender. Sprinkle buttered crumbs over the top before baking for a nice topping. Serves 4-6.

Buttery Baked Potatoes

Slice raw potatoes evenly and thinly (less than ⅛ inch), dry well in a towel, then lay them in a lavishly buttered baking dish—an iron skillet, for example. Salt and pepper. Pour melted butter over them and mix with your hands making sure that each slice is nicely coated. Place in a 400°F oven. If the layer is thin, the potatoes will cook and become crisp in surprisingly little time. When they are done, pour off the excess butter. Serve in the baking dish so that they will stay warm.

Note: You will need at least two tablespoons butter for each potato, but you will recover a good deal of that in the form of clarified butter, which is excellent to refrigerate for future frying.

Minty New Potato Soup

This dish is today generally served as a soup, but long ago, when food was not as plentiful or varied, it was a main course.

Scrape small new potatoes and turn into an ovenproof dish. Cover with milk and season with salt and pepper. Add a large quantity of mint sprays or leaves, enough to give the mint flavour you desire. Bring to the boil and simmer gently for 15-20 minutes. Take care that the milk doesn't boil over (do not put the lid on tight).

Potato Soup

2 cups mashed or left-over potatoes
3 tbsp butter
4 cups milk
celery salt
onion seasoning
pepper
salt

Cook potatoes and milk in double boiler to boiling point. Beat with rotary beater; add seasonings to taste, butter, serve very hot with a sprinkling of paprika.

Potato Biscuit

1 cup mashed potato
1 cup flour
3 tsp baking powder
1 tsp salt
2 tbsp fat
⅔ cup water or milk (about)

Sift together flour, baking powder and salt. Work in the fat with fork or knife. Add potato and mix thoroughly. Then add enough liquid to make a soft dough. Roll the dough lightly to about ½-inch in thickness. Cut into biscuits and bake 13 to 15 minutes in hot oven (400°F).

Potato Flour Muffins

2 eggs
3 tbsp ice water
1 tbsp sugar
½ cup white potato flour
¼ tsp salt
3 tsp baking powder

Beat egg white stiff and dry. Beat egg yolks; add sugar and salt. Sift flour and baking powder twice. Add egg yolks to whites, beat in dry ingredients thoroughly; add ice water last. Bake in hot oven 400°F 15 to 20 minutes. Serve warm.

Irish Potato Cakes

2 cups mashed potatoes
2 cups flour
4 tsp baking powder
1 tsp caraway seed
1 tbsp butter
1 tsp salt
½ cup milk

Mix and sift dry ingredients; work in butter; add seeds, mashed potatoes and lastly the milk. Roll about as thick as biscuits and cut in squares. Cook in a small amount of fat in a frying pan, over a slow fire. Serve hot, split and spread with butter.

Potato Pancake

6 raw grated potatoes
3 whole eggs
pinch baking powder
1 tsp salt
2 tbsp flour
a little milk

Peel large potatoes and soak several hours (or overnight) in cold water. Grate, drain and for every pint, allow 2 eggs, about 1 tablespoon flour, ½ teaspoon salt, a little pepper. Beat eggs well and mix with the rest of the ingredients. Drop by spoonfuls on a hot buttered spider (frying pan), in small cakes. Turn and brown on both sides. Or bake in a hot oven in one pancake until crisp and brown, allowing 15 minutes for baking each side. Serve with applesauce.

Settlement Cookbook

Potato Stuffing from "Up West"

5 large potatoes, boiled
¼ cup milk

4 tbsp butter
5 cups dried bread cubes
2 eggs
1 large onion, chopped fine
¾ cup celery, diced
1¼ tsp salt
1 tsp poultry seasoning
black pepper
2 tbsp chives, chopped fine

Drain boiled potatoes and mash with butter and milk. Cool. Soak the bread cubes in cold water and squeeze excess moisture out. Beat the eggs and stir them and all other ingredients into potatoes until all blended.

Bacon and Potato Balls

From a clipping dated Jan. 8, 1938

4 oz scrap bacon
8 oz mashed potatoes
1 tsp Chutney
1 tsp Worcestershire Sauce
pepper
dried bread crumbs
1½ oz flour and water (batter)
margarine or butter (to mash
 the potatoes)

Well mash some potatoes (either cold or freshly cooked), adding margarine. Mince the scrap bacon and mix the chutney, Worcestershire sauce, pepper and salt to taste in the potatoes. Roll the mixture into balls, using well-floured hands. Make a thick coating batter by adding a little cold water to the flour and mixing it into a smooth thick paste; then thin it down with a little more water until it is of the consistency of cream. Drop the balls into this batter, then roll them in bread crumbs. Then drop each ball into deep boiling fat and fry it until it is a rich brown. Drain well before serving.

Fruits

"Because the Micmac was a nomad and because he returned year after year to his same favourite camping places, there grew up around these sites a unique combination of shrubs trees and plants, known as the "Indian Orchard".

The Micmac would pick berries, nuts, etc., and carry them in bark baskets or the leather bag at his waist. As the family sat around their home they would eat these and spit the seeds upon the ground. In time, there grew around their encampment those species of berries, nuts, etc., which formed their diet. Thickets of raspberries, gooseberries, wild roses, haws, wild cherries, chokecherries, cranberries, and hazelnuts grew up wherever the Micmac rested.

Centuries later the tangled profusion of food plants around the campsite came to be one of the clues for searchers which indicated the presence of a former Indian encampment, thus the name 'Indian Orchard'."

Abegweit
was their Home

Apples

Anyone who doubts the popularity of the apple tree in rural Island homes can simply take a drive out in the country, especially down the old clay roads in Central Queens County and count the number of apple trees still producing fruit. They seem to be outnumbered only by the wild roses growing along the roadsides and like the roses are, in many places, free for the picking.

The earliest accountings of settlement tell of the creation of orchards, and virtually everyone mentions apple trees so it is a certainty that they have always played an important role in feeding Island families—just as they do today. Back in 1939-1940 war time shipping difficulties cut down seriously, or even cut off, export of Canadian apples, so the government began a campaign of education, distributing apple recipes, pointing out that the old adage about "an apple a day" was founded on truth. Some of those recipes were so delicious that they were saved and used over and over through the years. A few are repeated below.

Apple Sauce

"Wherever apples are grown, apple sauce is a staple on the farmer's table, so it seems unnecessary to say anything about how to make it. But here are a few suggestions that may be new to some readers:

Unpared Apple Sauce: Wipe, quarter and remove blossom ends, but do not pare or core, eight sour apples. Cover with boiling water. Cook until very soft, rub through a coarse sieve and add 1 cup of sugar. Cooking skins and all gives unusual flavor.

Almond Apple Sauce: Pour apple sauce into a flat serving dish. Sprinkle thickly with chopped almonds and cinnamon. Serve hot or cold, with or without cream"

Farmer's Magazine,
January, 1940

Apple Sherbet

Boil 1 quart of apples in 1 pint of water until soft. Rub through a sieve. Add the juice of 1 orange and 1 lemon, 1 cup sugar and 4 cups water. Beat well and freeze. When it becomes like a slush; add the well-beaten white of 1 egg and finish freezing.

Apple Pandowdy

Slice five or six apples into a deep dish. Add 3 tbsp sugar, 4 tbsp molasses, nutmeg, cinnamon, and salt to taste and mix all together. Cover and bake in a moderate (350°F) oven until soft, then cover with a rich baking powder biscuit crust, extending over the sides and bake for 15-20 minutes longer. Serve by cutting the crust into the apple and smothering with cream.

To Dry Apples

Slices of apple should be suspended on long strings in the attic or across the ceiling of the kitchen or pantry until quite dry. (Try to choose as dust free a place as possible.) Pack away in boxes and store in a cool dry place. To use in an apple pie, etc., plump up by soaking in water overnight. To make sauce, add sugar and cinnamon or maple syrup and simmer. You can also dry slices in the oven, set low (150-200°F), for a couple of hours. When done they will be soft and pliable. Store in plastic bags. Good snacks.

Sausage and Apple Rings

Core but do not peel large tart apples. Cut in ¾-inch slices or rings and fry in fat when sausages are almost cooked. Serve as a garnish for the sausages.

Sweet Apple Cider

Use fully ripened apples free from decay. Wash them thoroughly and remove all leaves. Crush apples and extract the juice or cider in a clean press. Place the juice in a large open preserving kettle, and boil it down until it is reduced to half, skimming it often. Pour at once into hot sterilized jars and seal; or pour the fresh juice at once in jars; put the covers in place loosely, without the rubber; stand the jars in a washboiler on a false bottom; surround them in a bath of warm water to within a few inches of the top of the jars. Cover boiler; place on fire and let water boil and steam one hour. Remove jars one at a time; put a new rubber in place and seal at once. Will keep indefinitely.

To Make Cider Vinegar

Let sweet cider stand in an open jug from 4 to 6 weeks and it will turn to vinegar.

Tarragon Vinegar

3 oz tarragon leaves
1 qt good cider vinegar (or white)

Strip the leaves from the branches of fresh or dried tarragon. Put in a quart fruit can and fill with the vinegar; close and let stand 20 days, then strain. Use for salads or sharp sauces.

Lamb's Wool

Boil 3 quarts of sharp cider down to 2 quarts and, while it is still boiling, add a teacup of brown sugar, also a teaspoon each of allspice, ginger, cloves and cinnamon; place the spice in a bag so it can be removed. Core and bake 6 good cooking apples until well done; scoop the apple out of the peel and put through a sieve. While the apples are still hot add them, with ½ teacup of brandy, to the cider and serve hot.

Tapioca Apple Bake

½ cup quick-cooking tapioca
½ cup sugar
¼ tsp salt
3 cups boiling water
6 medium apples, peel and slice
2 tbsp butter
½ tsp nutmeg

Combine tapioca, sugar, salt and water and bring to boil, stirring constantly. Remove from heat. Place apples in a casserole; dot with butter; sprinkle with nutmeg and then pour the tapioca over top. Bake at 375°F 45 minutes, or until apples are tender. Serves 6-7.

Apple Roly-Poly Pudding

Pare, core and slice sour apples; roll a rich biscuit dough ½-inch thick. Lay the sliced apples on the dough and roll as for jelly roll; tuck in the ends and prick deeply with a fork. Place on a plate dredged with flour; cover with a cloth and steam 45 minutes. Serve with sugar and cream or a sauce.

Coddled Apples and Apple Porcupine

The apples may be pared, cored and left whole or quartered. For 8 apples make a syrup of 2 cups boiling water, 1 cup sugar; add ginger root, or a few cloves and boil 5 minutes. Put apples in the syrup in a shallow dish; cover closely and simmer until tender. Lift the apples out; add a little lemon juice to the syrup and pour over the apples to serve. To make Apple Porcupine, stick apples with pieces of blanched almonds cut in spikes.

Apple Pie

Line pie pan with pastry, fill with thin slices of apple, sprinkle with $\frac{1}{2}$ cup sugar which has been mixed with 1 tsp flour and a pinch of salt. Dot with small pieces of butter. Cover with upper crust and bake in a moderate oven until apples are tender. Cinnamon or nutmeg may be sprinkled over apples when the apples have lost flavour late in the season.

Deep Fried Apples

2 medium-to-large sour apples
powdered sugar
lemon juice

Batter:
$1\frac{1}{3}$ cups flour
2 tsp baking powder
1 egg
$\frac{1}{4}$ tsp salt
$\frac{2}{3}$ cup milk
fat for deep frying

Heat fat for deep frying. Core, pare and cut apples in $\frac{1}{3}$-inch rounds or slices. Sprinkle with powdered sugar and a few drops of lemon juice; cover and let stand one-half hour. Prepare batter by mixing and sifting dry ingredients. Add milk gradually and the well-beaten egg. Drain apples; dip pieces in batter and deep fry in the hot batter. Drain. Sprinkle with sugar and cinnamon to serve.

Other fruit can be used—pineapple, fresh peaches, apricots or pears—and canned fruit that has been drained.

Apple Dumplings

1 cup flour
$\frac{1}{4}$ tsp salt
$\frac{1}{8}$ cup water or milk
2 tsp baking powder
2 tbsp shortening
4 apples
$\frac{1}{2}$ cup sugar

Mix and sift the flour, baking powder and salt. Cut or rub in the shortening; add the liquid, mixing to a soft dough. Roll on a well-floured board to ¼ of an inch thickness. Wipe; pare and core apples. Cut dough in squares; place apple in centre of square and fill the centre with sugar and cinnamon. Moisten edge of dough. Draw dough up around apple to cover. Pierce with fork to allow steam to escape. Steam or bake until apple is tender. Serve with sugar and cream or lemon sauce.

If using apples that do not cook quickly, it is better to slice the apples; sprinkle with sugar and cinnamon; pile on the square of dough and proceed as with whole apples.

Pickled Apples

½ peck apples
1 ounce stick cinnamon
whole cloves
2 lbs brown sugar
1 pt cider vinegar
1 cup water

Boil sugar, vinegar, water and cinnamon 20 minutes. Wipe, quarter, pare and core Canadian-grown apples; if large cut in eighths; stick 2-3 whole cloves in each piece of apple. Put into syrup, cook slowly, until tender, being very careful not to break. Put in only enough apples to cover the bottom of the saucepan. When these are finished remove and continue in the same way until all are cooked. Pour syrup over them in jars.

Even though apples keep very well in a cold cellar, almost every cook preserved some for use during the winter and spring.

Apple Chutney

12 apples
2 cups cider vinegar
1 cup raisins
1 tbsp salt
1 tsp ground ginger
1 tsp cinnamon
1 large onion
4 stalks celery
2 cups sugar
½ tsp pepper
⅛ tsp ground cloves

Wash, quarter and core, but do not peel apples. Chop apples, onion, celery and raisins. Add vinegar and pepper. Cook slowly one hour, stirring often. Add other ingredients. Cook until very thick. Seal in sterilized jars.

Apple Stuffing

(This stuffing is nice for "wild" or gamey birds with more fat than a store-bought chicken.)

10 sweet apples
1 cup currants

Apples are peeled, quartered and mixed with the currants and used as a stuffing.

Bananas

Bananas it seems began to be quite common on the Island around the year 1900 depending, of course, on how close you were to a sea port. In some areas they were more plentiful than oranges.

Banana Whip

1 cup milk
1 cup sugar
2 egg whites
2 tsp gelatin
3 bananas

Scald milk in double boiler; add sugar and when dissolved, stir in gelatin (which has been dissolved in a little cold water). Cool; add pulp of bananas; fold in gently the stiffly beaten egg whites and serve with whipped cream as a garnish. Serves 6.

Guardian, April 7, 1932

Banana sandwiches

I remember my cousins mashing bananas to eat in sandwiches. They used a sprinkle of sugar with theirs.

A very ripe banana, mashed and put between slices of buttered bread makes a very nutritious and appetizing sandwich. Mixed with chopped nuts its delicious.

Shaved chocolate is also a wonderful combination with bananas for sandwiches.

Jam Making

Jam making is a pleasant occupation and not difficult, provided certain rules are carefully followed. Weighing and measuring must be absolutely accurate, and the jam must be boiled till a good set is secured. A common failing of homemade jam is that it is too runny, and preparations are on the market for putting into jam to make it set. This should not be necessary. Certain fruits, such as strawberries, cherries and marrow, for example, are deficient in pectin—the acid which makes jam set—but it is easy to counteract this by adding the juice of fruit rich in pectin, such as lemon, gooseberry or red currant. The juice of the two latter can be extracted by boiling them with a little water till tender and then straining the juice into the other fruit. Green gooseberries, too, cooked with sugar the skins strained off, are excellent with strawberries. Use half and half, and a delicious jam results.

About Jam Making

— Choose a large size preserving pan with plenty of room for jam to boil.

— Make the sugar hot by spreading out on dishes in the oven, let it get very hot, but not enough to colour it. Sugar goes further this way.

— Always use good fruit, freshly picked on a fine day if possible. Wash harder fruits. Go through it carefully and remove any bad or blemished ones.

— Tough fruits should be simmered in a little water till tender before the sugar is added. Tender fruit can have the sugar added at once. Care must be taken that it does not burn before the juice comes out of the fruit.

— Always stir jam once the sugar is in. Do not let the mixture boil until the sugar has dissolved. Use a wooden spoon for stirring.

— When the sugar is dissolved boil the jam rapidly. A large amount of scum will come to the surface. Wait until the jam is nearly done before removing it, as a large part of it will boil back into the jam; the rest can easily be removed with a shallow spoon.

— Test Jam as it thickens and the fruit becomes clear. Test the juice to see if it will set by dropping a very little on to a china plate and putting it by the window for a minute. Touch the drop lightly with one finger. If the surface crinkles the jam is done. Always remove the pan a little from the fire before testing lest the jam get overdone.

— In some jam the fruit is apt to rise to the surface, leaving only syrup at the bottom of the jars. In this case, let the jam cool a bit in the pan and stir before pouring it out.
— Bottle according to the Canada Department of Agriculture's recommendations. (For generations jams, jellies and pickles have been bottled and stored by traditional methods such as covering over with "white kitchen paper, first dipped in milk, and well drained of moisture;" topping with wax or greaseproof paper. (For the safety of your family use the well-researched methods of today.)
— Jam should keep perfectly for a year if stored in a cool, dry place. Never store jam in a cupboard where hot-water pipes run up the walls. In every batch of jam use one glass jar. You can then see if that batch of jam is keeping. The jam cupboard should have air holes bored in the door to ensure ventilation.

About Jelly Making

— It is essential to have a good jelly bag. Various kinds can be bought, but it is quite easy to make one's own. Use strong muslin, and make the bag wide at the top and taper to a point. Sew on loops. A broom handle threaded through them can be balanced on two tables over the basin. Always scald jelly bags before using.
— The fruit should be put in the preserving pan with water and simmered till tender.
— The whole contents of the pan should then be put into the jelly bag. Let it drip all night into a basin. Never squeeze the bag nor try to hurry up the dripping process. If you do, the jelly will be cloudy instead of clear.
— The next day measure the juice and add the sugar. Let the sugar dissolve; then boil rapidly till the jelly will set, stirring all the time. Skim towards the end if necessary.
— Test as for jam, but the drops should keep their shape, as well as crinkling on the surface.
— Pour jelly into the jars as soon as it is done. Do not stir after it leaves the fire.

Marmalade Making

Marmalade can be made very successfully at home and is very economical. February is the best month in which to make marmalade as the fruit is then at its best and cheapest. For those who find the cutting up by hand too laborious, a special cutter can be bought or hired, but with practice one can do it very quickly by hand. The secret is to have a very sharp knife.

This handwritten information has been in my possession for more than 25 years. It was prepared by me for a home economics assignment with a lot of help from my grandmother—and her favourite cookbook. As you can guess I copied it. The teacher failed me for copying but said it was something I should always keep for the good information it contained!

Blackberries

Having always loved blackberries over all fruits, it was with great joy that I discovered them growing wild in the Maritimes. Probably planted many, many years ago by industrious farm women, they still flourish near our home. Probably the best thing I have ever tasted on bread was a blackberry, red currant and apple jelly which my good friend Helen and I made one summer using apples from the family's "Jelly Apple Tree." We have never quite duplicated its wonderful taste—but keep trying combinations of the three fruit searching for the elusive taste.

Blackberry Jam

Many people don't like using blackberries because of their seeds. This jam recipe removes them.

Heat one quart berries very slowly, then mash them through a sieve. Have 3 cups sugar heated in a moderate oven. Pour the blackberry juice and pulp into a kettle; bring to a boil and then add the sugar. Stir both together, boil very rapidly and watch carefully that it does not burn. Boil until it sets or "wrinkles" when a little is taken out in a dish and placed on ice.

If you do not want the seeds removed from the berries, put them at once into the kettle; stir and crush with a wooden spoon and boil thirty minutes; then add sugar and proceed as above. Put in small tumblers and cover tightly.

Mrs. Falconer's People's
Home Recipe Book

Helen's Blackberry Batter

Here is an interesting sweet to make which is the perfect accompaniment for a traditional English Sunday dinner of roast beef and Yorkshire pudding.

Peel and take the cores from the centres of some apples. Fill with blackberry jam and place in a deep dish. Make a batter as for Yorkshire pudding and put in a pie dish till level with the apples. Bake for 45 minutes in a fairly hot oven.

Blackberry Jelly

Wash the berries, measure, and to every quart of berries add 1 cup water. Place in a preserving kettle, and heat slowly but thoroughly. Pour into a jelly bag and drain. Boil the juice rapidly for 5 minutes; measure it; put it into a clean preserving kettle, and add an equal amount of sugar. Continue the rapid boiling until the liquid forms a jelly when cool. Pour into jelly glasses and cover it with melted paraffin.

Blackberry and Apple Jam

8 lbs blackberries
4 lbs cooking apples
12 lbs sugar

Peel and core apples and slice them rather coarsely. Stalk the blackberries and put them with the apples in the preserving pan. Add sugar and heat slowly till it is dissolved, stirring all the time. Then bring to the boil, and let it continue boiling till the jam will set when tested.

Home Management
1934

Blackberry Sauce

Prepare 1 cup of Bechamel sauce without salt or pepper. Stew 2 cups blackberries, add sugar to taste after they have been rubbed through a sieve, then mix the purée with the sauce, stir well, and reheat. Serve with plain pudding, custard, cake or ice cream.

Blueberries

Blueberries, or Whortle Berries, grew in great abundance to the delight of settlers arriving in the 1700s. So much so that they were reported, "in such plenty as to furnish the swine with their chief food for several weeks". John Stewart reported in 1806 that a gallon of spirits resembling gin in flavour, had been distilled from a bushel of Whortle Berries. People of the day seemed to take extraordinary pleasure in stocking up with such spirits. It was said in the early days of the railroad in P.E.I. that the train stopped at everyone's back door. Trains were indeed noted for their slowness. One story related by Gertrude Pendergast tells that the train stopped so long at stations and water tanks that the passengers got off and picked blueberries, "enough for several pies."

About Blueberries

— Make sure blueberries are plump, clean and firm with a silvery bloom which is a natural protective waxy coating. Berries that are past their prime are shrivelled or split open.

— Fresh berries keep longer than any other berry if kept dry and cool, as long as 2-4 weeks. Do not wash until ready to use, wet berries spoil quickly.

— Very versatile in cooking. Delicious raw with sugar and cream. For a quick dessert serve with custard or ice cream.

— Often confused with huckleberries—they both belong to the heather family. Sometimes when picked they are both dropped in the same pail and even sold together.

— Blueberries were harvested by native Indians for food who were in fact drying them like raisins for use throughout the winter long before Europeans arrived.

— To dry, spread thinly on trays and place in sun during the day and a warm room at night for about one week. When thoroughly dry, the berries rattle. Pack in airtight containers. Berries will keep for 12 months and can be substituted for raisins or currants in recipes.

— Add one cup blueberries to your biscuit dough or to pancake batter after all ingredients are mixed.

— Blueberry Cream: combine fresh blueberries, sour cream spiced with nutmeg and a touch of orange marmalade.

Blueberry Buckle

Base: ¼ cup shortening
½ cup sugar
2 eggs
1½ cups flour
½ cup milk
2 tsp baking powder
½ tsp salt
½ tsp nutmeg
¼ tsp cloves, ground

Blend shortening, sugar, eggs and milk. Stir in flour, baking powder, salt, nutmeg and cloves. Spread in a 9- × 9-inch pan.

Filling: Spread base with 1 pint fresh blueberries (or 10-oz frozen dry pack).

Topping: ⅓ cup sugar
⅓ cup flour
½ tsp cinnamon
¼ cup butter

Combine ingredients; mix until crumbly. Sprinkle over top. Bake at 350°F for 45 minutes. Serve warm with whipped cream if desired.

Annie's Blueberry Grunt

1 qt blueberries
½ cup sugar
1 cup water

Boil berries, water and sugar in a large saucepan until there is plenty of juice.

Sift together:
2 cups flour
4 tsp baking powder
½ tsp salt
1 tsp sugar

Add sufficient milk to make a soft dough (a generous ¾ cup), like biscuit dough. Drop by tablespoon over berries. (Use less if you like more juice.) Cover closely and cook for 15 minutes. Serve with cream.

Blueberry Sauce

Serve over ice cream, cream puffs, sponge or angel food cake, puddings, baked custard or pancakes.

½ cup sugar
2 tbsp cornstarch
dash salt
½ cup water
1 pt blueberries
1 tbsp lemon juice
1 tsp grated lemon rind

Combine sugar, cornstarch and salt in saucepan. Stir in water. Add blueberries. Bring to boil; simmer until clear and thickened, about 4 minutes. Remove from heat and add lemon juice and rind. Chill.

Blueberry Tart

Pastry (Try using the Whole Wheat Crust in the baking section or a puff pastry.)

4 cups blueberries
3 tbsp flour (Use whole wheat if using that crust.)
4-6 tbsp maple syrup
Cinnamon to taste

Measure out 1 cup of blueberries and set aside for topping. Press pastry into a straight sided nine-inch tart pan or pie plate. Place three cups of blueberries into the crust and sift the flour over the berries and drizzle with syrup. Lightly dust over with cinnamon if desired. Bake at 350°F for about 50 minutes, until berries are thickened and crust is browned. Remove from the oven and pour the remaining blueberries on top. Dust with icing sugar and serve while still warm. Delicious served with cream or ice cream.

Cherries in Currant Jelly

Delicious!
2 qts currant juice
8 lbs sugar
2 qts stemmed and pitted cherries

Wash, mash and cook slowly at first as many currants, with stems as will make 2 quarts of strained juice. Let juice come to a boil; add sugar and skim; add cherries and cook slowly and steadily for 10 to 15 minutes. Pour in jelly glasses.

Cherry Preserves

5 lbs cherries
5 lbs sugar

Wash cherries carefully and stone. Place in preserving kettle alternating layers of sugar and fruit; let stand overnight. Bring slowly to the boiling point and boil rapidly until thick and clear. Substitute raspberries.

Baked Cherry Preserves (also good with cranberries)

4 qts sour cherries
4 qts sugar
1 gallon stone jars

Stone cherries so they remain whole. Place a tablespoon hot water in a covered casserole, dish or jar, not too full, then alternately in layers cherries and sugar (end with sugar), cover tightly. Bake in a slow oven 2 hours, at 250°F, basting with the syrup several times. Place in hot jars and seal.

Cherry Toast

1 egg
day-old bread
pinch salt
3 tbsp sweetened cherry juice

Dip bread in blended mixture, fry in little hot fat. Serve with a few spiced cherries.

Crab Apple

Only once did I see reference to these small sour apples which had been so much a part of my childhood. We used to pelt each other with them in mock indian battles that raged for days on end. My love affair with cowboy and indian games ended one sunny day when I, as official "white guy" of the day, was tied to a stake (the washing line pole) and forced to eat fried worms. Then and there I realized solitary expeditions to catch minnows and lizards were for me. For that I needed no ammunition so left the crab apples to the birds.

Mamie MacPherson, born in Breadalbane in 1882, remembers her mother serving fresh crab apples, presumably stewed.

Baked Crabapple Preserved

½ peck crabapples
4 lbs sugar
1 gallon stone jars (optional)
1 tbsp water

Wash, wipe and remove the blossom ends of perfect, large, red crabapples. Pour water in bottom of a covered dish or jar, then place in alternate layers of apples and sugar, not too full, (with sugar on top). Cover. Bake 2 or 3 hours in a slow oven, 250°F, basting 3 or 4 times with the hot syrup. Place in sterilized jars, or glasses and seal.

Cranberry

The cranberry has always played an important role in Island kitchens. Readily available they were very simple to store and could easily be exported to Europe for our larger fruit was, and is, much desired. In the early days of sailing ships they were packed in barrels and simply covered with water, where they would remain in good condition for the length of the long sea voyage. Even today, some people keep cranberries in jars covered with water; in this way the berries remain good for months in the refrigerator.

They can also be preserved in jars by boiling them with a little water and sugar until they burst—about 10 minutes—and then sealing them in sterile jars. No heat treatment is necessary. Portions for Cranberry Sauce are 2 cups berries to 1 cup sugar and 1 cup water.

To test cranberries for freshness drop one; fresh, unbruised fruit will bounce. Cranberries will keep up to 8 months in the refrigerator.

Candied Ruby Berries

An old method of making a delicious snacking food.

Spread berries on a cookie sheet; sprinkle with sugar (about 2 cups to a pound of berries). Let stand for half an hour or so; stir; cover and bake at 350°F for $\frac{3}{4}$ hour. Stir gently once or twice. Cool before eating.

Cranapple pie

This is a deep dish pie and delicious.

pastry for one deep dish pie
6 apples, peel, core and slice
2 cups cranberries
$\frac{3}{4}$ cup maple sugar (or
substitute brown sugar)

Mix apples, cranberries and sugar and put into buttered baking dish. Cover with dough and then sprinkle it well with sugar and cinnamon. Bake at 375°F for 30-40 minutes.

Spiced Cranberries

5 lbs cranberries
$3\frac{1}{2}$ lbs brown sugar
2 cups vinegar
2 tbsp ground cinnamon and
allspice
1 tbsp cloves

Boil all together for two hours. Serve with hot or cold meats.

Cranberry Jelly

1 qt cranberries
2 cups sugar
1 pt boiling water

Boil berries and water about 15 minutes; strain. Add as much sugar as juice and boil 10 minutes. Pour into mold. Grated orange rind may be added to sugar if desired.

Cranberry Ice

1 qt cranberries
2 cups water
2 cups sugar
Juice of 2 lemons, strained

Cook cranberries and water 8 minutes; force through sieve. Add sugar, lemon juice and cool using a hand freezer. Today we can substitute a blender for the sieve and chill in the fridge.

Carol's Cranberry Preserves

It seems that preserving was often done in the oven instead of on the stove top. This habit came about when people would light the wood or oil stove on crisp fall days and simply took advantage of having a hot oven.

4 qts cranberries which are perfect
equal sugar

Place a tablespoon hot water in a covered casserole then alternately layer cranberries and sugar, ending with sugar. Cover closely and bake two hours at 250°F, basting from time to time. Put into hot jars and seal.

Mock Cranberry Frappe

Presumably called mock because a true frappe was a drink either made with partly frozen fruit juice, or poured over crushed ice. I believe this was a recipe from an old Watkins book.

2 level tsp gelatin
1 qt cold water
1 qt cranberries
2 ½ cups granulated sugar
½ cup boiling water
Juice of 2 lemons

Soak gelatin in 1 pint cold water. Cook cranberries in the other pint of cold water and when soft press through a sieve. Add boiling water to gelatin then add it, sugar, lemon juice and chill overnight.

Dried Fruit

Dried fruits such as apricots, peaches, apples, prunes, and also the smaller fruits such as currants, raisins, figs and dates have made a comeback in recent years. Today we are fortunate to have good quality dried fruit which is generally clean and free of debris. Some varieties of raisins and sultanas, however, need to be cleaned and have seeds removed. Place these in a colander and rinse well with cold water, picking through as you go. Shake out as much water as possible then spread on a cloth to dry overnight. You may even have to place in a warm oven if dry fruit is needed for baking. This used to be done when dried fruit was brought home from infrequent visits to the store. When completely dried the fruit would be packed away in jars. Wet fruit will not keep and, if used in cakes or puddings, will sink to the bottom.

A trick for cleaning the small currants is to mix in a little flour then rub in a sieve. Stalks and dirt will, I am told, come off with the flour.

To Stew Dried Fruits: apricots, pears, prunes, apples, etc. should be rinsed then soaked overnight in fresh cold water. In the morning cook them in the same water. Here taste comes into effect. I can easily bring to mind the tantalizing aroma of stewed fruit simmering on the stove as my mother prepared a potful for my father who loves it. As I recall she just simmered it gently until it was soft and tender with no sweetener. You can, of course, add sugar to taste, and even a shaving a lemon rind for flavour. Dad likes his with Birds Custard.

For home drying see index.

Canned Elderberries (Excellent)

Add 2½ pounds of sugar and 1 pint of pure cider vinegar to 7 pounds of elderberries; boil 1 hour. Then seal in jars. This will make four jars and is excellent for pies.

Gooseberry

The Gooseberry was one of the shrubs noted by Cartier on his first visit. It was very common along the edges of forests and often sprung up on land that had been cleared. Coming early in the spring, they were available for baking, for which they are very good, before any other fruit. They also preserve well in jams and jellies.

Gooseberry and Currant Tarts

1 can (No. 2) gooseberries
1 can (No. 2) red currants
1 tbsp cornstarch
6-8 baked tart shells
½ cup whipped cream

Drain juice from fruit. To the juice add cornstarch and cook until clear and thick, stirring to keep the mixture smooth. Add sugar to sweeten, if desired. Add drained fruit and cool. Pour into baked tart shells. Top with whipped cream.

Watkins 1933

Gooseberry Jam

5 lbs gooseberries
1 pkg seedless raisins
5 lbs sugar
4 medium-sized oranges, peel
  and cut up pulp

Partially cook gooseberries, oranges and raisins, then add sugar. Cook until right consistency for jam, then seal in sterilized jars.

Spiced Gooseberries

3 qts gooseberries
4 lbs sugar
1 pt vinegar
2 tbsp cinnamon
½ tbsp cloves
1 tbsp allspice

Remove stem and blossom; wash clean; make syrup of sugar and vinegar. Add berries; boil until thick. Add more sugar if necessary. When almost done, spice with cinnamon, cloves and allspice. Boil as thick as for apple butter. Seal in sterilized jars.

Fruit Jam

1 qt gooseberries
1 qt raspberries

1 qt cherries
1 qt currants (red or black)
sugar

Wash; crush fruit; mix thoroughly; add sugar; blend together. Add 1 pound sugar to 1 pound fruit; boil until sufficiently thick. Seal in sterilized jars.

Lemons

With the arrival of ships from the West Indies lemons and oranges became available in homes. What useful items they were. As well as being a valuable source of vitamin C, a wonderful flavoring and delicious to eat; they had many other uses:

To soften and whiten hands:
Take three tablespoonfuls of lemon juice, strained through a piece of muslin to remove pips and pulp, and shake up with one tablespoonful of glycerine.

For the arms:
Many women suffer from a red, goose-fleshy look on the upper arms in winter time. Here is a very good soothing and bleaching lotion which is inexpensive and easy to make up. Take equal parts of Hydrogen Peroxide, strained lemon juice and glycerine. Pour into a perfectly clean bottle and shake up thoroughly. Store until required, shaking the bottle afresh every time it is used. It should be applied at bedtime and rubbed thoroughly—the rubbing helps by stimulating the circulation.

To remove tan, lighten hair, soften elbows are just a few cosmetics used for lemons and their peel.

Thin slices of peel in hot water make an excellent steam to inhale for soothing the nasal passages when stuffed up with a cold. A hot drink of lemon and honey cannot be beaten for soothing the throat and the well being. Taking lemon juice was also recommended for cold sores on the lips and sores in the mouth.

Lemon Dessert

1 small can evaporated milk
2 eggs separated
½ cup white sugar
⅓ cup fresh lemon juice
Grated rind of 1 lemon

Pour evaporated milk into tray and chill in refrigerator until crystals form around edge. Separate eggs, beat yolks until thick and lemon-colored. Add sugar and beat until well blended. Add lemon juice and grated rind. Beat egg whites stiff. Then lightly fold in yolk mixture. Turn chilled milk into bowl and beat until stiff peaks form. Fold the egg mixture into the milk, and pour into ice cube trays. Freeze quickly at high control. For a Sunday dinner or special company dessert this sherbet-like mixture is delicious served over plain sponge or angel cake.

To Keep Lemons

They will keep and also be more juicy if kept covered with cold water. The water should be changed each week.

Lemon Sauce

1 lemon rind and juice
2 cups hot water
1 cup sugar
2 tbsp cornstarch
2 tbsp butter

Mix the sugar and cornstarch; add the boiling water gradually, stirring all the time. Cook 8 to 10 minutes; add lemon juice and butter. Serve hot over pudding or cake.

Zest of Citrus

Zest originally applied to the tough outer skin of a walnut but now is referred to as the thin, oily outer skin of citrus fruits such as lemon or orange which contain flavouring oils. A thin shaving of peel (the colored part) is pared off. Sometimes it is rubbed off onto lumps of sugar. (Handy little shavers can be be found in gourmet shops.)

Crystallized Lemons and Oranges

Boil together for one-half hour one cupful of granulated sugar and one of water. Dip the point of a skewer or darning needle in the syrup after it has been boiling the given time and then in water. If the thread formed breaks off brittle, the syrup is done. Pare the fruit, divide into eighths and wipe free of moisture. Pour part of the hot syrup into a cup, which keep in boiling water. Take the pieces of fruit on the point of the large needle and dip them in the syrup. Place them on a dish that has been buttered lightly. Care must be taken not to stir the syrup as that spoils it.

Fruit Glace is made with the syrup above. Take any prepared fruits desired, (grapes, pineapple, cherries, etc.) on the point of a darning needle; dip them in the syrup; when cold they are ready for use. Decorate with them—lovely on cakes and such.

> *"J. Bowes, merchant, announces having received, per the Sir Walter Scott (arrived at Three Rivers) the remainder of his winter supply, consisting of a variety of 'fur caps, elegant silk shawls and ladies' handkerchiefs, cravats, cotton wool, violin strings, etc., a small assortment of perfumery; also wine, gin, olives and brandy fruits, in cases; walnuts, almonds, currants, lemons and oranges; sealing wax and wafers; an assortment of large and elegant framed pictures; knives and forks, needles and buttons; almanacs; a few boxes of real Spanish cigars, wine corks, prime sole leather, and other articles; also on hand, teas, groceries, a pipe of Port wine, seal and codfish oils, etc."*
>
> *P.E.I. Register*
> *March 11, 1828*

Lemon Brandy

1 pt brandy
rind of two small lemons
2 oz sugar
¼ pt water

Peel the lemons rather thin, taking care to have none of the white pith. Put the rinds into a bottle with the brandy, and let them infuse for 24 hours, when they should be strained. Now boil the sugar with the water for a few minutes, skim it, and, when cold, add it to the brandy. A dessert spoonful of this will be found an excellent flavouring for boiled custards.

"Mrs. Beeton's Book
of Household Management
1861"

Melon

The Musk Melon, one of those delicious juicy importations from the sunny south—right? Not so. Jacques Cartier, credited with discovering Prince Edward Island, repeatedly stated in his diary that the Indians at Hochelaga (Montreal) cultivated cucumbers and melons (musk). In fact, experts have used this statement as proof that the Spaniards discovered Canada. According to Robert W. Boyle, a writer in Canadian Geographic:

> *"The Spaniards were the first who discovered Canada; but at their first arrival, having found nothing considerable in it, they abandon'd the Country, and call'd it Il Capo di Nada; that is A Cape of Nothing; hence by corruption springs the word Canada, which we use in all Maps."*
>
> *A New Discovery of a Vast Country in America, by the Flemish Father Louis Hennepin, published in 1668 in London.*

Just to add another twist to our melon tale, it could have been the Vikings who introduced both melons and cucumbers to the St. Lawrence Valley.

> *"They were avid disseminators of all manner of horticultural, forest and metal products."*
>
> *Robert W. Boyle, Canadian Geographic*
> *November 1984*

Oranges

Oranges were not as readily available as lemons or even, it seems bananas. Many fond memories of finding one tucked at the very end of a Christmas stocking avail.

If you wish to use oranges for cooking purposes, or anything in the kitchen, drop them into a pan of boiling water for a few minutes, and you will find they can be peeled ever so easily. And. if this is done, there will be no bother with the white pith inside, for it comes away with the peel.

Ambrosia

Because the fruit used in this dessert was expensive, the family usually enjoyed such a treat at Christmas. Ambrosia would be served at a yule gathering where the food was meant to please and impress. A banana can be added for a nice touch.

4 large oranges, peel, seed and section, remove all white pith
6 tbsp sugar
3½-4 oz flaked coconut
3 tbsp orange juice
2 maraschino cherries (optional)

Slice the orange into thin slices and cut the cherries into eighths; make two-three layers or orange sprinkled with sugar and coconut and a tablespoon of orange juice over each layer. Cover and chill for several hours. Garnish with maraschino cherries.

This is nicest when made in a fancy glass bowl and taken to the table to be served.

Grated Peel

To grate lemon or orange peel, take washed, and dried, fruit and rub with short strokes across the small section of a fine grater. Grate only the coloured part of the peel, for the white can be bitter. A medium orange will give about 2 tablespoons of grated peel, and medium lemon about 1 tablespoon.

Orange Gin

1 fine large Seville orange
6 cloves
1½ pt gin or rectified spirit
1¼ lb sugar

Stick the cloves into the orange; put it into a jar with the gin or spirit; cover and let remain for a month; boil the sugar quickly with half pint of water; when cool add it to the jar and leave for another month, then filter through blotting paper; pour into bottles; cork securely and store for use.

Note: a coffee filter is excellent to replace blotting paper.

San Diego Orange Marmalade

6 Naval Oranges
3 lemons
7 cups water
Sugar

Cut off the ends of the oranges and lemons and throw away. Peel thin oranges and lemons round and round like an apple and then cut with shears very fine. Remove the white skin and cut pulp into fine pieces. Cover the pulp and shredded peel well with cold water and let stand 12 to 24 hours. Drain; add the water and cook until reduced one inch or until the rinds are tender. Add equal amount of sugar and cook until it jellies.

Peaches

Peaches have not, that I have been able to find, been successfully grown on the Island. They have, however, been available in cans, and fresh when in season. I heard with interest from a fellow in his 80s that he remembered his father bringing home a crate of peaches from a train trip to Ontario. He was just a young lad at the time and spent several days helping his mother make jam and preserves. He says he didn't mind working in the kitchen while the other boys were outside, because he got to eat all the parts that were cut out as not suitable for preserving.

Dried fruit, including peaches, was an important item in the larder of yesteryear.

Peach Jam

3 lbs dried peaches
9 pts water
9 lbs sugar
Juice of 2 lemons

Cut the peaches into pieces. Stand them in the water for 24 hours. Add the lemon juice and boil slowly till the fruit is tender. Add the sugar; let it dissolve and then boil rapidly till the juice will set when tested. Pour it into warm dry jars.

Anne's Peach Salad

Arrange halves of fine large peaches, hollow side up on salad plates covered with lettuce or endive. Chop heart of celery and sliver almonds; moisten with mayonnaise and fill in the cavity of the peach. Garnish with cranberry jelly and greenery such as parsley.

The lady who gave me the two recipes that follow said that it was a family favourite for it was so good. She related that she lost the original material from whence they came but thought it was dated in the mid 1800s and came from a doctor's book. Fortunately for us she had written out these and some other recipes for her sister, and years later when going through old papers found them, so was able to start making the relish again. Peaches she said were not often to be had, and when obtained had to be well used. Preserving them this way meant "more use was got out of the fruit."

Mrs. Doucette was well into her late years and has passed away since we talked. Typical of many Islanders, she was born up west and spent some years in New England before returning to her native land to raise a family "up west of Summerside." She represented to me the greatest treasure to be found in the province—the storytellers, those elderly people with so much tradition and heritage in their memories. It is the essence of what makes Prince Edward Island the unique community it is. People still take the time to talk, to listen and to value the ties of family and neighbour.

Mrs. Doucette's Pickled Peach Relish

Using a brush, take the down from the skin of ripe, sound clingstone peaches. Make hot a gallon of good vinegar; add four pounds of coarse brown sugar; boil it down and skim it clean. Stick four or five cloves in each peach, put them into a stone jar, and strain the vinegar over them whilst hot. Cover the stone jar and set it in a cold place for a few days, but less than a week. Drain off the vinegar; make it boiling hot again; strain it over, and set them away. (Bottle them.) Freestone peaches can be used instead.

Brandy Peaches (for special occasions)

Drop peaches in hot water, until the skin can be ripped off. Make a thin syrup (sugar and water) and let it cover the fruit. Boil the fruit until they can be pierced with a straw (this is the farm straw not the plastic drinking kind). Take the fruit out and make a very rich syrup. Add, after it is taken from the fire, yet while still hot, an equal part of brandy. Pour this liquor, while it is still warm, over the peaches in the dish so that they are all covered.

Peach Port Wine Sauce

4 medium peaches, peeled,
 pitted and sliced
¼ cup port
2 tbsp sugar
1 tsp cornstarch

In a medium saucepan, combine peaches, port and sugar. Cook, covered, over a medium heat, stirring occasionally until peaches are tender. Blend cornstarch with a little cold water and stir into hot peaches. Continue cooking for 1-2 minutes, stirring gently until fruit sauce has thickened slightly. Cool. (Note: although the recipe says to cool, I love this served warm over white cake.)

Pears

Some early references to pears growing in orchards confirms that this fruit has long been enjoyed on the Island. Since they can be picked when mature, but not ripe, they store quite well and would last into the fall.

As pears ripen from the inside out, they should not be kept until soft on the outside. If they become soft, keep cool and humid and use as soon as possible. If cooking, baking or bottling use firm, slightly under-ripe fruit.

Adrianne's Pear Tourtiere

pastry for a two-crust deep dish
 pie (9-inch)
1½ lbs lean ground pork
½ cup onion, finely chopped
½ cup beef broth

1 clove garlic, minced
1½ tsp poultry seasoning
¼ tsp ground nutmeg
¼ tsp black pepper
¼ tsp ground allspice
¼ tsp salt
3 pears

In large frypan combine pork, onion, broth, garlic, poultry seasoning, nutmeg, pepper, allspice and salt. Cook over medium heat 15 minutes or until pork loses its pink colour and liquid has almost evaporated, but mixture is moist. Set aside to cool.

Line pie plate with pastry. Spread half of meat mixture over pastry. Peel, core and chop pears; layer over meat. Top with remaining meat. Cover with top crust. Seal pastry and flute edges. Cut slits in top. Bake at 425°F for 25-30 minutes until crust is golden.

Pear Butter

Delicious served with toast cooked on an open fire in the cool crisp days of fall.

5 medium pears, cut into
 ½-inch cubes (about 4 cups)
¾ cup sugar
1 stick cinnamon
¼ cup chopped almonds
2 tsp fresh lemon juice

Combine pears, sugar and 2 tbsp water in saucepan. Heat to boiling point over medium heat. Reduce heat and simmer 30 minutes, stirring frequently. Remove cinnamon stick. Remove pear mixture from heat. Mash until smooth. Stir in almonds and lemon juice. Cook over low-medium heat, stirring constantly, until consistency of thick applesauce. Chill. Makes about 2 cups. Serve in a crock.

Pear Sauce

12 pears
¼ cup water

Wash pears; cut into quarters and core. Place in large saucepan; add water and cover. Cook over low heat, stirring occasionally, until pears are tender, about 20 minutes. Pass through a food mill (or use a blender) until smooth. Serve warm or cold as dessert or as a condiment with pork or chicken.

Sweeten with honey or spice with cinnamon if you desire.

Pear Sauce Gingerbread

1-2 pears
½ cup butter
½ cup brown sugar
1 egg
½ cup molasses
1¾ cups all-purpose flour
1 tsp baking powder
½ tsp baking soda
1 tsp cinnamon
½ tsp ground ginger
½ tsp salt
⅔ cup Pear Sauce (See Preceeding Recipe)

Peel and core pears. Slice lengthwise. To prevent browning, submerge in salted water using ¼ tsp salt to 2 cups water. Drain well just before using.

Cream butter and sugar together. Add egg and molasses; beat thoroughly. Sift together flour, baking powder, baking soda, spices and salt; add alternately with pear sauce.

Arrange pear slices in an attractive pattern on bottom of a 9-inch round greased baking pan. Pour batter over pears and bake at 350°F for 35-40 minutes or until a knife inserted in center comes out clean.

Allow to cool 5 minutes, then invert onto a serving plate. Serve warm with whipped cream. Serves 8.

Prince John Pears

canned pear halves
red wine
cinnamon stick
fresh or powdered ginger
saffron

Drain pears, retaining liquid. Measure liquid and add an equal quantity of red wine. Add a small stick of cinnamon, a half-inch knob of green ginger, peeled (or ¼ tsp powdered), ¼ tsp saffron. Boil down quickly until reduced to half. Pour over the pears. Cover and allow to cool in their own liquid. Serve warm or chilled in your very best glass goblets.

Spiced Baked Pears

4 fresh pears
¼ cup sugar
1 tbsp grated orange rind
½ cup fresh orange juice
2 tbsp fresh lemon juice
1-inch stick cinnamon
2 whole cloves

Peel and core pears. Arrange in greased baking dish. Combine remaining ingredients and pour over pears. Cover and bake in moderate oven (350°F) 20-25 minutes or until tender. Remove cinnamon stick and cloves. Serve hot or cold with cream if desired. Serves 4.

Plums

Some of the earliest accounting of orchards make mention of plum trees being planted along with cherry and apple. Variety is rarely mentioned, but it would seem from recipes found that the majority were the blue or purple plum. Numerous varieties were found growing wild in North America and cultivated by ambitious newcomers. They make excellent jams and preserves.

Plum Conserve—a very old recipe

5 lbs blue plums
2 oranges
1 lemon
1 lb raisins, chopped
½ lb walnut meats, chopped
3 lbs sugar

Wash, peel plums and remove stones. Chop orange with peel. Add grated rind and juice of lemon. Add raisins and walnuts. Mix thoroughly in a heavy bottomed pot and boil until quite thick. Seal in pint jars.

Stewed Plums

Plums can be stewed more quickly on the top of the stove, but they tend to burst their skins. This method lessens the tartness of plums. Lovely served with thick or clotted cream, or ice cream.

1½ lbs plums
½ tsp ground cinnamon
¾ cup sugar
5 tbsp water

Melt the sugar and cinnamon in the water in a covered casserole, placed in the oven. Add the fruit and bake at 350°F for 20-25 minutes, or until tender. Turn over carefully once or twice during cooking.

Plum Tart

½ cup butter
½ cup sugar
1 egg, slightly beaten
2 cups all-purpose flour
1 tsp baking powder
25 prune plums
1½ tsp sugar

Cream butter and sugar together. Add egg and mix well. Stir flour and baking powder together then blend into creamed mixture. Roll into a ball, wrap in waxed paper and chill at least an hour. This makes enough for two nine-inch pastry shells. Roll out half of the pastry to line each pie plate. Reserve one for a second tart, or later use.

To prepare the plums, start cutting lengthwise, from the midpoint on one side all around to almost meet again. This will leave a 'hinge' on the plum. Remove pit. Close plum and make a one-inch slit down from the top so when it is reopened the tops fan slightly. Each plum should look like two petals.

Arrange a row of plums, partially standing, flesh side up around outer edge of pie shell. Continue to build attractive rings of semi-upright plums into centre of pie shell. Place half a plum cup side up in centre.

Bake at 325°F for 20 to 30 minutes until plums are tender and crust is cooked. To prevent excessive browning cover with greased paper (or a strip of aluminum foil) for the first half of baking time. After removing tart from the oven, immediately sprinkle with sugar.

Plum Loaf

Makes two tasty loaves

2 lbs prune plums (about 34)
4 thin slices lemon
4 whole allspice
2-inch cinnamon stick
¼ tsp ground nutmeg
1 cup sherry
2 tbsp dry bread crumbs
3 cups all-purpose flour, sifted
1 tsp baking soda
1 tsp mace
½ tsp salt
1 cup butter
2 cups sugar
4 eggs
½ cup milk
zest of one lemon, grated (see index)
3 tbsp lemon juice
2 cups walnuts, coarsely chopped

Wash plums and place in a large saucepan along with lemon slices, allspice, cinnamon stick, nutmeg and sherry. Heat until hot but not boiling. Reduce heat to very low and poach 10-15 minutes until skins of plums begin to split. Turn plums over halfway through. Drain and reserve ½ cup liquid. Discard lemon slices and whole spices. When plums are cool, pit and cut into eighths.

Grease two 9- × 5-inch loaf pans and sprinkle the sides and bottom with dry bread crumbs. Sift flour, soda, mace and salt into a large bowl. Cream butter in a separate bowl. Gradually beat in sugar until light and fluffy. Add eggs one at a time, beating well after each.

Fold half of flour mixture into creamed mixture. Stir in milk, add remaining flour and reserved plum-sherry liquid. Add lemon zest and lemon juice. Fold plums and walnuts into batter.

Pour into prepared pans and bake at 350°F for 50-60 minutes or until knife inserted in center comes out clean. Cool on wire racks before cutting.

Prunes

Prunes (dried plums) have been a winter staple for generations and certainly should not be overlooked today. Stewed they were most often served with custard or junket for dessert. Of course, we all know about prunes for breakfast to aid in "keeping one's system clean and well working." They can also be liquidized or pushed through a sieve to make a purée to use in cold sweets. Soaked, cooked, puréed and mixed with cream they make excellent ices (place in trays in freezer and stir frequently to make a 'slush.' (See index under dried fruit for directions on stewing prunes.)

Raspberry

In 1806 John Stewart wrote that the raspberry found growing wild on the Island

> *"is equal to any I ever saw in England, though growing wild, I never saw the white species produced but in one spot of small extent, at first I was inclined to think they had been imported, but upon enquiry, I was convinced they were like the red, the indigenous production of the soil, though they appeared to be as fine flavoured, and large as any I ever saw."*

Because raspberries must ripen on the cane for good flavour, it is often difficult to get good ones in the stores. Check the bottom of the container to see if there is any red juice stain. If there is, the berries have likely begun to rot. It is almost impossible to buy a pint or quart of raspberries without some mildewing. Lift those berries out with a toothpick to avoid contaminating the rest. The best way to get raspberries is to pick them just before you plan to use them, or visit a farm and buy freshly picked ones.

Raspberries and Cream

Like the other garden berries, raspberries are hard to beat served with heavy cream and a sprinkle of sugar. Ladies fingers, white cake and shortbread biscuits are as nice with these as strawberries.

Puréed Raspberries

If the seeds bother anyone at your table, push the berries through a sieve to make a sauce and serve over ice cream with cake.

Raspberry Cordial

Originally a spirit sweetened and infused with fruit or other agent to add flavour and scent cordial today is usually non-alcoholic and often concentrated so that it can be watered down to drink.

There is no question that raspberry cordial with a "punch" was to be found in Island homes, as any fan of Anne of Green Gables will know. One of the most popular scenes in the stage version of Lucy Maud Montgomery's novel is the "has Anne's young friend Diana imbibing in cordial"—much to the delight of the audience.

To one gallon juice add two pounds of loaf sugar, one-half ounce of cloves, one ounce of nutmeg, cinnamon and allspice; boil 25 minutes; add one quart of brandy when cold. Good with blackberry or raspberry.

Raspberry Shrub

A non-alcoholic drink:

Place raspberries in stone jar, cover with good cider vinegar, let stand over night; next morning strain and to one pint of juice add one pint of sugar; boil ten minutes; bottle while hot. Use about one-half glassful of shrub to one-half glassful of pounded ice and cold water. Delicious drink for summer.

An alcoholic drink:

One quart of red or black raspberry juice (make as you would for jelly), one-half pound of loaf sugar. Dissolve, then add one pint of good Jamaica rum. Mix thoroughly and bottle. To make a glassful of raspberry drink use one tablespoon of the shrub, the same of sugar, and fill glass with ice water.

All from Canada's Favourite Cookbook

Wild Raspberry

These recipes are best made with wild berries and are a real incentive to pack up the family and head out to the countryside to pick wild berries. The wild berries can be treated in just the same manner as cultivated, however, any connôisseur will tell you that nothing can equal wild raspberries. Just remember if you pick them along the roadside, they will be dusty and need washing well. We have a good friend who picks wild berries each year and makes the most delicious jams ever tasted. She always brings us a supply which we save for special treats.

Wild Raspberry Jam

8 cups raspberries, crushed
6 cups superfine sugar

Wash berries in cold water and pick them well for leaves, insects, etc. Using a large enamel or stainless steel saucepan, crush the berries then heat through over medium heat. When hot, add the sugar, stirring constantly until it is all dissolved. Continue cooking until it is thick, like jam, then bottle in sterilized jars.

Wild Raspberry Pudding Mold

1 qt raspberries (good clean berries only)
1 cup sugar
6 slices white bread (homemade type is best for old-fashioned flavour)
1 cup heavy cream

Wash in cold water and shake berries dry. Mix berries and sugar in a bowl, gently, until sugar turns to juice. Line the bottom of a deep bowl with the bread, then the sides overlapping the bread. Pour in the fruit and cover the top completely with the rest of the bread. Press by placing a flat plate on the mixture and a weight on the plate. Leave in cool place overnight (at least 12 hours). Unmold by inverting quickly onto a cold serving plate. Whip the cream until it holds peaks then cover the molded pudding with the cream. Garnish with fresh berries and serve well chilled. I usually double this recipe as we like it so well. Just remember the trick is to take the time lining the mold fully, with no gaps.

Raspberry and Apple Butter

Also good made with blueberries

1 qt raspberries
1 qt apple pulp
3 lbs sugar

Use tart apples. Remove stems; cut in quarters. Add enough water to cover and cook until soft. Put through a strainer. Measure apple pulp and raspberries and take an equal amount of sugar; cook until clear and thick. Place in clean, hot jars and seal.

Spring Storehouse

Mamie MacPherson, born in 1882 remembers her mother making mostly apple, rhubarb and custard pies. She stored the apples in barrels in the cellar. In those days you could only preserve fruit in jams. One thing her father did that was not very common was that when the sugar got low from making jam and preserves, her mother would cook raspberries until they ran and then her father would put it in a crockery jar and seal the top and then he would go down to the brook and dig a hole deep enough so that the water ran over the top and that would stay there for the winter and be just as good in the spring.

Rhubarb

Rhubarb, first valued for its medicinal properties, gained popularity in the nineteenth century as a food, particularly valued as the first fruit of spring. It was natural that it quickly joined the gardens of Islanders. Even as a simple remedy for cleaning pots (just stew the stalks) it was worth cultivating.

The best flavoured, and the most tender, rhubarb is the early pink stemmed spring plant that has been forced. It is easily done by using straw and bottomless buckets to promote early growth.

To Cook

Stewed rhubarb: Place rhubarb, cut into one-inch pieces; sugar and a small amount of water in a pan and simmer until tender. For delicious flavour add strawberries, or a few drops of strawberry extract when almost done.

Baked Rhubarb: Place rhubarb and sugar (sparingly; one-half cup per pound of rhubarb) in an oven-proof dish and bake at 350°F for about 25 minutes.

With fish serve puréed rhubarb (stewed) for a French touch.

Rhubarb leaves should never be eaten as they can be poisonous.

Rhubarb Jelly

Cut enough rhubarb to fill a quart basin (in small pieces). Place it and ½ pound sugar in a stewpan with the strained juice of half a lemon and the grated lemon rind. Add about a tablespoonful of water to prevent burning and cook over moderate heat until it is a soft pulp, stirring from time to time. Dissolve ½ ounce powdered gelatin in enough hot water to cover it and stir it into the pulp. Pour into a wet mold and leave until set. Turn out and decorate with strawberries and nuts. Serve with custard.

Rhubarb Short Cake

4 cups flour
2 tsp cream of tartar
1 tsp soda
1 tbsp sugar
1 tsp salt
½ cup butter
1 egg
1 cup (large) milk
Stewed rhubarb
Sugar

Sift together flour, cream of tartar, soda, sugar and salt. Rub the butter into the dry ingredients. Beat the egg and add the milk. Stir lightly and quickly into the prepared flour. Roll in two sheets ½-inch thick, laying one sheet on top of the other. Bake in a hot oven. While hot separate layers, spread stewed rhubarb between layers sandwich fashion. Sprinkle sugar on top and serve hot.

Strawberry shortcake can be prepared the same way spreading chopped strawberries and sugar between layers and on top.

To Cut a Shortcake: Take a firm hold of a piece of silk thread at either end as you would a knife. It will not make it soggy like using a knife. Especially good for splitting hot shortcake.

Baked Rhubarb Pudding

2 cups flour
½ tsp salt
2 cups rhubarb, cut into pieces
½ cup shortening
2 tsp baking powder
1 lemon (grate rind and squeeze
   juice from half)
6 tbsp brown sugar
water
½ cup white sugar

Brown the white sugar in a pan over medium heat, then coat the inside of a smooth-sided pudding bowl with it. Sift together flour, salt and baking powder, then rub the shortening into it. Mix this to a smooth dough by adding cold water. When it forms a ball, remove to a floured board and cut off one third to set aside. Roll out the rest until it will line the bowl (probably about twice the size of the top of the bowl). Line the bowl by gently lowering the dough into it and patting against the sides until all is even and laps over the edge. Put in rhubarb, lemon juice and rind, brown sugar and 3 tbsp water. Roll out reserved pastry to cover top. Wet edges and seal. Cut slits in top. It is best if you can cover with a piece of greased paper or brush top with milk and watch you don't burn it. Bake at 350°F for one hour. Turn out to serve. Nice topped with custard sauce or milk.

Short Day's Pud

This dish was so called because it could be made from stale bread and rhubarb from the garden on the days before money was due into the household funds.

1 lb rhubarb, cut in cubes
4 oz granulated sugar
Stale bread
½ pt custard

Line a basin with stale bread, stew the rhubarb with the sugar and very little water. Put a layer of rhubarb in the lined basin, then more bread, continuing until the basin is full. Cover with bread; pour in the juice. Cover with a plate with a weight on it. Leave for some hours. Then turn out and serve with custard.

Strawberries

Jacques Cartier mentioned strawberries in his accounting of landing on the Island in 1534. John Stewart in 1806 wrote that the berry is very common. "They are all of the scarlet kind, and though small, are well flavoured, and in some situations, grow large and in great plenty; it has been remarked that wherever the strawberry grows before the soil is cultivated, it afterwards throws up white clover in great abundance."

By 1918, a trade amounting to about $12,000 was being done with neighbouring provinces in strawberries according to

Heaton's Annual. It reported farmers planting small plots and predicted good things for commercially grown strawberries. The success predicted is with us today, providing the cook with an abundance of luscious red berries which are put down as frequently today as ever. For it is so simple to do.

Summer Pudding

An old fashioned sweet best made with a mixture of fruits. Strawberries and gooseberries used to be a favourite because they usually ripened at the same time. Black currants, gooseberries and raspberries or raspberries and currants are good combinations. In fact, when black currants are not available a tablespoon of black currant jam adds the right tang. The fruit must be cooked and sweetened.

Line a bowl or basin with slices of stale bread that have been buttered well. The bowl should have been buttered first. Cut a round piece to fit the bottom and lay it in. Pour in some of the fruit juice, then alternate layers of stewed fruit and bread and butter until the basin is full. Cover the top with a slice of bread and butter with the butter down. Cover with a plate and put a weight on it to press. Refrigerate. The next day turn out of the pudding basin onto a plate and top with whipped cream.

Crushed Berries

"Use all good berries. Mash with silver fork. (Don't let tin touch them.) To one cup berries add one cup sugar. Soak overnight, stirring frequently. Bottle and wax. These will keep all winter without freezing. (Where it says 'soak', means let the mixture stand.)

My mother-in-law used to do these. Those were the days before electricity in the country. They were put in mason jars, and kept either in the porch cupboard, or cellar, along with jams."

Strawberry Cordial

Slightly sweeten big, perfect strawberries with caps removed. At serving time spoon into goblets and splash with orange-flavoured liquor.

Caps On

The caps, or leaves of berries should not be removed before washing strawberries you wish to serve whole as they prevent the water from soaking into the berry and diluting the flavour and changing the texture. To serve with caps on try these:

— dip berries into powdered sugar and eat
— dip into sour cream, (or yogurt) and then into brown sugar

Preserved Strawberries in Wine

"To every quart bottle allow ¼ pound of finely pounded loaf sugar and sherry or madeira.

Let the fruit be gathered in fine weather and used as soon as picked. Have ready some perfectly dry glass bottles, and some nice soft corks or bungs. Pick the stalks from the strawberries, drop them into the bottles, sprinkling amongst them pounded sugar in the above portion, and when the fruit reaches the neck of the bottle, fill up with sherry or Madeira. Cork the bottles down with the new corks, and dip them into melted resin."

Mrs. Beeton's Book
of Household Management — 1861

Strawberry Angel Delight

Base:
1 angel food cake

Filling:
1½ cups sliced strawberries, sweetened
1 small package of strawberry jelly powder
1 cup boiling water
1 cup cold water
1 cup heavy cream, whipped

Topping:
1 cup heavy cream whipped

Note: You can substitute prepared whipped topping if desired.

Cut a one-inch layer from the top of the cake and reserve. Carefully remove cake to make a hollow tunnel, leaving at least an inch around the sides and bottom. Dissolve the jelly powder in the boiling water. Stir in cold water and chill until almost firm (about 2 hours). Beat jelly until foamy then fold in the whipped cream and strawberries. Fill the angel food cake and replace the top.

Ice with cream reserved for topping. Chill at least two hours before serving, and garnish with fresh strawberries.

The Mighty Maple — more than a sugar bush

One of the things that always puzzles me in life is how people decided to do something the first time around. Take pork, who would have thought of eating a pig. It's not enough to say people had always eaten meat. No matter what someone had to be first. The story with pork is that some early Europeans came upon a fire than had taken the lives of several pigs. One man, thinking the carred corpse was a person reached out and touched it. The flesh was hot and burned his fingers. He jerked back in natural reaction and put his fingers in his mouth to suck away the hurt. Those fingers, of course, had some of the flesh of the pig stuck to them, and that was how man first came to savour roast pork.

Maple syrup now was another mystery to me. How in heaven's name did the Indians think of puncturing a hole in a tree, catching the sap and boiling it down to make maple sugar. I was spouting the sad tale of my absorption with such puzzles to an old neighbour one day when he said it was fairly obvious to him. He went on to relate a tale about a mighty maple in the woods which came crashing to the ground during an ice storm. The following day Indian women and children went to the tree and began to gather the wood. The tree was smashed and broken in several places and had bled sap which in the cold weather turned into icicles. The children put these to their mouths, as children will do, and were delighted with the sweet taste. It didn't take the women long to discover that the sap was seeping from the tree and could be gathered, nor did it take them long to try boiling it down so that they had a more concentrated syrup. The tale I'm told came from Maine as Indians were harvesting from the maple long before they came to Minegoo.

The contribution of the maple tree in the form of maple sugar and syrup, has long been accepted as a valuable one to Canadian kitchens. However, enterprising folk of years gone by derived more from these stately trees as was outlined in Heaton's Annual 1918.

> *"In the Maritime Provinces the yearly output has seldom exceeded 500,000 lbs. The trees are generally tapped in the latter part of March and April. Moderately warm days followed by freezing nights are ideal conditions to promote flow. From the product of 1,000 tapped trees, 25 to 30 gallons of very fine vinegar can easily be made from materials that are usually thrown away: to this may be added in some seasons a quantity of "buddy" sap that will not make food sugar. As the boiling of maple syrup is continued a sediment of "sugar sand" deposits—1,000 trees should yield 40 to 50 lbs., in a season—from this can be produced malic acid and bimalate of lime, the best known acid constituent for baking powder."*

French Toast with Maple Syrup

Beat together eggs and milk (two eggs to ½ cup of milk — amount to suit your needs). Pour into a wide bottomed bowl and soak slices of bread thoroughly (each side). Brown in dripping or butter in a frying pan. Serve with maple syrup as you would pancakes.

Eggs Cooked in Maple Syrup

I had often enjoyed French toast but never in my wildest imagination did I ever dream of cooking eggs in maple syrup. In my journeys to Island homes I was told of this family favourite which is from Quebec.

In a large frying pan boil two cups of maple syrup. Drop eggs into it, one at a time, and cook until they are done. The only thing I wonder is if this was a dessert, breakfast or snack.

Maple Sugar

When you have fresh berries try this very old dessert. It called for saving the cream from the top of the milk, but today you will have to buy cream and chill it very cold.

Pour top cream which has sat on ice over thick slices of bread, and cover with maple sugar which has been scrapped from a block. Top with fresh berries and a tablespoon more cream.

Maple Cinnamon Buns

3 cups flour (sifted)
6 tsp baking powder
4 tbsp butter
2 tbsp sugar
1 tsp salt
1 egg
⅔ cup seedless raisins
¾ cup cold water
cinnamon
grated maple sugar

Caramel Syrup:
4 tbsp butter
½ cup dark corn syrup

Sift together flour, sugar, salt and baking powder. With a pastry knife cut shortening into flour as for pie dough. Beat egg in cup adding three-fourths or more of cold water to make 1 cup. Blend the ingredients, turn on a floured board and knead to a smooth dough. Roll ½ inch in thickness. Spread thickly with softened butter; sprinkle with raisins, then grated maple sugar, then cinnamon. Roll as for jelly roll. Cut in pieces 2-inch thick. Dip biscuits in a caramel syrup and bake for about 30 minutes in a 400°F oven or until done. Remove from oven; invert immediately.

For Caramel syrup melt 4 tbsp butter with ½ cup dark corn syrup in a heavy skillet.

Maple Toast

Spread buttered toast with soft maple sugar; heat under broiler; serve at once.

Maple Stuffed Apple to serve with meat

Serve with ham, sausage or roast.

Core tart apples. Fill cavity with 1 tbsp brown granulated maple sugar, or maple syrup and ½ tsp of butter. Shredded pineapple or mincemeat may be used. Bake in oven; add a little water and apple cores to base while cooking.

Watkins Cookbook, 1933

Maple Cream Candy

½ cup sweetened condensed
milk

½ cup water
1 cup granulated sugar
¾ cup maple syrup
1 tbsp butter
¾ cup pecan meats cut into
small pieces
½ tsp vanilla

Blend milk, water, sugar and syrup; dissolve thoroughly; heat slowly to boiling point; cook slowly to soft ball stage when tested in cold water. Remove from fire; drop in butter and flavouring; do not stir. When luke warm beat until creamy, add nuts, spread in buttered pan.

Maple Taffy

1⅓ cups sweetened condensed
milk
½ cup maple syrup
pinch salt
vanilla or maple flavouring

Cook milk, syrup and salt together in heavy pan. Stir over low fire until hard ball forms when tested in cold water. Add flavouring. Pour into buttered pans; cool and pull. Cut with scissors.

Maple Duff

1 20-oz can peaches or pears
with as little sugar content as
possible
4 or 5 apples, peeled, cored and
cut in eighths and dropped
into a cup of boiling water
with 3 tbsp sugar and
simmered until barely fork
tender
1 cup liquid (fruit juice plus
water to make 1 cup)
½ cup maple syrup
½ tsp grated nutmeg
1 tbsp quick cooking tapioca

Peddlers, or door-to-door salesmen like Wildred Bovyer were crucial to many Island homemakers. This photo was taken outside Mr. Bovyer's home in Bunbury c1910.

(Public Archives of PEI accession 2767)

2 eggs yolks
1/4 tsp salt
6 tbsp white sugar
2 egg whites
1/4 tsp cream of tartar
1/2 tsp vanilla
6 tbsp all-purpose flour

Heat oven to 325°F. Put fruit in lightly buttered 9- × 9-inch baking dish. Combine liquid, maple syrup, nutmeg and tapioca. Bring to a boil over moderate heat and cook slowly for 5 minutes stirring constantly. Pour over fruit.

Beat egg yolks, salt and sugar until thick and lemon coloured. Beat egg whites and cream of tartar until they stand in peaks. Fold in egg yolk mixture. Add vanilla and fold flour in gently. Pour over fruit mixture. Bake 30-35 minutes until lightly browned. Serves 6.

Dried Fruits and Nuts

In days gone by, dried fruit and nuts were very important to the homeowner, particularly during the long winter months when fresh products were very high priced. They were easy to store, easy to use, nutritious and added wonderful variety to the diet.

The art of drying fruit is one deserving of a book of its own, however, a couple of examples will show how easily this art of food preservation could be fit into the regular homemaker's chores.

Drying Berries

Blueberries, currants, gooseberries, raspberries, cherries and grapes can be dried. The length of time required is from 6 to 8 hours. Use only sound, unbruised fruit; wash clean and drain on platters and dry in oven. Be careful that the oven is not too warm in the beginning. A low temperature, 110°F, at first, will be about right. If this is gradually raised to 130°F or 140°F, the best results will be produced.

The drying should be stopped as soon as the berries fail to stain the hand when pressed, but not so hard that they will rattle. This will take from 4-5 hours.

To Cook Dried Berries — Soak 4-5 hours, using 1½ parts of water to 1 part of berries. Cook in the same water 20 minutes and sweeten to taste. Use the same as fresh berries.

Settlement Cookbook

Nut Salad Sandwiches

These and the following sandwiches hark back to the days when nuts were valued for their easy storing. A fine spread of sandwiches could be served to guests or family using nuts.

Grind English walnuts or hickory nuts in your meat grinder, mix with an equal quantity of celery chopped extremely fine and add to this mixture mayonnaise made with plenty of lemon juice. Have white bread cut thin, brush lightly with melted butter; lay on a crisp lettuce leaf; spread this with the nut and celery mixture; lay the second slice of bread upon it and serve at once.

Filling for Sweet Sandwiches

(Keeps for a week)

Pint of milk, 1 cup sugar, 3 eggs, half a teacup of flour. Mix sugar and flour thoroughly, then stir into the milk. Cook in double boiler to a thick paste. Add the eggs, well beaten, just before removing from the fire. Let stand until cold. It is then ready for use for any kind of sweet sandwiches.

For instance, take a small portion of the paste and stir in a little vanilla and freshly grated coconut, chocolate, preserved ginger or any kind of ground nuts. Black walnuts and roasted almonds are especially good. Jams, marmalade and orange may also be used in this way. Coconut and orange make a delicious combination. Raisins and chopped nuts also go well together. The sandwiches may be made of crackers and wafers or white and brown bread.

Fig Paste for Filling

Three-quarters of a pound of figs cut into small pieces, 3/4 pound brown sugar, 1/4 pound seeded raisins, 1 cup water and the juice of half a lemon. Stew on the back of stove until very soft; remove and add a dessertspoon vanilla. Then put all through meat-grinder, and to clear grinder use 2-3 crackers. If desired the cracker dust may be stirred into the paste. It is then ready for use and will keep indefinitely. Delicious between thin, delicate crackers or thin slices of brown bread. It may also be put on thin slices of bread buttered in layers and cut down like cake.

Sugar and Spice Nuts

"Gather nuts and shell, any type will be satisfying. Mix together in a deep bowl ½ cups sugar, 2 tablespoonfuls cinnamon and ¼ teaspoonful nutmeg. In another bowl beat one egg white. Drop the nuts in the egg white a few at a time and coat thoroughly. Then plunge them into the sugar mixture and coat thoroughly. These should be baked in a warm (300°F) oven on a cookie sheet that has been buttered. Thirty minutes baking will suffice." V.M.

Nature's Chewing Gum

Long before confectioners thought of chewing gum, early dwellers' children had found their own treats in the woods. This excerpt from Lucy Maud Montgomery's book "The Alpine Path" was written while she was enjoying her honeymoon trip in Britain.

"Thursday afternoon we had a delightful little expedition to Homecliffe Glen and its deserted old mill. It might serve as a scene for a ghost story. In the midst of the ravine we came upon a clump of spruce trees literally loaded with gum, the first I had seen since leaving home. Spruce gum and the delight of picking it seem quite unknown in Scotland. We spent a half-hour picking it. To me and my husband the gum tasted delicious, but neither Mr. M. nor Miss A liked its flavor declaring it was 'bitter'."

Lucy Maud Montgomery
York, England
August 27, 1912

Herbs and Edible Wild Plants

Many settlers brought with them herbs, plants, small trees, as well as seed, and so on to start their gardens in the new land. They also foraged for edible wild plants and used some unexpected ones from the garden.

Bayberry

A small shrub, seldom rising above two and a half feet, it yields a strong aromatic perfume and from the fruit which clings together in little green clusters, a fine green wax which makes excellent scented candles.

This bush grows prolificly along the north shore where the harsh winds of the Gulf of St. Lawrence deter other plants. The first thing I did after settling in our Island home was to gather leaves and dry them for soups and stews in the coming winter. These leaves can be used in stews, soups, with a roast of pork or when cooking tomatoes for a delightful flavour.

Various people have told me how they use bayleaves in cooking: in a bouquet garni, stock, fish stews, boiled beef, ham, pickled pork, tongue and poultry, pot roasts, marinade for meat, sauces and even in milk pudding.

Bouquet Garni

The classic bouquet garni is composed of a small bay leaf, three to four sprays of parsley (including the stalks) and a sprig of thyme all tied together in a piece of muslin for extraction before serving. You can add any other herb required for a particular dish. These bags can be dried, or better yet frozen.

Dandelion

This flowering plant we have all come to hate as a weed was more valued in years past. The tender, young greens were eaten in salads, the flowers used to make wine, the white "milk" used to remove warts and dried and roasted roots to make a drink which was substituted for coffee.

Garlic

Garlic is not something we consider common to Canadian gardens. Yet, it seems early gardeners valued this bulb not only for the flavouring of various dishes in the kitchen. It was also said to cure colds and lung infections (bronchitis and pneumonia and such) and discourage aphids from attacking roses, if planted nearby.

Ginseng

Ginseng is found in great plenty in the forest, where the timber is large, and the soil good, no attempt that I know of, has ever been made to ascertain its value.

John Stewart
1806

Kitchen Bouquet

A sprig each of parsley, savoury, and thyme, one small leaf of sage and a bay leaf tied together in a muslin bag to flavour stews. You can also buy in liquid form. Often used for flavouring sauces and soups.

Mace

We often see reference to mace and mace leaves in old recipes yet it is difficult to find on spice racks today. Mace is the membrane which surrounds the shell of the nutmeg. Its general qualities are the same as those of the nutmeg although it is harder to grind because it is very oily. (To solve that problem mix with other less oily spices to mix, or with raw rice.) Mace is used in baking, and to add flavour to chocolate dishes, oyster stew, stuffings and jellies.

Mint

Said to grow like a weed once it took hold, mint is used as a flavouring. Added to new peas or potatoes when they are cooking it gives a delightful taste. And, of course, it is made into a mint sauce to serve with lamb or mutton. Also try mint added to oatmeal, fruit salads, apple dishes and drinks.

Mint was also added to bath water and the last rinse when washing hair to give the skin and body a clean, fresh smell.

Mint Sauce

¼ cup chopped mint leaves
½ cup cider vinegar
1 tbsp finely powdered sugar
or
½ cup strained honey

(Note: In my own opinion, the sugar is not needed in mint sauce, however, this is an original old method of preparing this traditional accompaniment for lamb or mutton).

Add sugar to vinegar; when dissolved pour over mint and let stand 30 minutes over slow fire to infuse. If vinegar is strong, dilute with water. Serve hot over hot lamb.

Or boil sugar and vinegar, throw in the mint leaves and let boil up at once. Set aside and serve cold with lamb.

Crystallized Mint Leaves

Boil sugar and water to a very thick syrup; roll in fresh mint leaves; dry them on buttered plates in the oven with door open; sprinkle with granulated sugar from time to time.

Savoury

This herb frequents the shop shelves today. It didn't take the early settlers long to realize it flourished in Island soil; as a result, it has become a true part of Island cooking.

Summer savoury (the more popular) has a more delicate flavour than winter savoury. Both have a peppery taste; the winter variety being quite strong, so use with care. Use sprigs for boiling with broad beans and all kind of green beans; chopped leaves in a sauce for beans, tomatoes, fish, poultry, stews, pork and veal chops, salads, pickled cucumbers, biscuit pastry for meat and vegetable pies. Try a sprinkle in creamed potatoes, scrambled eggs and hamburger.

Savoury was once used in poultic for easing pain from wasp or bee stings.

Nasturtium Sandwiches

Wash the fresh flower and lay the petals in ice water for a few minutes. Spread the bread with mayonnaise and place on a thick layer of the petals; or, omit the dressing and spread the petals on buttered slices. If possible, serve these sandwiches with a few of the fresh blossoms and leaves scattered loosely over the plate.

From the Dairy

When the milk man came to call with fresh milk, butter, cheese and eggs, many housewives would create wonderful main dishes, desserts and savouries from those basic ingredients. It is only in recent years that the ordinary family began to expect meat at every meal.

We would all be fortunate to again savour these simpler things.

Many homes in rural areas had their own cow and hens so that supplies of dairy products were reasonably steady and plentiful.

May MacNab of Grand Tracadie, born in 1893, recalls that her family had two milking cows which they milked. They would place the milk container in a cold stream and allow the cream to come to the top. Then they would skim off the cream and use it for butter making. The milk that was left they called skimmed milk although it did contain some fat. Before skimming the milk they would take out the whole milk that they needed for that day's baking.

It was apparently the responsibility of the women and children to see that home cows were milked; men seldom looked after this chore.

Custard

Custard is one of our family's favourite desserts enjoyed most by itself or topping a trifle. My husband prefers his cold; I like mine hot, poured over raspberry jam. I must admit to always using that old favourite, Bird's Custard Powder at home, even though we love the kind that is made from scratch over a double boiler or egg custard baked in the oven.

Here are a number of custards and variations.

Soft Custard

1½ cups milk
2 eggs or 4 yolks
¼ cup sugar
dash salt
1 tsp vanilla

Place milk in top of double boiler. Scald over direct heat. Set aside. Beat together eggs, sugar and salt. Stir a little of the hot milk into the eggs, then slowly stir egg mixture back into remaining milk. Return to double boiler and cook over simmering water, stirring constantly until mixture coats a metal spoon; test frequently to avoid overcooking. Cool. Blend in vanilla. Serves 4.

Note: If soft custard takes on a curdled appearance, it is an indication that it has been overcooked. Should this happen, immediately remove from the heat, set the pan in cold water and beat rapidly with a whisk until custard becomes smooth.

Custard and Fruit

Soft custards such as the above are often used as sauces poured over fruit and/or cake. Drain any fruit such as peaches, raspberries, pears and place in serving dishes then pour custard (hot or cold depending on your preference) over to serve. This is a grand way to use up stale cake which can either be softened with a little jam or juicy fruit, or simply let stand covered with custard sauce for a few minutes.

Mandarin oranges can be drained, divided between six serving dishes, and topped with soft custard in which you have substituted 1 tbsp orange-flavoured liquor and ¼ tsp grated orange rind for the vanilla. Truly delicious.

Creme Renversee au Caramel

(Caramel Custard with Raisins)

¾ cup granulated sugar
2 eggs
3 egg yolks
⅛ tsp salt
2 vanilla beans, split and scraped out or 1 tsp vanilla extract

$1\frac{1}{2}$ cups milk
1 cup white raisins

Melt sugar over moderate heat until it browns, then slowly stir in $\frac{3}{4}$ cup boiling water, a little at a time. Simmer 3 or 4 minutes, then pour into a one-quart baking dish. Pick up the dish (be careful of the heat) and tilt it all around to coat the sides with the caramel. In a mixing bowl beat eggs, egg yolks, salt and vanilla thoroughly. Heat the milk without boiling, and pour slowly into egg mixture, beating all the while. (An electric mixer makes this task easy.) When all the milk is blended, remove the mixer and stir in the raisins. Preheat oven to 250°F. Pour custard into the baking dish, place in a shallow pan of water and bake for one hour. Custard is ready when a knife or needle inserted in the centre comes out clean.

This can also be made in individual custard cups by evenly dividing caramel and custard and reducing the cooking time.

To serve, run a knife around edges to loosen then reverse onto serving plate.

Custard Ice Cream

3 eggs
2 cups milk
3 tbsp sugar
Vanilla

Add milk, sugar, vanilla to beaten eggs. Cook the mixture in a double boiler until the custard thickens. Pour the custard, when it has cooled into an ice cream freezer and freeze it.

Snow Pancakes

"Freshly fallen snow can be used instead of eggs in making batter for pancakes. Care must be had that the snow is as pure as possible. The batter should be made rather thick, and the snow mixed with each pancake, just before it is put into the pan. Two tablespoons of snow will be equal to one egg."

Canada's Cook Book
undated

Old Time Pancakes

Remember those times when you were hungry and mom, or grandmother, would whip up something delicious to eat out of nothing. I asked many older folk what they remembered as some of the best eating they did in the old days. For one country man it was his mother's deep fried potatoes and for another thin pancakes that they would spread with jam.

Going by his memories, and my own favourite form of pancakes we came up with this. My mom used to serve them on Pancake Tuesday with lemon juice and sugar.

His mother used to shake the batter in a jar. I use a blender. The secret to success is the pan. The heavier and thicker the base is, the better the result because the batter cooks at an even temperature. You simply cannot beat the old cast iron pans. You can toss these, or just flip them over gently.

Pancake Batter

2 oz plain flour
pinch salt
1 egg
½ pt milk

Sieve the flour and salt into a bowl and beat in egg. Then beat in the milk until you have a smooth batter. (With a mixer or blender you can beat the flour, salt and egg then gradually add the milk.) Brush a heavy-based pan with a thin layer of lard (or oil). Heat until almost sizzling and then pour in 2 kitchen spoonfuls of batter. Swirl the mixture around to coat the bottom of the pan evenly and thinly. Cook for about 3 minutes before turning. Cook for a further 1 or 2 minutes so that both sides are golden brown. Put on a serving plate and top with filling. There is no need to roll although you can roll or fold over. To keep a number of pancakes warm while you are cooking, layer them on a plate with kitchen or grease-proof paper between them. Cover and place in a warm oven. Makes 6-8 pancakes.

Note: You can make batter ahead and store in a jar in the refrigerator. You can also freeze layered pancakes and thaw by heating in a low oven.

To Serve:

— squeeze lemon juice over and sprinkle with sugar

- with syrup or jam
- for dessert use fruit such as peaches, a chocolate sauce and ice cream
- applesauce and cinnamon, top with sieved icing sugar
- add half a cup of very finely chopped spinach to batter when making pancakes then top with chicken and a white sauce made using part white wine as liquid
- treat them as crepes and experiment

Variations:

- add a little extra flavour to the batter by beating in 2 tsp finely grated orange or lemon rind, or 1 tsp mixed herbs or curry powder.

Queen Bread Pudding

4 slices buttered bread
1 cup brown sugar, packed solid
½ tsp cinnamon
2⅓ cups milk
2 eggs
½ tsp nutmeg
1 tsp vanilla

Put brown sugar in bottom of baking dish. Break bread over sugar. Beat eggs, milk and vanilla. Pour over all, sprinkle spices over top. Bake in moderate oven until puffed up to top and brown. Sugar forms sauce for pudding. Serve hot or cold.

Mom's Impossible Pie

Named for me because it was the first pie I learned to make—it makes its own crust. Crunchy custard-coconut.

4 eggs
2 cups milk
½ cup margarine or butter
¼ tsp nutmeg
1 cup flour
1 cup sugar
1 cup coconut
2 tsp vanilla

Mix thoroughly by hand (or you could use a blender). Pour into greased 10-inch pie plate. Bake at 350°F for 50 minutes or until centre tests firm.

Sour Milk or Cream

Many, many of the old recipes called for an ingredient that seems strange to us today, sour milk. Of course, in the days before refrigeration, sweet cream which had been skimmed off milk all too often soured before it could be used. Not to be daunted by such a mishap, early cooks developed many ways to use up, rather than waste sour cream. Once they discovered the special taste it gives, many a housewife would deliberately leave a bowl of heavy sweet cream on the back of the wood stove till it became thick and sour tasting. Today we generally purchase sour cream partly because our milk is not the same as that brought into the home years ago. Believe me, you cannot leave a quart of 2 per cent milk in the refrigerator for a few weeks and come up with the same product as our ancestors created. Should you wish to try making your own sour cream at home try the following procedure. The end result will be a bit thinner than that you buy in stores and can readily be used in recipes calling for sour milk. Some of the old recipes tell you to add vinegar to the milk to sour it. If substituting, eliminate both the milk and vinegar from the recipe.

Homemade Sour Cream

2 cups whipping cream
2 tbsp buttermilk

Pour cream and buttermilk into a sterile glass mason jar. Screw on the lid tightly and shake well. Let jar stand in a warm place until the cream is thickened and sour, about 24 hours in warm weather and 48 hours in cool. After the cream has cultured, cover it and chill overnight before using. You can whip it slightly for a smoother texture, but do not overbeat.

Makes two cups.

Butter Making

I grew up with a family story about my grandfather shaking cream in a milk bottle until he had made a small amount of butter for my grandmother to enjoy on a Sunday morning. This was during the lean war years in Britain, when such a deed must have made Nanny feel like a queen. If you would like your children to sample this type of butter making and learn a little about the process try this.

Pour 1 cup cold whipping cream into a clean jar with a tight—fitting lid. Shake jar until butter forms (about 50 minutes). Pour off buttermilk (the liquid that separates from the butter). Wash butter with cold water. Press butter against side of jar with spatula to work out excess liquid. Pour off water and repeat until water remains clear. Be sure all excess water is worked out. Add salt and mix well.

Cheesemaking has been part of Island life for many years with factories located in communities such as Orwell and Mount Stewart.

(Public Archives of PEI Accession No. 2930)

To Sour Fresh Milk

Measure 1 tbsp lemon juice or vinegar into a 1 cup container. Add milk to fill container.

To Whitewash a Wall

To keep the whitewash from cracking and being washed away, mix enough unslaked lime into a gallon of sweet milk to make it thicker than cream, stir in a teacup of turpentine and put on at once with a paint brush. It will stick to smooth wood. If you want a color, add earth colors and stir well.

Cheese

Back in the 1890s and on through the 1900s Grace McPhail remembers their family always had cheese. It came in big rolls. "Father would cut off a good slice and we could taste it. Cheese and crackers and tea was night lunch in the country."

Cheese factories sprung up around the Island, one was located in Orwell. Shop owners would buy the rounds to sell in their stores and by 1910 or so most people bought it. Florrie Steele recalls her mother making cottage cheese.

Welsh Rarebit

Have ready one pound of rich cheese, grated. Rub the bottom of a dish with a piece of onion. Put in the cheese, add one tablespoonful of tomato catsup, one tablespoonful of Worcestershire sauce, one half tablespoonful of salt, four shakes of cayenne pepper and two level tablespoonfuls of butter. Stir until it begins to melt, then add gradually four tablespoonfuls of ale or beer. When it is soft, smooth and creamy, pour it over toasted bread or crackers.

Ramequins of Cheese Pastry

When you have puff pastry left over, roll it out lightly, and sprinkle over it grated cheese. Fold the pastry in three and sprinkle every fold with the cheese. Cut shapes out with an ordinary pastry cutter. Brush them over with the beaten yolk of an egg, and bake in a quick oven.

Cheese and Egg Strata

10 slices white bread
6 eggs
3 cups milk
2 tbsp chopped parsley
1 tsp dry mustard

1 tsp salt
2 cups shredded cheddar cheese
½ small onion, finely chopped
2 cups cooked ham, chopped
(optional)

Remove crusts from bread and cut bread into 1-inch cubes. In a large bowl beat together eggs, milk, parsley, mustard and salt. Stir in bread cubes, cheese, onion and ham. Pour into 12- × 8-inch baking dish. You may refrigerate up to 12 hours before baking. Bake at 350°F uncovered for 1 hour or until centre is set. Serves 6.

Homemade Cottage Cheese

clabbered milk (sour milk that
is solidified) must be whole
milk
salt
paprika
melted butter or sweet cream

Do not attempt to make this with less than two quarts of milk, which should be turned, but not bitter. Place the utensil containing it in a pan of hot water and beat until the curd separates. Do not let the water boil. If it becomes too hot, the cheese will be tough. When well separated, strain through cheesecloth and season the curd with salt, paprika and melted butter or sweet cream.

Cheddar Scallop

1 lb potatoes, pared and sliced
½ lb sharp cheddar cheese,
sliced
1 lb onions, peeled and sliced
salt and pepper
½ cup milk
½ cup bread crumbs
4 tbsp melted butter

Layer potatoes, cheese and onions in a greased casserole. Sprinkle each layer with salt and pepper. Cover with milk; sprinkle with bread crumbs; cover with butter and bake at 350°F for 45 minutes or until potatoes are tender and browned.

Tomato Cheese Puff

$\frac{1}{4}$ cup butter
$\frac{1}{4}$ cup flour
1 tsp Worcestershire sauce
$\frac{1}{2}$ tsp dry mustard
$\frac{1}{2}$ tsp salt
1 cup milk
1$\frac{1}{4}$ cups cheddar cheese, shredded
4 eggs, separated
6 slices bread, toasted with crusts removed
2 large tomatoes, sliced thin

Preheat oven to 425°F. Melt butter over low heat; gradually add flour, stirring until smooth. Add Worcestershire sauce, mustard and salt; blend thoroughly. Stir in milk. Blend in cheese. Continue cooking until cheese melts and sauce boils and thickens. Remove from heat and set aside. In large bowl beat egg whites until stiff but not dry. Set aside. In medium mixing bowl beat egg yolks until thickened and lemon coloured, about 5 minutes. Slowly stir cheese sauce into yolks.

Gently fold egg-cheese mixture into beaten egg whites. Arrange toast on bottom of a lightly greased 8- × 12-inch baking dish. Top with tomato slices. Pour egg-cheese mixture evenly over tomatoes. Bake 15-20 minutes or until puffed and golden. Serve immediately. Enough for 6.

Rink-Tum-Diddy

If any recipe marks how eating habits have changed, it is this World War II creation. We forget that the simplest things as nourishing and filling.

Toast as many slices of bread as necessary. Melt 1 tbsp butter in frying pan; sauté 2 slices of onion; add 1 can tomato soup and stir well. Add 1 cup grated cheese and 1 beaten egg. When thoroughly mixed pour on toast and serve at once.

Mexican Rarebit

3 tbsp butter
1 small onion
3 tbsp flour

2 cup canned tomatoes
1 tsp Worcestershire sauce
salt and pepper
2 cups corn, macaroni or
   spaghetti may be added with
   tomatoes

Cook chopped onion slowly in butter for 5 minutes. Stir in flour. Gradually add tomatoes and cook until mixture thickens. Add grated cheese and seasonings. Cook very slowly until cheese melts. Serve at once on toast.

Eggs

Hens, being the contrary creatures they are, go through spells when they don't lay. At other times eggs are supplied in such copious numbers it can distress the cook. Steps, of course, had to be taken to preserve the surplus for times of want. Eggs could be packed in salt or charcoal (always with the small end down of course) and were said to keep from two-to-three years this way. Another method of preservation was to pickle them. They could be used as a snack, garnish or part of a meal. My husband's grandmother used to make them, and he would often take one to fill the hollow spots between meals.

About Eggs:

- store eggs with the large end up. They keep best in the carton, in the refrigerator.
- to thicken sauces, 1 whole egg, 2 yolks or 2 whites can replace 1 tbsp of flour or 2 tsp of cornstarch.
- to judge freshness of an egg, break it onto a flat surface. If the white is thick and the yolk stands up the egg is fresh. Watery white and flat yolk mark an old egg.
- when beaten eggs are added to hot mixtures they may coagulate too rapidly and form lumps. Stir a small amount of the hot mixture into the eggs to warm them and then stir the warmed egg mixture into the remaining hot mixture.
- fold heavy mixture into beaten egg whites rather than whites into the mixture, as less air is forced out of whites in the process.
- do not use cracked eggs in meringues, egg nogs, uncooked sauces or icings. Instead use them so that they are thoroughly cooked. To determine whether an egg is hard cooked, spin it. If it spins round and round, it is hard cooked. If it wobbles and will not spin, it is raw.

- to hard cook eggs, place in a pan and cover with cold water. Bring to a boil, and remove pan from heat. Cover and let stand 20 minutes. Immediately rinse with cold water. The eggs will be tender with no grey ring. For easy shelling, gently roll the eggs back and forth in the pan containing a little cold water. The cold water creeps into the cracks and facilitates peeling.
- the secret to extra high meringues, souffles or any recipe calling for beaten egg white is a stable white foam. Always use a glass or metal mixing bowl. You may add 1 tsp cream of tartar for every cup of whites, for extra stability. (Note: 8-10 whites = 1 cup, 12-16 yolks = 1 cup or 5 large whole eggs = 1 cup.)
- the water from boiling eggs contains many nutrients that are good for plants.

While today we put our trust for fresh eggs into the store, our forebearers were not quite so trusting. They knew that a stale egg rises in water; fresh eggs are heavy and sink to the bottom. They also remembered to wash eggs before using and rather than boiling, they placed eggs in cold water and removed from the heat just before the boil. Leave in the water at least 20 minutes. (You can tell an egg is cooked by lifting it out of the hot water on a spoon—it will dry immediately if it is cooked.) This method will prevent tough eggs, with dark yolks.

Goldenrod Toast

4 hard cooked eggs
6-8 slices toast
2 cups white sauce

Separate the yolk and white of egg and chop the white. Put the yolk in a warm place. Make a White Sauce; add the whites to the sauce. Heat thoroughly, and pour the mixture upon the toast. Press the yolk over the whole, though a fine strainer, and garnish with toast points and parsley.

Eggs in a Nest

Separate whites from yolks; beat whites until dry. Butter a small baking dish in which eggs are to be served; sprinkle fine bread crumbs in the bottom. Place beaten whites in dish, make hollow and slip in the yolks, set bowl in sauce pan containing boiling water, cover and cook until white is firm. Set in hot oven for 1 minute or hold dish under flame in broiling oven.

Eggs make excellent appetizers, snacks and additions to buffets.

Pickled Eggs

12 hard cooked eggs
1½ cups white vinegar
½ cup water
1 tsp salt
2 tsp mixed pickling spice

Shell eggs and place in a large jar. Place remaining ingredients in medium glass or stainless steel saucepan and bring to a boil. Reduce heat and simmer for 5 minutes. Pour through a strainer over hard cooked eggs. Cover and refrigerate. Let stand at least two days before using.

Note: A combination of any of the following may be substituted for pickling spice: mustard seed, peppercorns, bay leaves, ginger root, celery seed, garlic. Use whole spices, as ground spices may discolour eggs. Sugar to taste may be added, if desired.

Scotch Eggs

12 hard-cooked eggs, peeled
½ cup flour
2 lbs sausage meat (no skin)
1½ tsp basil
1 tsp sage
1 tsp salt
¼ tsp pepper
1 egg
1 tbsp water
2-3 cups fine bread crumbs (or seasoned coating mix)
deep fat (or vegetable oil) for frying

Roll eggs in flour. Combine sausage meat with basil, sage, salt and pepper. With floured hands cover each egg with sausage mixture. Prepare egg wash by beating together egg and water. Dip each sausage covered egg in wash and roll in crumbs. Refrigerate 10-15 minutes to allow crumbs to dry. Fry in deep fat 350°F until golden brown. If preferred, Scotch eggs may be cooked in shallow fat or baked in a moderate oven, 350°F, until sausage meat is thoroughly cooked.

Serve hot with a tomato or mushroom sauce, or serve cold. For hors d'oeuvres, use 12 small eggs to 1½ pounds sausage meat.

Devilled Eggs

6 eggs
1 tbsp ham
½ pimiento
1 tbsp melted butter
Salt and paprika to taste

Put the eggs into warm water and bring to the boiling point which is 212°F. Lower to about 200°F and keep them there for thirty minutes. Put into cold water. Shell, cut into halves lengthwise and remove yolks; put them into the bowl, add melted butter, the pimiento and ham chopped fine; add the other ingredients, refill the whites and fasten the corresponding halves together with toothpicks. Dip first in egg and then in bread crumbs; repeat once more and fry in hot fat. Serve wrapped in tissue paper, the ends fringed and tied for picnics, or, put on hot platter and pour white sauce around (or a hotter tomato sauce is nice) when served at home.

The People's Home Recipe Book
Toronto, 1919

Curried Eggs with Rice

6 eggs
3 onions
1 tbsp butter
1 tbsp bacon fat
1 tsp curry powder
1 tsp flour
1 cup stock or water
Rice, steamed

Put the eggs into boiling water and let cook just below the

boiling point for thirty minutes. Put at once into cold water and when cool, peel and slice thin around a mound of rice on a hot chop plate (platter). Have the onions peeled and sliced very thin and put with the fat into a double boiler. Cook until the onions are soft and yellow; now add all the remaining ingredients, stir until boiling and the desired thickness. Strain this curry sauce and serve at once by pouring over rice. Garnish with sweet red peppers cut into fancy shapes.

Eggs Baked in Tomatoes

Take an equal number of eggs and tomatoes, butter, parsley and butter toast. For this effective dish large tomatoes and small eggs are best. Cut large tomatoes in half, remove the centres, seeds and juice; sprinkle a little salt, pepper and caster sugar into each. Break an egg into a cup and carefully pour it into the hollowed tomato, which should be placed on a greased baking tin. Place in a hot oven and cook until the whites are set, testing every few minutes with a little melted butter. Just before serving scatter a little finely chopped parsley over each. They may be served on rounds of buttered toast.

Columbus Eggs

Peel the shells from a dozen hard-boiled eggs and cut each egg in two around the centre. Also cut a little off one rounded end so they can stand on end as did the famous egg which Columbus handled. Pulverize, or mash, the yolks and mix with some finely minced chicken, smoked tongue or lean ham, moistening with a little fresh butter or vinegar and seasoning to the taste with salt, pepper and mustard. Fill the empty egg whites, taking care not to break them. Press the two parts together and stand on a platter so that they will have the appearance of eggs that have not been dissected. These are fun at a gathering of friends.

Kentucky Egg Nog

The following came home with horsemen who had been "away" buying standardbreds for harness racing.

Stir ⅔ of a cup of sugar into 6 eggs that have been beaten until light. When dissolved add 12 tablespoons of best whiskey. The whiskey is intended to cook the egg and the quantity used depends upon its strength. Mix a pint of rich cream with the other ingredients. This makes 6 glasses of egg nog. Grate a little nutmeg over the top of each glass when filled.

Beef fat or drippings, lard, vegetable oils, butter or a mixture of several fats can be used for frying such goodies as fritters or doughnuts.

Rendering Butter

Before our modern storage and refrigerators such commodities as butter often would not retain their freshness until they could be used. Obviously, these things could not be discarded at every turn, so steps were taken to preserve them—extend their life.

Any butter that is unfit for table use may be made good for cooking and baking purposes and will last for months. Place butter in a deep, iron kettle, fill half full, set on the fire, where it will simmer slowly without stirring for several hours. Watch carefully that it does not boil over, and when the fat is clear, and the sediment at the bottom is just browning, take it from the fire gently, so as not to disturb the sediment. Let cool a little, strain through cloth into a stone crock; cover and keep in a cool place.

From the Home Kitchen

To the stranger from away it would seem certain that Island cooks would be renowned for cooking seafood. With all those wonderful oysters, scallops, lobster and fresh fish right at the door step, it would be a natural assumption. It would not, however, be a correct one.

It is the squares, the fresh bread, the cakes and the wonderful sweet things that reign as their most wonderful creations.

Tea Parties

Islanders, it seems, have always taken great delight in gathering together for some fun and festivities, mixed with lots of good food and entertainment of course. In the early days gatherings were small with only those in the immediate area, and perhaps a traveller or two in attendance. Around about 1850, however, roads improved, and with them communications, bringing about a new form of gathering called a "Tea Party." James and Gertrude Pendergast described tea parties in the book *Folklore.*

> *"At first they were all-day affairs. People brought their entire family in a truck-wagon loaded with supplies for dinner and supper. The men built the booths which were festive with their canopies of green-leafed saplings. Stoves were set up and wood was cut to cook the dinner and make large pots of tea. (Does anybody recall the smoky taste on the tea?) There were also booths where fruit, tobacco, cider, lemonade and candy were sold along with ice cream."*

Merry-go-rounds, wheels of fortune, bowling and dancing were often featured as part of the day's festivities.

"While the men set up the booths, etc. which we have described, the women were busy setting up the dinner tables. Each district in the parish was assigned a particular table, and there were great rivalries to have the best appointed table.

Down the center of the tables were rows of gaily decorated fruit cakes to be sold by auction as evening closed in. One group of ladies heard rumors that their cakes were in danger of being wrecked by a rival district when they were taking them to the parochial house the previous night. To ensure safe delivery of their cakes they disguised their horse by putting a large white handkerchief on the horse's face held in place by his bridle. Their rivals hiding in the bushes saw this white-faced horse and thought he belonged to some stranger and let them pass unmolested. You see everyone in the district knew all the horses in their own neighbourhood and many in the adjoining districts."

These tea parties often ended in brawls, making for exciting entertainment which attracted crowds. There was little concern about the fights, however, for most often than not combatants were better friends after settling their differences and peace and harmony quickly restored.

"It is believed that one of the first tea parties was held at Rustico in 1867 the day Father George Belcourt drove his horseless carriage. When dinner was ready the Master of Ceremonies rang a large bell and called in a loud voice "Dinner is now being served; all you strangers and people from distance come first; all you men and women of Rustico come last." This exemplifies the modesty and hospitality of the Acadian People.

Folklore
James and Gertrude Pendergast

It should be noted that this same Father Belcourt designed and built the very first automobile in Canada. He also established a marvelous library and is credited with helping many of the people in Rustico, a small and relatively poor fishing village, develop to their utmost and assume positions of great importance in the development of the country.

Marian's Cottage Pudding

This is a modern variation of an old recipe and, like so many in this book, can be used in a variety of ways. It is my firm belief that the good cook with a fine reputation is the one who mastered a number of basic recipes, then uses them in various ways.

¼ cup shortening or butter
⅔ cup sugar
1 egg
1 tsp vanilla
1½ cups sifted pastry flour
½ tsp salt
2½ tsp baking powder
¾ cup milk

Cream the shortening, gradually adding sugar. Blend well. Add the egg and beat until light and creamy. Add vanilla. Sift together dry ingredients. Add alternately with milk, beating slightly after each addition. Beat for one minute and pour into a greased 8-inch square pan. Bake at 375°F for 25-30 minutes. Cake is done if it springs back when lightly pressed with fingertips.

Variations:

Fruit: Before pouring the batter into the pan, layer 2 cups of fruit in the bottom (apples, canned cherries, plums, pineapple, lightly stewed rhubarb, all work well). Extend the baking time to 40 minutes. Serve with cream, milk or hard sauce. The cake can be carefully turned upside down on a platter to serve and is lovely warm.

Sauce: Cut in squares and serve hot with a brown sugar or Hot Cherry Sauce (see index), or applesauce.

Jelly: Cut into squares and slice each in half. Spread a layer of jam or jelly on bottom half, replace top and dollup on whipped cream.

Hazel's Boiled Dark Cake (War Cake)

Very economical cake—butterless, eggless and milkless—simple to make. These were often referred to as war cake because rationing made the technique necessary.

1 lb seeded raisins (sticky)
½ cup shortening (Crisco)
2 cups sugar
2 tsp salt
2 cups water

Combine above five ingredients in a saucepan and place on medium—high burner. Boil together for five minutes. Turn off heat and with a serated or slotted spoon, remove raisins to a large mixing bowl. Strain liquid through a fine mesh or cheesecloth (this removes seed, stems, and any sand that was in the raisins). If your raisins contained lots of seed and stem, pick them over. Add the liquid and 2 tbsp cinnamon.

Allow to cool to lukewarm. Prepare pan by lightly greasing and heat oven to 350°F.

Mix together:
1 tsp baking soda
3 cups flour (a little more if needed)

Add to fruit mixture and stir only until mixed thoroughly (be quick). The mixture may foam or fluff up at this stage—do not beat down, just quickly place in a tube pan for cooking and pop in the hot oven. Cook for 45 minutes.

(Note: this type of cake often calls for a combination of allspice, nutmeg and cinnamon. But we prefer this version.)

One thing that I have noticed about the old-time cooks was their ability to have basic recipes, (which they used for a number of very different dishes)—Johnny Cake and Upside Down Sausage, Cornbread, Yorkshire pudding, in a number of forms, even as a dessert. One basic biscuit or cake mix was used in a variety of ways. This is something that today's cook tends not to do and should in fact be doing. For it becomes a great time saver when you have a basic recipe which you know works.

Cakes

About Cake

- always bake cakes in the middle of the oven on the centre rack
- cool cake in pan on wire rack 15 minutes if pan is greased and floured, 5 minutes if pan is lined with waxed paper. Remove from pan and cool completely.

Johnny Cake

"Two cups Indian, one cup wheat,
One cup sour milk, one cup sweet,
One cup good eggs that you can eat,
One-half cup molasses, too,
One-half cup sugar add thereto,
Salt and soda, each a spoon,
Mix up quickly and bake it soon."

The People's Home Recipe Book
Imperial Publishing Company
Toronto, 1919

Or, a slightly easier-to-follow recipe:

1⅓ cups sifted all-purpose flour
⅔ cup fine cornmeal
3½ tsp baking powder
½ tsp salt
2 eggs, well beaten
⅔ cup milk
⅓ cup corn syrup
¼ cup melted shortening

Sift dry ingredients. To well-beaten eggs, add milk, corn syrup and melted shortening. Combine the two mixtures; beat till smooth; pour into oiled pan, 8 × 8 × 2 inches. Bake in hot oven (400°F); serve hot with butter and corn syrup.

Tumbler Cake

2 tumblers of brown sugar
1 tumbler butter
1 tumbler molasses
1 tumbler sweet milk
5 tumblers flour
2 tsp (small) soda
1 tsp cloves
1 tsp cinnamon
nutmeg to taste

Above makes a good fruit cake by adding 1 pint raisins and 1 cup currants.

Boiling Water Cake

Uses no milk—handy when it is scarce.

3 eggs, well beaten
1 cup sugar
1 cup flour
3 tsp (small) baking powder
4 tbsp boiling water

Have oven at good baking heat and water boiling before starting to make this cake, as it must be made quickly. Pans should be oiled ready to receive it. It will be found good either as a layer, plain, or roll jelly cake.

Beat eggs well, and beat in the sugar. Have ready the flour with the baking powder sifted in. Add 4 tablespoons boiling water to eggs and sugar, stirring constantly. Add the flour, beat well and bake at once from 10 to 15 minutes, according to heat of oven and size of baking pan. The thinner it is spread, the shorter time it takes to bake.

The life of a woman and her family was often reflected in her baking. Consider:

Scriptural Cake

4½ cups flour, 1 Kings iv, 22
1 cup butter, Judges v, 25
2 cups sugar, Jeremiah vi, 20
2 cups raisins, 1 Samuel xxx, 12
2 cups figs, Nahum iii, 12

2 cups almonds, Numbers xvii, 8
½ cup sour milk, Judges iv, 19
3 tablespoons honey, 1 Samuel xiv, 25
pinch of salt, Leviticus ii, 13
6 eggs, Jeremiah xvii, 11
2 teaspoons soda, Amos iv, 5
season with spices to taste, 2 Chronicles ix, 9

Follow Solomon's prescription for making a good boy (Proverbs iii, 12) and you will have a good cake. Bake in slow oven.

Sugarless, Eggless, Milkless, Butterless Cake

Mrs. Ann Marie Gallant of North Rustico gave me this recipe from a book put out during World War II—a time when making do with what you've got, or less if you could manage it, was the order of the day.

¾ cup corn syrup
⅓ cup shortening
¼ cup chopped dates
¼ tsp allspice and nutmeg
pinch of salt
1 tsp cinnamon
1 tsp cloves
½ tsp lemon
1 cup hot water

Boil together for three minutes. Cool.

1¾ cup flour
½ tsp baking powder
1 tsp soda

Sift the above ingredients and add to first mixture. Bake 1 hour in moderate oven. This makes a good fruit cake if eggs and butter are scarce.

Filling for Cakes

Many types of filling can be put between layers of cake. The simplest is a custard filling which can be varied by the addition of melted chocolate, flavour extracts such as orange, strawberry or lemon, or a cup of almond slivers and a drop of almond extract.

¾ cup sugar
⅓ cup flour
⅓ tsp salt
2 eggs
2 cups milk or cream
1 tsp vanilla

Mix dry ingredients; add the scalded milk and pour gradually on the slightly beaten eggs. Cook in double boiler, stirring constantly until thickened; cool and flavour.

Raisin Filling

1 cup water
⅔ cup sugar
1 cup light syrup
1 cup raisins
1 egg, slightly beaten
½ tsp lemon extract

Seed and chop the raisins; add sugar, syrup and water and cook until raisins are soft. Remove from fire; add egg; cook over water until thick, stirring constantly. Flavour, cool and spread.

Icing or Frosting on Cakes

Seldom did I find recipes that included icing or frosting on cakes. Of the many men and women in their 80s and 90s interviewed, none made mention of it and a few commented that it was very uncommon.

Loaf cakes or cakes in puddings were, it seems, more favoured than our frothy presentations of the 1980s.

Cocoa Icing

¼ cup butter, softened
2 cups icing sugar
2 tbsp cocoa
3 tbsp coffee (cold, strong and black)
½ tsp vanilla

Cream the butter. Mix the icing sugar and cocoa together then slowly add to the butter, alternating with small amounts of coffee. Add the vanilla as above or to taste.

Brown Sugar Frosting

1½ cups brown sugar
¼ cup cold water
½ tsp vanilla
2 egg whites

Boil sugar and water until syrup spins a thread. Beat egg with wire whip, on a platter until dry and add hot syrup slowly, beating all the time. When almost creamy, put between layers and on top of cake.

Fancy Breads and Loaves

The following fancy breads or loaves used to be kept on hand in a cake tin so that any caller or hungry worker could be quickly offered a slice or two.

Nut Bread Loaf from Cardigan

2 eggs
4 cups all purpose flour
4 tsp baking powder
1 tsp cinnamon
½ cup granulated sugar
1 tsp salt
1⅝ cups milk
¼ cup melted shortening or dripping
1 cup broken nut meats (any kind)

Beat the eggs; add the dry ingredients which have been sifted together; next add the milk and shortening and lastly the nuts. Mix, transfer to an oiled bread pan and let stand twenty minutes; then bake about 40 minutes in a moderate (350°F oven).

Nanny's Banana Bread

½ cup shortening or butter
¾ cup sugar
1½ tablespoons buttermilk (or milk + ¼ tsp vinegar)
2 eggs, well beaten
2 cups flour
1 tsp lemon juice
½ tsp baking soda

2 tsp baking powder
3 ripe bananas mashed with a fork
$\frac{1}{4}$ tsp salt

Mix enough to moisten. Bake slowly in 300°F oven.

Lemon Loaf

$\frac{3}{4}$ cup white sugar
$\frac{1}{2}$ cup butter
2 eggs
1$\frac{1}{2}$ cups all-purpose flour
$\frac{1}{2}$ cup milk
2 tsp baking powder
$\frac{1}{2}$ tsp salt
grated rind and juice of 1 lemon
$\frac{1}{3}$ cup sugar

Cream butter, add sugar and continue creaming until fluffy. Add well-beaten eggs, then lemon rind. Sift flour with baking powder and salt. Add alternately with milk. Bake one hour in a slow oven, 325°F. When done, remove. Mix the $\frac{1}{3}$ cup white sugar with the juice of the lemon until dissolved and pour over the bread in the pan while still warm. Let stand in the pan about 15 minutes before removing.

Orange Bread from Mina

Cut fine rind from 2 oranges, add 2 cups cold water and simmer one half hour. Change 3 times and drain the last off. Add $\frac{1}{2}$ cup sugar and a little water, not more than 2 tbsp and cook until it becomes syrup. Remove from stove and cool.

Combine:
$\frac{1}{2}$ cup sugar
1 cup milk
3 tsp baking powder
1 egg
2 tbsp melted butter
2$\frac{1}{2}$ cups flour

Add orange to flour mixture after it is cool. Put in pans and let rise 20 minutes. Bake from 40-60 minutes in moderate oven.

Spicy Ginger Bread

— taken from a 1932 edition of TRUE STORY MAGAZINE lovingly kept all these years

2 eggs
¾ cup brown sugar
¾ cup molasses
¾ cup melted shortening
2½ cups flour
2 tsp soda
2 tsp ginger
1½ tsp cinnamon
½ tsp cloves
½ tsp nutmeg
½ tsp baking powder
1 cup boiling water

Add beaten eggs to the sugar, molasses and melted shortening then add the dry ingredients which have been mixed and sifted, and lastly the hot water.

Bake in small individual pans or in a shallow pan in moderate oven (350°F) 30-40 minutes.

Gingerbread was certainly popular in the late 1800s. Handwritten recipe books such as Mrs. Shaw's from Covehead, dated 1880, contains five gingerbread recipes. It also appeared in some variation in many others of the era. Gingerbread was commonly served to company, with whipped cream.

Before our modern modes of transportation made replenishing the larder as easy as sitting in an arm chair while being propelled to the grocery store, one of the most popular visitors to any home was the travelling salesman. Whether they were selling fish in town or canned goods and spices in the country, these men and their wares were very welcome callers. One of those most fondly remembered is the Watkins man who brought a wonderful array of spices and extracts and gave cooks the opportunity to introduce dozens of new flavours to their families. In 1936 the J. R. Watkins Company put out a cookbook and one of them came into the possession of friends in Cavendish. Judging by the spatters and well-worn pages, it was a popular edition to the home. The next three recipes are from that old book.

Spiced Gem Muffins

⅔ cup butter
1 cup sugar
3 eggs, separated
1 cup molasses
⅓ tsp salt
1 cup sour milk
½ tsp cinnamon
½ tsp nutmeg
½ tsp soda
3 cups flour, sifted
2 tsp baking powder

Cream butter; beat in sugar. Add egg yolks and molasses. Sift dry ingredients; add alternately with milk. Add beaten egg whites. Fill muffin tins two-thirds full. Bake about 20 minutes in a 425°F oven.

Cinnamon Rolls

1 cup milk (scald)
1 tsp salt
2 tbsp sugar
4 tbsp butter
1 compressed yeast cake
3 cups sifted flour or little more if needed
½ cup currants or raisins may be added if desired

Topping:
5 rounding tbsp sugar
1 tsp cinnamon

Place milk, salt, sugar, butter in mixing bowl; blend. Add broken yeast cake and half of the flour. Beat; add remaining flour; knead. Place dough in greased bowl; spread with melted butter. Cover; let rise to double its size, 2 to 3 hours. Knead and roll ½-inch thick; brush with melted butter. Sprinkle with topping. Roll as for jelly roll. Cut in one-inch slices. Place rolls together in a greased pan; brush with melted butter. Cover; let rise one hour. Bake in hot, 400°F oven about 20 minutes.

Mincemeat Cookie Bars

Mincemeat
½ cup butter
1 cup light brown sugar, packed
1 tsp vanilla
1½ cups flour, sifted
2 tsp baking powder
¼ tsp salt
1¾ cups rolled oats

Cream the butter thoroughly; slowly stir in the sugar, vanilla and flour, baking powder and salt sifted together. Then add the rolled oats. Mix thoroughly. Take one half of the mixture and pat into a buttered square pan. Spread with a layer of mincemeat. Crumble the remaining cake mixture and sprinkle over the mincemeat; press gently in place. Bake about 25 minutes at 325°F. Cut into two-inch bars while warm and remove from pan. Keep in air-tight tin when cold.

Molasses Bran Muffins

1 cup sifted flour
1 tsp baking soda
1 tsp salt
1 egg, well beaten
1 cup sweet milk
½ cup molasses
2 cups all bran
2 tbsp melted shortening (or cooking oil)
Raisins or chopped dates, if desired

Sift flour; measure; add soda, salt and sift again. Combine egg, milk, molasses and bran; add to flour mixture; mix only until blended. Add shortening. Bake in greased muffin tins in hot oven, 425°F, 20 minutes. Makes 12 muffins.

Iva's Fruit Muffins

1 cup brown sugar
1 egg
1 tsp cinnamon
¼ tsp cloves, ground
½ cup shortening
1¾ cups flour
½ tsp ginger
½ tsp salt
Vanilla
¾ cup raisins
¼ cup mixed peel
1 tsp soda

Pour one cup boiling water on last three ingredients. Cool. Add other ingredients. Cook in muffin tins at 350°F until done.

Fritters

I was given two methods of making fritters, both good with slightly different ingredients. Sliced bananas or apples can be added if desired.

Annie's Fritters

3 eggs (beaten separately)
3 cups flour
2 cups sour milk or buttermilk
1 tsp soda
1 tsp salt

Dissolve the soda in the milk; stir in the egg yolks, then the sifted flour and salt, and lastly the whites beaten stiff. Have kettle of boiling fat ready; drop the batter in by spoonfuls, and cook to a light brown.

Carol's Fritters

2 tbsp butter
6 tbsp sweet milk
1 tsp baking powder
flour to roll

Roll thin, cut into small squares, and fry in hot lard. Serve with maple syrup.

Note: Fat in which fritters are fried should be very deep and boiling hot. When done, remove like doughnuts and drain well. Transfer to hot platter covered with folded napkin and serve at once.

Potato Doughnuts

Doughnuts were very popular in the 1890s and many handwritten recipes can be found for them. They were easy to make and could be chilled to allow for other chores to be done. Lard was very common which would increase the popularity.

4 cups flour
3 tsp cream of tartar
1 tsp salt
1 cup mashed potatoes
1¼ cup sugar
½ cup butter
1½ tsp soda
2 tsp nutmeg
⅔ cup milk
3 eggs
½ tsp vanilla

Combine flour, soda, cream of tartar, nutmeg and salt. Set aside. Beat milk and potatoes together until smooth. Beat eggs with sugar and melted butter until light. Add vanilla. Blend in dry ingredients gradually, alternating with milk mixture beginning and ending with dry ingredients. Chill 1½ hours. Roll half the dough at a time, chilling the rest. Roll out to ⅜-inch thick. Cut. Fry in fat at 190°C (375°F) until brown, turning once. Drain and set on rack. Dip in sugar if desired.

Cookies

Helen's Old Fashioned Oatmeal Cookies

This is an old Scottish recipe for a crunchy, oat bar which is excellent for dipping in tea or coffee, delicious served with raspberry jam and lovely on its own.

Use a very large bowl for mixing.

Combine together dry ingredients:

2 cups sugar
5 cups flour
5 cups oatmeal (Ogilvie Scotch-type Oatmeal)
2½ tsp salt
1 tsp baking powder

Rub in (as for pie crust):
1 pound Maple Leaf Tenderflake Lard

(This takes perseverance, keep rubbing until there is no evidence of fat having been added, no lumps, and all a fine, even texture.)

Mix together:
⅛ cup water
1 tsp baking soda

Keep mixing so that the soda doesn't settle and sprinkle over dry mixture. Blend in.

Preheat oven to 425°F.

Push most of dry ingredients to one side of mixing bowl. Add 1 tablespoon water and work in to part of the dry ingredients to form a ball of dough the right consistency to roll. Remove that ball; roll on board lightly dusted with flour using a rolling pin which has also been lightly dusted. Roll until even and less than

¼-inch thick. Trim off broken sides; cut into squares. Using a lifter, place on ungreased baking sheets and pop into a hot oven. Watch them carefully for being so thin they can easily burn. Cook 10-12 minutes until golden brown. Remove from pan immediately when taken from the oven. Repeat the procedure until all dough is used. This makes a large tinful of bar cookies which keep extremely well.

"Oh, weary mothers mixing dough,
Don't you wish that food would grow?
Your lips would smile I know to see
A cookie bush or a pancake tree."

The People's Home Recipe Book
1910

Chocolate Biscuit

"especially appropriate for afternoon tea"

Cover three large baking pans with paper that has been well oiled with washed butter. Over these dredge powdered sugar. Melt in a cup one ounce of chocolate. Separate the whites and yolks of four eggs. Add to the yolks a generous one-half cupful of powdered sugar, and beat until light and firm. Add the melted chocolate, and beat a few minutes longer. Beat the whites of the eggs to a stiff, dry froth. Measure out three-fourths of a cupful of sifted flour, and stir it and the whites into the yolks. The whites and flour must be cut in as lightly as possible, and with very little stirring. Drop the mixture in teaspoonfuls on the buttered paper. Sprinkle powdered sugar over the cakes and bake in a slow oven for about fourteen or fifteen minutes. The mixture can be shaped like lady fingers, if preferred.

Canada's Cook Book

Scotch Oat Cakes

1 cup boiling water
½ tsp salt
1 tbsp shortening
oatmeal
¼ tsp soda

Add salt, soda, shortening to boiling water, then stir in oatmeal until dough is stiff enough to knead. Roll very thin; cut into squares; bake slightly on griddle, then dry in slow oven.

Sweetheart Cookies

½ cup butter or butter and shortening mixed
⅓ cup white sugar
⅓ cup brown sugar
2 cups flour
½ tsp baking powder
¼ tsp salt
1 egg
1 tsp vanilla
¼ tsp almond extract

Cream sugars and butter. Add egg, vanilla and almond flavouring. Add flour, baking powder and salt. Mix well. Roll out thin and cut with heart-shaped cookie cutter. Bake in 350°F oven until lightly browned.

Spiced Ginger Mounds

¾ cup butter
1 cup sugar
¼ cup molasses
1 egg
2 cups flour
1 tsp baking soda
1 tsp cinnamon
1 tsp nutmeg
¼ tsp salt

Cream butter and sugar. Add molasses and egg, creaming well together. Add dry ingredients. Roll in balls and place on ungreased cookie sheets. Bake at 350°F for 15-18 minutes.

Fruit Drops

1 cup butter
1½ cups sugar
3 eggs
1 tsp soda
1 tbsp hot water
3¼ cups flour
1 tsp cinnamon

1 cup walnuts, chopped
½ cup currants
½ cup seeded raisins

Cream the butter; add the sugar gradually and eggs, well beaten and the soda dissolved in the water, and then mix in half the flour with the cinnamon sifted in it. Lastly add walnuts, fruit and the remaining flour. Drop by teaspoonfuls at least one inch apart and bake in a moderate oven.

Mrs. Falconer's Scotch Cake

½ cup brown sugar (light)
1 cup butter
2 cups flour

Cream butter; add sugar, then work in flour using hands. Knead in bowl (keep creaming with hands) for 10 minutes, working constantly. Put in an 8- × 8-inch ungreased pan. Pat down level so that it is an even thickness all over. Prick with a fork in rows, right to the bottom (these lines will enable you to break the shortbread apart). Cook in a 275°F oven until lightly brown and receding away from the sides of the pan. This recipe can easily be doubled and a larger pan used (or two pans).

This old recipe for shortbread sounds simple, but the creaming of butter and sugar must be done well. Kneading must also be done well for at least 10 minutes or you will not have good shortbread cake. The working is crucial. If you don't knead, shortbread will be tough, short of grain, instead of light, fluffy and of the melt-in-your-mouth variety. Learn to do this properly through practice and you will be on your way to being a cook as good as those of the golden days of the kitchen.

About Molasses

If there is one thing that can be said to be an integral part of the Island life it is molasses. Being connected by the sea routes to the West Indies meant that Maritime Canada had easy access to this wonderful sweetener—so much so that it was used with as much frequency, if not more, than we use white sugar today.

Homemakers baked with it, it was used to make illegal booze, why farmers even fed it to livestock—as we still do today.

But most important of all, it was just there on the table after a hard day of work. An older gentleman described the joy he experienced all his life at sitting down to the kitchen table after his day's work was done. In early years it was school work, then labouring on the farm. Hot biscuits, spread with butter and molasses drizzled over would be served with a cup of tea (strong and black as tar I imagine) during this, his favourite time of day. Family members would stop and chat he said, and everyone would share each other's news, gossip about neighbours and generally get caught up on what was going on around them.

Even today in many homes, the best, most carefully prepared meal with a scrumptious dessert, will be followed by bread, molasses and a cup of good strong tea, just the excuse needed for a relaxing time out to chat before heading back to chores.

Jackie's Soft Molasses Cookies

¾ cup butter
1 cup sugar
1 egg
1 cup molasses
1 tsp soda
¾ cup hot water
4 cups flour
1 tsp cinnamon
¼ tsp ginger
1 tsp salt

Cream butter; add sugar, well beaten egg, molasses and hot water, then the mixed and sifted dry ingredients. Drop from spoon in warm buttered pan; bake 8 minutes in moderate oven (350°F), or take only enough water to make dough that may be rolled out and cut with cookie cutter.

Grandmother's Soft Molasses Cookies

This is an easy and convenient recipe because it must be chilled. It could be mixed up in the evening and then cooked in the morning. You can also substitute any kind of fat. These soft chewy cookies are usually large.

¾ cup shortening or other fat
1½ cup molasses
1 tsp salt
½ cup hot water
2 tsp ginger

½ tsp cinnamon
½ cup brown sugar
1 egg
5 cups flour
4 tsp soda
½ tsp nutmeg
½ tsp cloves

Cream shortening, add sugar, eggs and molasses; beat well. Add 2 cups flour. Mix well. Add water. Add remaining flour with spices. If still soft add up to one more cup flour. Chill two to three hours. Roll to ⅓-inch thickness and bake for 8-10 minutes at 375°F.

Range Top Cookies

Mix in a saucepan:
1½ cups sugar
2 tbsp cocoa
½ cup milk
½ cup margarine

Boil 1½ minutes, stirring occasionally. Remove from heat and add:

1 tsp vanilla
½ cup peanut butter
3 cups quick cooking oatmeal

(You may add ½ cup raisins or shredded coconut, with peanut butter if desired.)

Mix well. Drop by rounded teaspoonfuls on waxed paper or spread in a greased pan and cool for a few hours before cutting.

Jolly Boys

Mix together thoroughly while dry, one and one-half pints of rye-meal, one-half of a pint of flour, one-half of a teacupful of cornmeal, two pinches of cinnamon, a little salt and two teaspoonfuls of baking powder. Add one egg, well beaten; two tablespoonfuls each of molasses and sugar, and cold water enough to make a thick batter. Fry in hot lard a heaping tablespoonful at a time and cook until well browned.

Canada's Cook Book

Butter Macaroons

Break four eggs, reserve the whites for some other use and drop the yolks into boiling water. Let stand where the water will keep hot without boiling about twenty minutes, then drain on a soft cloth. Beat 1 cup of butter to a cream; press the egg yolks through a sieve into the butter; beat in thoroughly then gradually beat in one cup sugar, ½ cups almonds blanched and chopped, the grated rind of a lemon, ½ teaspoon of cinnamon and 3 cups flour. Break the dough into pieces about the size of a hickory nut. Roll these in the hands into balls and press on a buttered baking pan into flat rounds, the size and shape of a macaroon. Baste over with slightly beaten egg white, dredge with granulated sugar and bake to an amber shade. This recipe makes 60 macaroons. The dough may be rolled into a sheet and cut into rounds with a small tin cutter, then finished as above.

Charlottetown Guardian 1932

Ragged Robins

2 egg whites
¼ tsp vanilla
⅛ tsp salt
½ lb dates (remove stones and chop)
½ cup glazed cherries
1 cup walnuts
1¾ cups corn flakes
½ cup white sugar

Beat egg whites until stiff, add vanilla and salt. Combine the rest of the ingredients and add to egg-white mixture. Drop from a spoon on to greased baking sheet. Bake in a slow oven (325°F) for 15 minutes or until lightly browned.

Purity Cook Book

Sand Tarts from Stanhope

½ cup butter
1 cup plus 4 tbsp white sugar
1 egg
1¾ cups sifted flour
3 tsp baking powder

1 egg white
1 tsp cinnamon
½ cup blanched almonds

Cream butter; add one cup of sugar gradually, and cream until light and fluffy. Add well beaten egg. Sift flour with baking powder and add to first mixture. Chill, then roll to ⅛-inch thickness. Cut in rounds, brush with egg white, and sprinkle with remaining sugar mixed with cinnamon. Split almonds and arrange on each tart. Bake on greased baking sheet at 350°F for about 10 minutes.

Purity Cook Book

Squares

Squares are perhaps even more popular with Island families than cake or cookies. Every gathering where food is brought along offers up a dazzling array of delicious creations which I'm sure have as much variety as cooks have imagination.

Raspberry Squares (also delicious using apricot)

½ cup butter
½ cup brown sugar, firmly packed
1 cup sifted flour
¼ tsp baking soda
¼ tsp salt
1½ cups rolled oats
1 cup raspberry jam (or try apricot)
¼ cup finely chopped almonds, blanched and skinned (optional)
1 cup grated lemon rind

Cream together butter and brown sugar until fluffy. Sift flour, soda and salt together and stir into butter, sugar mixture. Add the oats and stir until thoroughly blended together. Divide this into two third and one third. To the one third add the almonds again mixing well. Put the larger portion into a greased square pan (9- × 9-inch) and press evenly over the bottom. Combine the jam and lemon rind then spread evenly over the oat mixture. Gently sprinkle the remaining oat mixture over the jam and pat lightly down. Preheat oven to 350°F and bake 30 minutes or until golden brown. Cut into squares while still warm for easy handling.

Mary's Raspberry Squares

¾ cup butter
¾ cup sugar
2 eggs separated
1½ cups sifted flour
1 cup walnuts, chopped
1 cup raspberry preserve
½ cup flaked coconut

Beat butter with ¼ cup sugar until light and fluffy; beat in egg yolks. Stir in flour until blended. Spread evenly in 13- × 9- × 2-inch pan. While this layer bakes, beat egg whites in a small bowl until foamy white and doubled in volume. Beat in ½ cup sugar until meringue stands in peaks. Fold walnuts into meringue. Spread raspberry preserve over layer in pan. Sprinkle with coconut. Spread over that the meringue. Bake at 350°F for 25 minutes or until lightly golden brown. Cool completely in pan. Also good with thickened rhubarb sauce.

Pineapple Squares

1⅓ cups flour
2 tbsp icing sugar
⅔ cup butter
1 cup crushed pineapple
1 6-oz bottle red cherries
⅓ cup white sugar
2 tbsp cornstarch
2 egg whites
4 tbsp white sugar

Make the first layer by mixing together flour, icing sugar and butter. Smooth out in a large square pan and bake 10 minutes at 350°F. Let cool. To make filling mix pineapple, cherries, ⅓ cup white sugar and cornstarch in a saucepan and cook at medium heat until thick. Let cool and pour over bottom layer.

Make the topping by beating egg whites until stiff, then adding 4 tbsp white sugar. Spoon over filling layer. Place in oven just long enough to lightly brown.

Hello Dollies

1 cup crushed graham crackers
$\frac{1}{4}$ cup melted butter
1 cup semi-sweet chocolate
  chips
1 cup pecans, chopped
1 cup coconut
1 can sweetened condensed milk

Mix crumbs and butter together and press into a greased 8-inch pan. Sprinkle crumb mixture with chocolate chips, then pecans, then coconut. Pour condensed milk over the whole mixture and spread lightly. Bake at 350°F for 30 minutes.

Speckled Squares

1 cup white sugar
2 cups flour
$\frac{1}{2}$ cup shortening
3 tsp baking powder
1 cup milk
1 tsp vanilla (or to taste)
2 squares semi-sweet chocolate
  (grated)
3 egg whites
$\frac{1}{2}$ cup (scant) sugar

Topping:
$\frac{1}{2}$ cup butter
$1\frac{1}{2}$ cups icing sugar
3 egg yolks
$1\frac{1}{2}$ squares chocolate

Combine the first four ingredients and then add to bowl alternately with milk and vanilla. Add the grated chocolate then the egg whites with the $\frac{1}{2}$ cup (scant) sugar beaten in. Bake at 350°F for $\frac{3}{4}$ hour. Cool and top with $\frac{1}{2}$ cup butter, $1\frac{1}{2}$ cups icing sugar, 3 egg yolks combined and spread on top. Melt chocolate and spread on icing.

Tea Squares

Lower Crust:

¾ cup butter, cream well
⅓ cup sugar
2 egg yolks, well beaten
1½ cups flour, sifted
1 tsp vanilla

Blend all and pat into a 9- × 9-inch pan. Bake in 350°F oven 12 minutes or until lightly browned.

Upper Crust:

2 eggs, beaten separately
2 tbsp flour
¼ tsp baking powder
1½ cups brown sugar
½ cup walnut meats
¼ tsp salt
1 cup shredded coconut,
moistened with little milk
1 tsp vanilla

Mix all ingredients and spread over partly baked crust. Return to oven and bake a further 20 minutes. Cool and cut in squares.

Black and White Squares

½ cup butter
3 tbsp icing sugar
1 cup flour

Rub to crumbs, put in 8- × 8-inch square pan. Pat down and bake 12 minutes.

2 eggs, beaten well
1 cup brown sugar
3 tbsp flour
½ tsp baking powder
½ tsp salt
3 tbsp cocoa

Slowly beat together until well mixed, then add:

½ cup nuts
1 tsp vanilla

Put on base; bake 20 minutes in a 350°F oven. Cool then ice with a white icing.

Mincemeat Oat Squares

An easy filling in an old-time favourite

1 cup whole wheat flour
 (substitute all purpose)
2 cups Robin Hood oats
1 cup lightly packed brown
 sugar
1 tsp baking soda
¾ cup melted butter
2 cups mincemeat pie filling

Combine flour, oats, brown sugar and baking soda in large mixing bowl. Stir well to blend. Stir in melted butter until mixture is crumbly. Pat half the oat mixture firmly into a greased 13- × 9-inch cake pan. Spread with mincemeat. Sprinkle remaining oat mixture over top. Pat lightly. Bake at 375°F for 20-25 minutes or until golden. Cool and cut into squares. Makes about 3 dozen squares.

Bread

Breadmaking is not an art that I have yet mastered—much to my family's regret. One of the most memorable winters of my life was spent with daily visits to a great friend, Jean K. in Sherwood. It was a winter of heavy snowfall and circumstance (and pleasure) led me to spend almost every day in her company, consuming vast quantities of tea, trying to lose weight and many a day making bread. I did get to the point where under supervision I could run out a not-too-bad loaf, but I have yet to solo. It is one of the things which I am saving to savour in my retirement.

Because of my own lack of skill I am indebted to friends who have passed along their own tried-and-true recipes. Breadmaking is to me an area of cooking where individual talents cannot be duplicated by simply following a recipe. A good loaf of bread is truly a baker's signature.

I decided to leave out most of the very old recipes simply because the ingredients today are different. Yeast, for example, used to be homemade, our milk is pasteurized and does not need the boiling which was often required. I did repeat below instructions for kneading, but I left out almost everything with instructions such as "add about a penny's worth of yeast."

Kneading Bread

"Set the whole mass (of dough) on a well-floured board. The hands are to be covered with flour also. The dough farthest from the operator is to be turned over into the middle of the mass a number of times, and then moved half-way around. The former procedure is gone through with, taking the dough farthest away and pressing it down into the center, either with the fingers or the ball of the hand. A rocking motion adds to the efficiency of the kneading.

At the outset flour is to be dusted on the board from time to time, until the sticky stage has been passed. As soon as the dough does not stick to the clean board, even when pressed down, the process is finished. It should take not less than a quarter of an hour, at the least."

Mrs. Rorer, well-known Eastern instructor, as quoted in Canada's Favorite Cook Book, undated

Good Old-fashioned Scotch Oat Bread

Take 1 cup standard oatmeal, 1 cup flour, 1 small teaspoonful salt, 1 teaspoonful baking powder. Rub in butter size of an English walnut or more. Into this pour enough cold water to make a stiff dough as dry as possible, just as if you were trying to make good pie crust. Spread on board by hand pressure, and keep the edges from parting by the support of one hand while you spread with the other. At the last, roll your rolling pin over it to smoothen the surface. Get it ¼-inch thick, cut in squares, put in moderate oven and bake until it is quite hard through.

Pumpkin Bread

1½ cups white cornmeal
1 cup boiling water
1 cup sour milk
1 cup baked pumpkin or squash
1 egg (well-beaten)
1 tsp salt
1 tsp (level) soda
1 tsp (heaping) sugar
1 tsp melted butter
1 tsp (heaping) baking powder

Scald ½ cup meal with 1 cup boiling water. Add sour milk, baked pumpkin, beaten egg, salt, balance of the cornmeal sifted twice with the soda and baking powder. Mix quickly and beat in well 1 heaping teaspoon sugar and 1 of melted butter. Stir and beat into a light batter. Pour into baking pan until it is about 1 inch in thickness. Bake quickly and serve hot.

Boston Brown Bread

2 cups sour milk or buttermilk
¾ cup dark molasses
1 tsp baking soda
1 cup graham meal
2 cups cornmeal
1 cup grapenuts
1 tsp salt
½ cup raisins, seeded (optional)

Combine the milk and molasses. Dissolve the soda in a tablespoon of warm water; stir it in; and then beat in the graham meal, cornmeal, grape nuts and salt mixed with the raisins, if used. Transfer to three one-pound well-oiled coffee or baking powder cans and steam for two hours (or steam for three hours if put in a larger container).

Boston Brown Bread, or steamed brown bread, is an easy recipe which could be cooked on top of the stove. It was often an accompaniment for baked beans which came up the coast from Boston. Cornmeal and molasses were staples in the cupboard. In the recipe below which was researched by U.P.E.I. students for use in the Heritage kitchens, it was found that 4 tbsp of bran could be substituted for the graham flour and that 2 tbsp vinegar would sour the milk.

Sour Milk Brown Bread

1 pt cornmeal
1 tsp soda
1 pt sour milk (2 tbsp vinegar)
1 pt graham flour (or 4 tbsp
  bran and 2 cups white flour)
1 tsp salt
1 cup molasses

Mix the meal with the flour. Add soda and salt. Add milk and molasses. Beat well. Place in a well floured cloth (see note). Place in rolling water and continue in this way for 3 hours. Cool before removing from the bag.

Note: To cook, the steamed brown bread mixture is placed in a floured bag and the bag is put into boiling water. This method of cooking gives the steamed brown bread its characteristic round or oval shape and mushy exterior (due to constant contact with water). The inside has a medium-golden color and a smooth texture. It can also be steamed in a greased round can.

Colonial Bread

3 cups sifted flour
3 level tsp baking powder
1 level tsp salt
2 tbsp shortening
2 tbsp sugar
1½ cups sweet milk
½ cup chopped nuts
½ cup chopped raisins

Sift flour, baking powder and salt together three times; add other ingredients and mix thoroughly with a spatula or the rounded side of a mixing spoon. Let stand ten minutes. Put in ungreased pan and bake one hour in slow oven (275°F). It makes much better bread if baked in round corrugated pans. Brush with melted butter after removing from oven.

Tea Bread

A yeast bread spiced with cinnamon and allspice and threaded with raisins. Slather it with butter and enjoy.

1 pkg yeast
¼ cup warm water
2 cups scalded milk, cooled
1 cup brown sugar
2 eggs
¼ cup melted butter
1½ tsp cinnamon
¾ tsp allspice
1½ cup raisins
6 to 6½ cups flour, divided

Glaze (follows)

Dissolve the yeast in the water. Put scalded milk in large bowl. Add yeast, sugar, eggs, butter and spices, mixing well after each addition. Mix raisins with 1 cup of the flour and add to egg mixture. Gradually add 5 more cups of flour. Place on floured board and knead until dough is smooth and not sticky (adding rest of flour if necessary), about 10 minutes. Place in an oiled bowl; cover and let rise until doubled (1 to 1½ hours). Punch down and let rise again about 20 minutes. Punch down and form into two loaves. Place in two greased bread pans; cover and let rise again (about 45 minutes). Bake in preheated 325°F oven about one hour and 15 minutes. Remove from pans and place on wire rack. Glaze (see below) while loaves are hot.

Glaze:

Mix together 1 cup powdered sugar, 2 tbsp milk and 1 tsp vanilla.

About Oats

Stories about oats and what people did with them filtered into many conversations with those who remember the turn of the century and early 1900s.

Sally MacKinnon, in her 80th year, remembers an older lady she knew in 1930 who used to still make oat cakes the old way. She would roll them out in a round circle and cut them in quarters, and they were stood up to finish drying in front of the fireplace and cook them on a griddle on top of the open fire. She did not have a stove, just an open fireplace with an oven on the side. She would put coals in a sider underneath and cook. It had a griddle on top.

Angus MacGowan, born 1906, recalls oats being taken to the mill for oatmeal. Cattle were fed oats and horses the round oats, the rest was sent to make oatmeal. They were dried at a kiln and then put through a grinder. The hulls would come off and then a blower would blow the hulls away. The remains were crushed.

Mamie MacPherson remembers oatbread made the same way—stood in front of the fireplace to dry. It was served with butter and molasses. She said this was the only bread they had (Mrs. MacPherson recalls that sometimes a loaf they would call a bannock was made. It was put in a round pan and covered with ashes to cook.

Porridge Bread

This is a very interesting and easy recipe. The left-over cornmeal and oatmeal porridge was used to make this bread. It is convenient to make because it could be allowed to rise overnight. Molasses, butter and flour along with the cornmeal and oatmeal were always in the house.

¼ cup yellow cornmeal	⅓ cup oatmeal
¼ cup soft butter	½ cup molasses
½ tsp salt	1½ cups water
1-1½ cups yeast (good)	10-14 cups flour

In a heavy 1-1½-quart saucepan bring water to a boil over high heat. Pour in the cornmeal and oatmeal in a slow thin stream stirring the mixture constantly with a wooden spoon so that the water continues to boil. Cook briskly for a minute or so, then remove the pan from the heat and beat in the butter, molasses and salt. Pour the cornmeal, oatmeal mixture into a deep bowl and cool to lukewarm. Add the good yeast to the mixture and mix well. Beat in about 8 cups of flour or more until the dough can be gathered in a compact ball. Place the dough on a lightly floured surface and knead. As you knead incorporate enough flour so that the dough is no longer sticky. This can be done by sprinkling the flour over the dough as you knead. Continue to knead for about 10 minutes or until the dough is smooth and shiny. After kneading, spread some softened butter over the inside of a large bowl. Place the dough in the bowl and turn the ball around to coat the surface. Cover with greased wax paper and a towel and place in a draft-free area until the dough has doubled in size. Grease 3 loaf pans and punch the dough down after rising. Knead dough 2-3 minutes more then divide and shape into loaves. Place in pans. Put the loaves in a draft-free area for about 40 minutes longer. Bake in a hot oven (400°F) for about 45 minutes to 1 hour or until the crust is light brown in color, and the loaves begin to shrink away from the side of the pans. Cool loaves before serving.

Porridge — Oatmeal

A very important staple in the Scottish diet, porridge was eaten every morning by many families in the late 1800s. Sometimes it was made one day and left on the back of the stove to cook all day and water was added. It would be eaten the next day and any left over used in recipes like the one above.

2 cups boiling water
⅔ cup oatmeal
1 tsp salt

Add oatmeal to boiling salted water gradually. Stir and set at the back of the stove. Porridge tastes better the next day.

Bannock

Very popular in Scottish communities.

Bannock was made by many different ethnic groups as a substitute for yeast bread. It was quick to assemble and cook and calls for few ingredients that can easily be substituted. Drippings from pork gave bannock added colour from the dark flecks in the fat. Sour milk, or sweet milk and cream of tartar could be used. Sugar can be added to make it sweeter for special occasions.

Bannock is usually cooked in the oven which allows it to rise well and take on a golden brown colour. If cooked on top of the stove, it can rise well, depending on temperature but the exterior tends to take on a darker colour because of the direct contact with the pan.

Usually it is cooked in a oval shape with cross marks on top. They are made with a knife so that serving size pieces can be broken off. Or, you can leave the cross marks and slice it.

3 cups flour
1 tbsp cream of tartar
¼ cup lard or dripping
1½ tsp soda
1 tsp salt
1 cup milk

Combine flour, soda, cream of tartar and salt in large bowl. Cut in fat. Stir in milk with a fork. Knead lightly 10-12 times. Roll out to one-inch thickness and cut squares in surface about ½-inch deep. Place bannock in hot cast iron pan lightly greased with lard. Cook for 4 to 5 minutes on each side. Serve hot or cold with butter and molasses.

Assize of Bread

Messrs. B. De St. Crois, Francis Longworth and Richard Yate, Justices appointed to regulate the Assize of Bread, announce the following regulations: the half- penny loaf of fine wheaten flour is to weigh 10 oz. 11 dr; the three-penny loaf, do, to weight 1 lb. 5 oz. 6 dr; the six-penny loaf, do, to weigh 2 lb. 10 oz. 12 dr; the shilling loaf, do, to weigh 5 lb. 5 oz. 8 dr.

P.E.I. Register,
March 11, 1828

And we complain about government regulations.

A well stocked Summerside store of yesteryear.

(Public Archives of PEI, Allan Rankin Collection Accession 2930)

Biscuits

One Dough with Many Uses

The biscuit dough which follows is one of those standby recipes which every good cook has tucked away in her mind. With it they can create all manner of desserts (recipes for several variations of use for this dough follow).

> *"When a flour mixture is moistened stuff enough to knead, it is called a dough; if thin enough to be beaten, it is called a batter."*

This dough can be prepared and cooked as biscuits, which are delicious with conserve, jam or jelly.

Biscuit Dough for Shortcake

2 cups flour
4 tsp baking powder
½ tsp salt
1 tbsp sugar
¾ cup milk
¼ cup shortening or butter

Mix dry ingredients; work in butter or fat with tips of fingers. Add milk gradually. Toss on flour board; pat; roll; cut with large biscuit cutter or roll to fit two pans and bake in a very hot oven, 450°F 12 to 15 minutes.

Strawberry Shortcake

Split biscuits and fill with crushed, sweetened berries. Allow 1-1½ cups berries to each shortcake. Serve with cream plain or whipped.

Blackberry Roll

1½ qts blackberries
1 cup sugar
Biscuit dough
2 tbsp butter

Toss above dough on board; roll ½-inch thick; spread with melted butter and strew half of the berries on top; cover with half the sugar and cinnamon, if desired.

Fold dough over on one side and roll; put in large well-greased pan, surrounded with the rest of the berries and sugar. Place in hot oven; bake 20 minutes or until crisp and well done. Cut in slices and serve warm with sauce in pan.

Apple Dumplings, Baked

Biscuit dough
6 apples, peeled and cored
1 cup sugar
1 cup water

Toss biscuit dough on floured board; divide in two parts. Roll dough in 6-inch squares; place on each an apple and 1 tablespoon sugar. Bring up corners; twist and pinch together and place side by side in a well-greased pan. Pour over water and the remaining sugar and bake in a hot oven about 45 minutes or until crisp and well done. Serve hot with sauce in pan.

Roly Poly

Make biscuit dough; roll out ½-inch thick. Spread with chopped apples, raisins, sugar and cinnamon or with jam; roll. Place it into a small baking pan; spread the butter over all and add 2 cups of cold water and bake in a hot oven, basting often with the sauce in the pan until done. Serve hot.

Kneaded Biscuits

Kneaded biscuits, referred to as hard biscuits, were referred to often during my travels. They can be cooked on the top of the stove or in the oven. Ingredients are very simple and would have been in any kitchen from the 1890s on. Butter or lard can be used depending on which is more available.

3 cups flour
1½ tsp salt
½ cup butter
½ tsp cream of tartar
¾ cup sour milk
½ tsp baking soda

Combine flour, baking soda, cream of tartar and salt. Cut in butter. Add milk; stir in with a fork. Knead 5 to 8 minutes. Roll out to ¼-inch thickness and cut into 2- × 2-inch squares. Prick the top with a fork three or four times on each square. Cook on top of stove in a heavy cast iron pan for 5 to 6 minutes on each side.

Rich Baking Powder Biscuits

2 cups cake or general use flour
4 tsp baking powder
1 tsp sugar
½ tsp salt
6 tbsp shortening
¾ cup milk

Sift the dry ingredients together and, with the back and edge of a spoon, cut in the shortening until the mixture looks flaky. Moisten with the milk and mix until blended. Transfer to a board dusted with flour. Pat out to one-fourth inch in thickness and shape with a biscuit cutter first dipped in flour. Transfer to an oiled baking pan and bake in a hot oven (400°F) for 15 minutes or until puffy and brown. These biscuits are very short and flaky. To make a biscuit with a bready texture, use general-use flour and only four tablespoons of shortening.

Note: Baking powder biscuits may be mixed, cut in advance, placed on oiled pans, and kept for hours in the refrigerator before baking.

Magic Almond Rolls

3 cups sifted bread flour
1 tsp salt
½ cup butter or other shortening
¼ cup milk

$\frac{1}{4}$ cup hot water
2 cakes compressed yeast
1 tbsp sugar
3 eggs
1 tsp vanilla
1 cup chopped almonds
$\frac{1}{2}$ cup granulated sugar

To 1$\frac{1}{2}$ cups flour add salt and butter, blending as for pie crust. Dissolve yeast in milk, water and sugar. Add to first mixture; beat until smooth. Cover; let stand 20 minutes. Add beaten eggs, beat vigorously. Fold in remaining flour; add vanilla; stir until smooth. Tie dough loosely in square of cheesecloth; drop into pan of warm water 1 hour until it rises to top of pan. Place dough on platter; cut in small pieces; roll in sugar and chopped almonds. Twist into figure 8; place in well-greased pan; let stand 5 minutes; bake in hot oven, 15 minutes.

1933 Rogers Cookbook

Pastry

Flaky Pastry

8 oz flour
Pinch salt
5-6 oz butter
Water to mix

Sift together the flour and salt. Divide butter into three portions and rub one portion into flour. Mix to a rolling consistency with cold water and roll out to an oblong shape. Cut second portion of butter into small pieces and lay on two-thirds of dough, leaving one third without fat. Take two corners and fold over second third to make an envelope with its flap open. Fold over top end of pastry, so closing the envelope. Turn pastry at right angles and seal ends. Rib at intervals with a rolling pin to give a corrugated effect, thus equalizing the pressure of air and so making certain the pastry will rise evenly. Repeat the process using the remaining butter and turning pastry in the same way. Roll out once more and put into a cold place for 30 minutes if it feels very soft and sticky. Fold pastry as before, turn, seal edges and rib again. Altogether the pastry should have three foldings and three rollings. Stand in a cold place for a little while, before baking, to make the pastry rise better. Sweets made with flaky pastry should be eaten within 24 hours.

Debbie's Fool-Proof Flaky Pastry

2 cups flour
1 tsp salt
⅔ cup Crisco shortening
2 tbsp butter, melted
5 tbsp cold water

1 tbsp vinegar

Mix flour and salt. Cut in Crisco and butter until mixture is like coarse crumbs. Add water and vinegar, mixing with fork. Form into ball and chill. Roll out into two crusts.

Whole Wheat Crust for Pies and Tarts

¼ cup butter or margarine
2 tbsp chicken fat
1 tbsp maple syrup (this is optional)
1¼ cups whole wheat pastry flour

Heat butter and chicken fat until foamy; remove from heat and add syrup if desired; cut in flour to make pastry dough. Press into a straight-sided 9-inch tart pan or a pie plate.

To Hot Up Pastry

If you want to reheat a meat or fruit pie, slip the whole thing into a grease-proof paper bag and then slip into the oven till thoroughly hot. If you do this, you will find that the reheating will not turn the pastry hard and uneatable.

(1936)

Puddings

Rum Runners Black Bottom Pie

With so many Island boats and crews involved in the fruitful business of running rum and other illegal beverages, particularly into the United States, it seems only right that they enjoy some of the goods they so carefully brought home.

4 tbsp butter
1⅓ cups graham crackers or
  vanilla wafers, finely crushed
6 ozs semi-sweet chocolate
2 tbsp strong black coffee
3 egg yolks
¾ cup granulated sugar
¾ cup milk
1 envelope unflavoured gelatin
¼ tsp salt
3 egg whites
2 tbsp brandy
2 tbsp rum
1 cup heavy cream, whipped

Melt the butter and add to the crumbs, stirring until evenly mixed. Using these cover the bottom and sides of a 9-inch pie plate, evenly. Melt 4 ounces of the chocolate in a double boiler, then add the coffee and stir. When mixed pour over the pie crust. Beat egg yolks slightly. Cook yolks, ½ cup sugar and milk in the double boiler until mixture is thick enough to coat a spoon. Remove from the heat and add the gelatin which has been dissolved in ¼ cup cold water. Cool until the mixture begins to set. Add salt to egg whites and beat stiffly. Fold egg whites and brandy into filling mixture and then pour filling into the crust. Chill. You can leave overnight refrigerated as long as you cover. Fold 2 tbsp sugar and the rum into whipped cream. Shave or sliver the remaining chocolate (a potato peeler is handy for this). Spread the whipped cream over the pie, cover with the shaved chocolate and serve.

Corn Flake Pudding

2 cups corn flakes
2 cups milk
½ cup molasses
½ cup sugar
2 eggs, beaten
little salt
⅓ tsp ginger
½ tsp vanilla

Place corn flakes in buttered baking dish. Blend all ingredients and pour over flakes. Bake in 350°F oven until mixture sets.

Steamed Fig Pudding

2 eggs
4 tbsp melted butter
½ cup brown sugar
½ cup chopped figs
½ cups chopped dates
½ cup chopped nutmeats
1 tsp grated lemon rind
1 cup flour (sifted)
¼ tsp salt
½ tsp soda
¼ cup milk
1 tsp baking powder

Beat eggs well, dissolve brown sugar in butter, add to eggs, add figs, dates, nutmeats and lemon rind. Sift flour once before measuring then sift with salt and add. Dissolve soda in milk and add last. Fill greased mold or pan two-thirds full. Cover with waxed paper and steam in a covered kettle 2 hours. Do not open kettle until through steaming.

Nut Cabinet Pudding

"Cabinet pudding is one of those fine old-time desserts that have come down to us with a never-diminishing aura of distinction about them. But modern culinary thought has dared even to paint this lily, and the addition of moist cocoanut to the delicate mixture is just one more delight. Do try this for a Sunday super treat or for your next guest dinner."

5 egg yolks, slightly beaten
5 tbsp sugar
¼ tsp salt
2 cups milk
1 tbsp gelatin
¼ cup cold milk
¼ tsp vanilla
Lady fingers or strips of cake
1½ cups apricots, sliced
1 can moist cocoanut

Combine egg yolks, sugar and salt with 2 cups milk, and cook in double boiler until mixture coats the spoon, stirring constantly. Soak gelatine in ¼ cup milk five minutes, and add hot custard. Stir until gelatin dissolves. Add vanilla. Strain custard into mold, filling 1½ inches deep. Chill until firm. Dip lady fingers into part of custard mixture and line sides of mold. Fill centre of mold with alternate layers of apricots, remaining custard and cocoanut. Chill until firm. Unmold. Garnish with additional apricot halves, whipped cream and strips of angelica.

Serves 8

Charlottetown Guardian
1932

Raisin-Almond Bread Pudding

1 cup brown sugar
3 slices white bread
3 tbsp butter
1 cup raisins (white are best)
¼ cup blanched slivered
almonds
1 tbsp grated orange rind
¼ tsp ground cinnamon

3 eggs
2 cups milk
1 tsp vanilla extract
Pinch of salt

Place brown sugar in a double boiler, spreading evenly across the bottom. Butter the bread, using all the butter, then cut into small squares and lay over the sugar. Sprinkle on the raisins, almonds, orange rind and cinnamon. Beat together eggs, milk, vanilla and salt. Pour over above without stirring. Cover and cook over simmering water for one hour. This can be served hot or cold. If it is to be served cold, cool in the same pan then transfer to a serving dish. If you wish to make ahead and reheat the next day, return to double broiler and keep over simmering water to heat through.

Sauces

"Sauces and soups are the fine art of cookery and the person who understands them must understand tastes and flavors and possess a trained palate."

"All sauces are made or derived from brown or white sauce and the flavoring makes the numerous changes. The basis for this is one rounding tablespoonful of butter, the same of flour and one-half pint (1 cup) of any desired liquid, such as stock, strained tomatoes, milk, cream, water, etc.

Certain sauces belong to some particular vegetable, meat, fish or dessert, such as brandy sauce with plum pudding, cranberry sauce with turkey, applesauce with pork, mint sauce with lamb, and caper sauce with mutton.

A general principle in uniting material for sauces is, rub butter or fat and flour together, and soften with a little of the hot liquid which is heating in the double boiler; stir all together until it is the desired thickness. In this way the flour is most thoroughly cooked, besides more digestible than when cooked in the fat.

The main standard seasonings are salt, pepper, paprika, onion, bay leaf, Worcestershire sauce, Tabasco sauce, mint, capers, and flavorings from meats, fish stock or vegetables. The thickening may be flour, bread crumbs, yolks of eggs, arrowroot, cornstarch or vegetable purée.

There are many fruit sauces very nice for puddings and ice creams made from crushed fresh fruits and the juice and sugar cooked to any desired thickness."

Serve a sauce as soon as possible as there is danger of separating.

If necessary to keep hot, set in a pan of hot water.

The People's Home Recipe Book
Toronto, 1919

White Sauce

1 rounding tablespoonful butter
1 rounding tablespoonful flour
1 cup milk
½ teaspoonful salt
¼ teaspoonful pepper

Rub the butter and flour together in a double boiler. When smooth add the milk, slowly. Stir over the fire steadily until it thickens. Add the seasoning and it is ready for use. This is the best of all sauces.

— one cup of strained tomatoes in place of milk or cream will make tomato sauce, adding a seasoning of bay leaf and onion when stewing the tomatoes.
— to make an egg sauce add four hard-boiled eggs, the yolks put through the ricer and the whites chopped fine. This sauce is very nice to serve either with chicken or boiled salt cod.
— for a butter sauce substitute boiling water instead of the milk or cream, adding it slowly beating all the while.
— for a mushroom sauce, make the white sauce then add ½ teaspoonful Kitchen Bouquet, 1 can mushrooms, drained and if desired, 1 sweet green pepper chopped. Stand the double boiler over a slow fire for ten minutes to heat. Nice served with warmed over chicken or sweetbreads.

Mrs. Kirk's Card Index
Cooking Recipes
1906

Bechamel (Foundation white sauce)

This sauce, just a little more elaborate than a plain white sauce is said to be one of the great sauces and actually serves as the foundation for other sauces. If the salt and pepper are left out and honey, sugar or syrup substituted then it can be turned into a sweet sauce by adding flavourings such as outlined below. This and the white sauce were commonly used in days past to turn an ordinary meat, vegetable, fruit or dessert into something more appealing. This is a very old recipe—the one I commonly use.

— equal quantities of flour and butter to make white roux

- salt and pepper to taste
- a dash of mace or a dash of grated nutmeg
- ½ pint or more milk (1 cup)
- an extra piece of butter

Put the butter into a perfectly clean saucepan; add the flour and stir with a wooden spoon for a few minutes to cook the flour, but do not let it brown. Now add the milk slowly, stirring meanwhile, and cook over a moderate fire for a quarter of an hour. Add salt and pepper, then at the last, when it is quite smooth and creamy like thick cream, take off the heat and stir in a little extra butter, the nutmeg or mace. Mix well together. This is now Bechamel sauce which may be used to surround vegetables like cauliflower or marrows, or as a foundation for other sauces.

Note: If a richer sauce is needed, a gill of cream stirred in after it has been taken from the fire, or the beaten yolk of an egg will make it delicious.

Variations: See white sauce and below:

- make a sweet sauce by substituting sugar, honey or treacle (I use golden syrup) to taste, and adding flavourings such as lemon juice and grated lemon rind, similar for orange, ginger syrup and a little cut-up preserved ginger, chocolate powder, marmalade or jam.
- shrimp sauce — use fish stock instead of milk for mixing, then add half a pint of shrimps, with their armour removed and chopped.
- anchovy sauce — add half a teaspoonful anchovy sauce or 2-3 anchovies rubbed through a sieve. Omit salt.
- lemon sauce (to serve with fowl) — add strained juice of a lemon, grated rind and the boiled liver of the fowl, minced fine.
- chutney sauce — add a gill of tomato purée and the same amount of chutney.
- crab sauce — cut up the meat from a crab (or use a small can), mix this with the white sauce, and add a dish of Worcestershire or other piquante sauce.
- onion sauce — cook one or more Spanish onions, chopped, pass through a sieve and add.

Hollandaise Sauce

2 rounding tablespoonfuls butter
1 rounding tablespoonful flour
1 tablespoonful grated onion
2 tablespoonfuls tarragon-vinegar or lemon juice
2 yolks of eggs
1 bay leaf
1 cup boiling water
½ teaspoonful salt
white pepper

Put bay leaf, onion and vinegar over the fire in a small stew pan; bring to the boiling point and cool. Rub the butter and flour together in the double boiler and add gradually the water; stir until thickened and the flour cooked. Now add the vinegar (or lemon juice) strained. Remove from the fire and stir in the yolks of the eggs one at a time, stirring gently. Reheat just a moment; add salt and pepper; strain and serve at once.

This is elegant for fish or used in many ways with vegetables being especially nice with brussels sprouts, spinach and asparagus. This sauce should be served as soon as made.

Mrs. Kirk's Card Index Cooking
Recipes 1906

Mustard Sauce

To serve with ham, corned beef, and such

1 clove garlic
2 tbsp butter
1 tbsp flour
¾ cup rich stock (or melt in a bouillon cube)
6 tsp prepared mustard
1 tsp each minced chives and chervil

Rub a saucepan with the garlic; melt the butter; add the flour and stock; stir until boiling, and add the remaining ingredients; more mustard may be added if desired. The sauce may be served hot or cold.

French Sauce

To serve with pork, stewed rabbit or roast mutton

1 apple
1 onion
½ oz butter
¼ pt good stock
Juice of 1 lemon
1 tsp prepared mustard
1 tsp sugar
little salt
little cayenne
1 dessert spoonful cognac, optional

Chop the onion and apple very small and fry them in butter till quite tender; bruise them to a pulp with a wooden spoon; add about a quarter of a pint of stock and the seasonings; stir over the fire till it boils; just before serving, if liked, the cognac may be added.

Parsley Butter Balls

A nice garnish that shows you took a little extra care

½ cup butter
1 tsp lemon juice
2 tbsp very finely minced parsley

Combine the ingredients in the order given and cream thoroughly. Chill and form into small balls with butter paddles.

Lemon Horseradish Butter

½ cup butter
¼ tsp salt
1 tbsp lemon juice
2 tsp horseradish
¼ tsp cayenne
paprika

Cream the butter; add the salt, lemon juice, horseradish and cayenne slowly. Chill and form into balls with butter paddles. Dust with paprika.

Chocolate Sauce for Ice Cream or Cake

1 square chocolate
1 cup sugar
1 cup boiling water
1 tsp vanilla
½ cup chopped nuts

Melt the chocolate in a double boiler. Add the sugar and water. Stir while adding the water, so as to form a smooth, glossy mixture as it cooks. Keep adding the water and the sugar until all is used. Boil until thick as desired. Remove from the fire, add vanilla and nuts and serve at once.

Lemon Sauce to serve over Hot Puddings or Cake

1 tbsp flour
1 cup boiling water
½ cup sugar
1 egg
1 tsp vanilla
1½ tsp lemon juice and grated
  peel of one lemon

Mix the flour and sugar well together in a double boiler and pour over quickly the boiling water, stirring all the time till it thickens. Remove from the fire and add the lemon juice and grated peel and pour while hot over the well-beaten egg. Mix well.

Hard Sauce

½ cup butter
1 cup powdered sugar
1 tsp vanilla
1 tbsp brandy

Wash the butter in cold water until it is elastic; put it into a bowl and heat to a cream. When light, gradually add the sugar beating all the while. Add vanilla and gradually the brandy. Put into an attractive dish to serve. Set on ice until wanted. Fresh strawberries are a nice addition to this, or a little grating of nutmeg over the top. The brandy may be omitted—add one teaspoonful of lemon juice.

Brandy Sauce

This is delicious served hot over plum pudding, bread pudding or ice cream.

1½ cups light brown sugar
1½ tbsp quick-cooking tapioca
⅓ tsp salt
2¼ cups boiling water
2 eggs
2 tbsp butter
3 oz brandy

Mix sugar, tapioca, and salt together in the top of a double boiler over boiling water. Slowly add the boiling water, stirring constantly as you pour. Cook five minutes, stirring constantly. Beat the eggs to a lemony froth. Stir the hot syrup into the eggs, a little at a time, then return to double boiler. Continue to cook and stir until it thickens. To serve, reheat in one pan and the butter and brandy in another. Pour the brandy mixture on top of the sauce; set it aflame to carry to the table and serve hot.

Hot Cherry Sauce

1 19-oz can pitted red cherries
1½ tbsp cornstarch
2 tbsp cold water
1 tbsp butter
¼ tsp almond flavouring or
  1 tbsp lemon juice
few grains salt

Drain syrup from the cherries and heat to boiling. Combine cornstarch with water to make a smooth paste. Stir into hot syrup and cool, stirring, until thickened and clear. Cook one or two minutes longer, stirring occasionally. Remove from the heat; add cherries, salt, butter and flavouring. Makes about 2 ½ cups. Serve over cake, pudding or ice cream.

Brown Sugar Sauce

1 cup brown sugar
2 tbsp cornstarch
2 cups boiling water
2 tbsp butter
1 tsp vanilla
few grains salt

Mix sugar and cornstarch thoroughly. Stir in boiling water and cook, stirring, until thickened and there is no taste of raw starch. Remove from heat; add butter and vanilla. Serve hot. Makes about 2 cups, enough for 8 servings.

Traditional Island fare served at Stanhope Beach Lodge is reminiscent of that served at frolics or weddings of days gone by.

Those Special Olden Days

A cause for a large gathering was a family wedding. Many were catered at home or in local halls by the women of the community, church or Institute.

Bride's Cake

1½ lbs butter
1¾ lbs sugar
2 lbs eggs (18) separate and beat yolks and whites separately
4 lbs raisins (seeded and chopped)
5 lbs currants (well washed)
1 lb citron (cut fine)
1 lb almonds, blanched and cut fine
2 lbs Five Roses Flour (sifted)
2 nutmegs
Mace (same bulk as nutmegs)
½ pt alcohol
1 tsp lemon essence (dissolved in the alcohol)
1 tsp soda

Weigh the butter and cut in pieces. Soften, but do not melt. Stir to a cream, then add the sugar and work until white. Add beaten yolks. Beat again. Beat the whites to a stiff froth and also add. Sift the flour over the fruit. Mix well, then add to the other ingredients. Last of all, put in the citron and nuts and also a teaspoon soda dissolved in a little water.

"This makes a three-story cake. Would cost $12 in a confectioner's—costs about $3.00. Lower story 1 foot in diameter."

Pour into cake pans for three tiers; bake in a moderate oven

(350°F) until it tests done (a straw or toothpick inserted in centre comes out clean).

Almond Icing for Bride's Cake

Put 8 ounces almond paste into a bowl, and add 16 ounces of crushed and sifted sugar. Then add enough egg whites, unbeaten to make a stiff paste. While working, add gradually 1 teaspoon rose water.

These cakes were often decorated with candied violets or other flowers from the garden.

Bridegroom's Cake

1 cup butter
1 cup sugar
1 cup sweet milk
3 cups flour
1 tsp baking powder
½ tsp vanilla
3 drops lemon extract
4 eggs
½ lb blanched almonds (shredded)
¾ lb citron
½ lb candied cherries
½ lb candied pineapple (shredded)

Cream the butter; add sugar and cream again. Add extract, part of flour and mix well. Add egg yolks beaten until light-coloured. Now add the remainder of the flour, into which sift the baking powder, and add the fruit. Then add the egg whites beaten until dry and stiff. Bake in moderate oven (350°F) 1 hour.

Ice the groom's cake in two colours to harmonize with colour scheme of table decorations.

Note: The Bride's Cake is distributed only to the attendants of the bride. It usually contains a ring.

The Groom's Cake is cut by him and given to his attendants.

This distinction is given so that mistakes may not be made. The wedding cake should be at least three months old before being cut to be at its best.

Yule Season

Preparations for the yule season began early. It was a special time in the home when tantalizing aromas of homemade mincemeat simmering and fruit cakes baking reminded everyone in the area of the kitchen that they had better start planning their gift making.

With frosts making harvesting of the garden a priority chore the excess green tomatoes, apples, pears and such were bottled for winter use. Because of the short growing season green tomatoes in particular were in abundance. It was natural that the skilled cook would make the best use of them possible.

Green tomato mincemeat was easy to make, and a much favoured replacement for the traditional mincemeat which had been developed to preserve meat. Aged to blend and mellow its rich, spicy flavour this mincemeat is delicious by Christmas.

Green Tomato Mincemeat from Helen

6 cups chopped peeled apples
6 cups chopped green tomatoes
4 cups brown sugar
3 cups raisins
1¼ cups vinegar
1 tbsp cinnamon
2 tsp salt
¾ tsp cloves
¾ tsp allspice
¾ tsp mace
½ tsp pepper (or to taste)

Combine all ingredients and bring to a boil, stirring constantly. Reduce heat and simmer, uncovered, until thickened, about two hours. Pour into hot sterilized jars and seal. Makes about 2 quarts. Store in a cool dry place for up to one year.

The Acadian Christmas

Christmas celebrations began with decorating the home. Midnight Mass drew everyone to church; those who lived close by walked and those from further away travelled by sleigh. If the night was dark, each sleigh would have a lantern to light up the way. Afterwards the congregation was soon homeward bound for the réveillon. Writer Georges Arsenault described the celebration recently for the newcomers of the 1980s those employed with the Federal Department of Veterans Affairs.

"Everyone looked forward to this traditional meal, especially since for many it marked the end of four weeks of penance when fast and abstinence were the order of the day. Pâté (meat pie) was always greatly appreciated, and especially rabbit pie. Often the réveillon was the first chance people had to taste the delicious blood pudding prepared during Advent when the pigs were slaughtered.

The réveillon was for the most part a family celebration but sometimes neighbours, relatives and friends would gather together. If there were musicians in the crowd, music and songs added to the fun.

Christmas in those days was centered more on the children, and they were the only ones who received gifts. On Christmas Eve the children hung their stockings near the chimney where St. Nicholas would find them and fill them with goodies. They would find them filled with treats—an apple, or sometimes only half an apple, a hard-boiled egg, a few hard candies, and an orange for the more fortunate children. Later the children would visit their godparents who always had a special Christmas present for them—usually a gingerbread man.

The main dish for Christmas dinner was always some type of stuffed fowl—very often a goose. The dessert could vary, but steamed pudding was always popular. As for sweets, they were not as abundant then as they are today. However, croquignoles, a kind of deep-fried bread, pork tarts and several kinds of cookies were served. Pâté was always a popular festive dish. People enjoyed it at the réveillon, and it was served for breakfast and for supper on Christmas day. Christmas afternoon, the families used to take the children to the church to visit the Christ child's crib.

All in all, Acadian Christmas celebrations were a family affair with celebrations of simple yet very religious nature, much as the Christmas of all Islanders, taking its beauty from great simplicity and appreciation for family and friends."

Christmas Log

Rather than a fruit cake one West Prince Family has always made a Christmas Log. A jelly roll was prepared and placed on a platter. This was covered by a cocoa icing (see index) which was scored in grooves with a fork so that it resembled bark. This was then decorated with green leaves and red berries, cut from prepared gelatin desserts. (You could also use candy leaves and berries or holly and maraschino cherries.) It is a nice addition to the Christmas table and lighter than many traditional cakes. Slices best when chilled.

Plum Puff

Helen Herring, who used to do a tv program, *Today at Home,* gave this recipe one Heritage Day, saying she got it from an old cookbook, the pages of which were yellowed with age.

Prepare filling by mixing together the following, cooking and set aside to cool:
1½ cups raisins
½ cup sugar
2 cups water
2 tbsp flour

Cream together:
1 cup brown sugar
½ cup butter

Add:
1 egg
¼ cup milk

Combine then add:
1 tsp soda
2 tsp cream of tartar
1 tsp salt

Add:
1 tsp vanilla

Use enough flour to roll out. Put half in pan, filling and rest for top. Bake 40 minutes at 350°F. If desired prick top when done, sprinkle with sugar.

Sugar Plums

(said to be a 200 year old recipe) A real Yule season treat.

1 pound almonds
½ pound raisins
½ pound dates
½ pound currants
½ pound figs

Mix together and grind with an old-fashioned meat grinder. After grinding form into one inch balls and roll in sugar. Wrap in coloured tinfoil.

Holiday Gifts from the Kitchen

The holiday season is a perfect time to share some special gifts from your kitchen. Any favourite cake, cookie or candy will be well received, not to mention a sampling of your pickles, jam or jelly.

In days gone by Christmas and the kitchen went together much more than today. Many extra special treats were produced for the family during the weeks before the festive season.

Molasses-Raisin-Nut Bars

¼ cup butter
½ cup sugar
1 egg
½ cup Molasses
2 cups flour
1 cup chopped raisins or dates
¼ tsp salt
¼ tsp soda
1½ tsp baking powder
½ cup sweet milk
1 cup chopped nuts

Cream butter; add sugar and beat until light. Add beaten eggs; mix well, then add molasses. Sift flour with dry ingredients and add alternately with milk to first mixture. Add chopped nuts and fruit last. Spread very thinly in shallow pan. Bake in moderate oven (350°F) 10-12 minutes. Cut in bars 3 inches long and 1½ inches wide. Makes 4 dozen.

Molasses Candy

2 cups brown sugar
1 cup Crosby's Gold Star
  Molasses
1 tsp flavouring
butter size of an egg
1 tbsp vinegar

Boil 10 minutes. Try in water until it cracks.

Ginger

To preserve: Wash and thoroughly scrape ginger root; throw quickly into cold water to prevent discolouration. Cover with fresh cold water; bring to boiling point and drain. Cover again with boiling water and cook slowly until the ginger is tender; drain, this time saving the water for use as a flavouring of other preserves, or it may be put aside for a ginger extract. Weigh the ginger and to each pound allow a pound of sugar and a half a pint of boiling water. Put the sugar and water in a preserving kettle; bring to boiling point and skim. Put in the ginger and cook slowly until each piece is perfectly transparent. The ginger may now be put away the same as other preserves, or drained free from the syrup, cut into thin slices and rolled in granulated sugar. The syrup may be used for flavouring preserves and is nice over white cake.

Ginger can be bottled in fancy containers for giving as a gift as can honey, jams, jellies and pickles.

Honey

A recipe from the days of World War II

5 pound white sugar
3 cups boiling water
½ tsp alum
18 red clovers
30 white clovers
2 roses

Boil sugar, alum and water 4 minutes. Pick over clover blossoms and roses, throw away the cores. Pour the boiled syrup over the blossoms. Let stand for 15 minutes; strain and bottle while warm.

Orange Brandy

I can always envision the adult members of a family sitting down in great anticipation to await their serving of Orange Brandy. It can be served as a drink, as is or over crushed ice or as a dessert, over fresh fruits such as pears or vanilla ice cream. This can also be made substituting a lemon for the orange.

1 orange (use peel only)
3 cups brandy
1 cup sugar

With vegetable parer, peel orange in continuous spirals. Place peel and brandy in jar with tight-fitting lid. Let stand one week; shake occasionally. Remove orange peel. Add sugar; shake until sugar dissolves, let stand 7 days longer.

Lemon Seasoned Pepper

6 lemons
4 oz ground black pepper
½ cup toasted sesame seeds
½ cup celery seeds
¼ cup onion salt
¼ cup salt
1 tbsp garlic powder

Grate lemons (to equal about 6 tablespoons peel). On baking sheet, spread peel in thin layer. Dry in oven at 200°F for 20 minutes. Cool. Combine lemon peel and remaining ingredients mixing thoroughly. Store in small jars with lids. Makes about 2 cups.

Lemon Herbed Vinegar

4 lemons
4 small sprigs fresh dill, basil or
tarragon
32-40 oz white wine vinegar

With vegetable parer, peel each lemon in continuous spiral. In each of four 8-10 ounce bottles with lids, place peel of 1 lemon and 1 herb sprig; fill with vinegar. Refrigerate for at least 2 days to blend flavours. Makes four 8-10 oz bottles.

This can also be varied as follows:

— omit herbs and add 1 or 2 cloves garlic, cut in half
— substitute orange peel for lemon
— omit the herbs and make Lemon vinegar — a treat on fish and chips.

Special occasions such as Christmas would be made more festive by unique additions to the general operation of things. While the effects might be minimal, these acts were those of love and caring which made the family unit strong.

Fireplace Frivolites

For the magical effect of blue and green flames in the fire collect and dry pine cones when they fall from the trees. Dissolve four pounds of bluestone and three pounds of coarse salt in 1 gallon of water, soak the cones in this mixture for three weeks and then dry. These make nice gifts when packaged up in a pretty fireside container.

A stoneware pot full of dried herbs kept by the hearth is nice to sweeten the air. For gifts use good herbs; for everyday use do as the practical older folk would have, and use the prunings from your herbs, such as lavender. For a fragrant fire on a winter night, just throw in a small handful.

As I sit and write this final section of my book of Island recipes the first signs of winter are outside. It's late this year, December 24th, and just a sprinkle of snow on the ground. The cedar growing in front of my office window has just a few icicles clinging to the top branches, today glistening in the sun. A flock of snowbirds have arrived and every so often still my fingers on the typewriter as they wheel and turn in the sky. Even more distracting is the sight of our new dog, Penny, a border collie who, in just three weeks has stolen into our hearts. A black and white bundle of energy, she has at last found a playmate who can keep up with her—the brisk winds of the windy Riverdale valley. They and a piece of bark which takes off each time she lets go of it are ideal companions who will perhaps leave her too tired to cart the gifts, from under the tree, all over the house tonight.

It somehow seems fitting that the last pages should be devoted to Christmas, signifying a glorious close to one year and a positive beginning to the next. A celebration of peace, goodwill and kinship is indeed the best way to end any event.

Index

Acadian
- Chicken Ragout with Dumplings 74
- Christmas 334
- Tourtiere 45

Ambrosia 225

Apple 201
- Blackberry and Apple Jam 211
- Chutney 206
- Marrow and, Chutney 184
- Cider, Sweet 203
- Cider, Vinegar 203
- Coddled Apples and Apple Porcupine 204
- Deep Fried 205
- to Dry 203
- Dumplings 205
- Dumplings, Baked -314
- Lamb's Wool 204
- Maple Stuffed to serve with meat 244
- Onions, and 168
- Pandowdy 202
- Pickled 206
- Pie 205
- and Raspberry Butter 236
- Roly-Poly Pudding 204
- Sauce 202
- and Sausage Rings 203
- Sherbet 202
- Stuffing 207
- Tapioca Bake 204
- Tarragon Vinegar 203

Artichoke 132
- Country-Style 133
- Pickled 133

Asparagus 133
- Cream of Soup 134
- Freda's Deep Fried Spears 134
- Marinade 135

Aspic
- Jelly 97
- Sherried 76

Bacon
- and Clam Pie 123
- Potato Balls 200

Bananas 207
- Sandwiches 207
- Whip 207

Bannock 311

Bayberry 251

Beans 135
- Baked from Maine 137
- Broad 138
- Dilled 138
- Dried — and Peas 131
- Dried, cooking 136
- String Bean Pickles 137

Beef 53
- Boiled Dinner 63
- Carol's Spiced 55
- Corn or Pickle 62
- Corned 62, 63
- Corned, Hash with Eggs 64
- Cornish Pasties 57
- Dill Steak Rolls 55
- Fillet 56
- Fricassee, Mrs. Gallant's 59
- Liver Loaf 61
- Liver and Onions and Gravy 61
- Norma's Beef in a Pot (pot roast) 53
- Ox-tail Soup 60
- Pickle 62
- Planked Steak 54
- Shepherd's Pie 57
- Spiced 55
- Tongue 63

Beets 139
- Greens 140
- Harvard 140
- 'N' Cheddar 140
- Spiced as Nanny Did Them 139

Biscuits
- Blackberry Roll 314

Chocolate 292
Dough for Shortcake 313
Kneaded 314
One Dough With Many Uses 313
Potato 198
Rich Baking Powder 315
Roly Poly 314
Strawberry Shortcake 313
Blackberries 210
and Apple Jam 211
Helen's Batter 211
Jam 210
Jelly 211
Roll 314
Sauce 211
Blueberries 212
Buckle 213
Grunt, Annie's 213
Sauce 214
Tart 214
Boiled Dinner 63
Bondinettes
Rabbit 68
Bouquet Garni 251
Brandy
Lemon 223
Orange 338
Peaches 228
Sauce 329
Bread
Assize of 311
Bannock 311
Boston Brown 307
Colonial 308
Kneading 305
Oat, Good Old-Fashioned
Scotch 306
Porridge 309
Potato 196
Pudding, Queen 259
Pudding, Raisin-Almond 321
Pumpkin 179
Sour Milk Brown 307
Tea 308
Broccoli 142
Ham Stratta 142
Piquant 143
on Toast 143
Brose, Mussel 125
Brussel Sprouts 143
Fritters, Sprout 144
Marinated 144
Tangy 144
Bubble and Squeak 145
Buckle, see Blueberry
Buns, see Rolls
Butter
Making 260

Parsley Balls 327
Pear 229
Rendering 272
Raspberry and Apple 236

Cabbage 145
Bubble and Squeak 145
Sauerkraut by the jar 146
Sauerkraut, cooking 146
Cakes (and loaves) 277
Banana Bread, Nanny's 282
Boiled Cake (War Cake), Mrs.
Falconer's 275
Boiling Water Cake 278
Bride's Cake 331
Bridegroom's Cake 332
Christmas Log 335
Ginger Bread
Pear Sauce 230
Spicy 285
Icing or Frosting on Cakes . . . 281
Brown Sugar Frosting 282
Cocoa Icing 282
Filling for Cakes 281
Raisin Filling 281
Johnny Cake 277
Lemon Loaf 284
Nut Bread Loaf from
Cardigan 283
Orange Bread from Mina 284
Plum Puff 335
Plum Loaf 233
Pork 43
Pumpkin Pecan Loaf 179
Rhubarb Shortcake 238
Scotch Cake, Mrs. Falconer's 294
Scotch Oat Cake 292
Scriptural Cake 278
Shortcake, Biscuit Dough for 313
Shortcake, Strawberry 313
Strawberry Angel Delight 241
Sugarless, Eggless, Milkless,
Butterless Cake 279
Tumbler Cake 278
War Cake, Hazel's Boiled
Dark Cake 275
Candy
Maple Cream 244
Maple Taffy 245
Molasses 337
Nature's Chewing Gum 249
Sugar Plums 336
Carrots 147
à la Hollandaise 148
Candied 149
and Celery Casserole 153
Honey's 148

Jam to imitate Apricot
  Preserve . . . 148
Cauliflower . . . 149
  and Tomato Casserole . . . 150
Celeriac . . . 150
  Hot Pot . . . 151
Celery . . . 152
  Braised . . . 153
  and Carrot Casserole . . . 153
  Leaves, dried . . . 131
  Meat Loaf . . . 152
  Sauté . . . 153
Cheese . . . 263
  Cheddar Scallop . . . 264
  Cottage, Homemade . . . 264
  and Egg Strata . . . 263
  Mexican Rarebit . . . 265
  Ramequins of Cheese Pastry 263
  Rink-Tum-Diddy . . . 265
  Tomato Puff . . . 265
  Welsh Rarebit . . . 263
Cherry
  in Currant Jelly . . . 214
  Preserves . . . 215
  Preserves, Baked 215
  Sauce, Hot . . . 329
  Toast . . . 215
Chicken . . . 71
  n' Corn Scallop . . . 73
  Glazed Liver Pâté . . . 76
  Mushroom Caps with
  Chicken Liver . . . 166
  in Oatmeal . . . 75
  Old Fashioned Pie . . . 74
  Paprika . . . 72
  Acadian Ragoût with
  Dumplings . . . 74
  Roll . . . 72
  Sandwich . . . 73
  Soup from a Carcass . . . 77
  Stuffed . . . 74
Chowder
  Clam 'n Corn . . . 156
  Clam, Mosser's . . . 119
  Crab . . . 110
  Cream Corn . . . 155
  Mussel . . . 124
  Salmon . . . 99
Christmas . . . 333
  Acadian . . . 334
  Fireplace Frivolites . . . 339
  Gifts, Holiday . . . 336
  Log . . . 335
  Mincemeat, Green Tomato . . . 333
  Plum Puff . . . 335
  Sugar plums . . . 336
Chutney — see pickle
Cider
  Sweet Apple . . . 203
  Vinegar . . . 203
Citrus
  Zest . . . 222
Clam, see shellfish
Conserve
  Plum . . . 231
Cookies
  Chocolate Biscuit . . . 292
  Fruit Drops . . . 293
  Jolly Boys . . . 296
  Macaroons, Butter . . . 297
  Mincemeat Cookie Bars . . . 287
  Molasses, Grandmother's
  Soft . . . 295
  Molasses, Jackie's Soft . . . 295
  Molasses-Raisin-Nut Bars . . . 336
  Oatmeal, Helen's Old
  Fashioned . . . 291
  Ragged Robins . . . 297
  Range Top . . . 296
  Sand Tarts from Stanhope . . . 297
  Scotch Cake (Shortbread),
  Mrs. Falconer's . . . 294
  Scotch Oat Cakes . . . 292
  Spiced Ginger Mounds . . . 293
  Sweetheart Cookies . . . 293
Cordial
  Raspberry . . . 235
  Strawberry . . . 240
Corn . . . 153
  Carol's Casserole . . . 157
  'n' Chicken Scallop . . . 73
  Clam and, Casserole . . . 122
  Clam 'n' Chowder . . . 156
  Cream, Chowder . . . 155
  Creamed Hot Pot . . . 157
  Hominy . . . 154
  Hominy with Carrots . . . 155
  Hominy with Cheese . . . 155
  Hominy, Cracked . . . 155
  Skillet . . . 158
Cornbread
  Upside Down Sausage . . . 50
Corned Beef . . . 62
  Boiled Dinner . . . 63
  Hash with Eggs . . . 64
Cornish Pasties . . . 57
Cottage Cheese, Homemade . . . 264
Crab, see Shellfish
Crabapple . . . 215
  Preserved, Baked . . . 216
Crackers, Souffled . . . 84
Cranberries . . . 216
  Candied Ruby Berries . . . 217
  Cranapple Pie . . . 217
  Frappe, Mock . . . 218
  Ice . . . 218

Jelly..................... 217
Preserves, Carol's.......... 218
Spiced.................. 217
Cream
Homemade Sour........... 260
Sour.................... 260
Creme Renversee au Caramel.... 256
Cucumbers.................. 158
Boiled.................. 159
Braised with Onion......... 159
Helen's Sweet Sliced Pickles 160
India Relish.............. 161
No-fail Mustard Relish...... 160
Vinegar.................. 159
Cures and Remedies
Cold..................... 170
Currant
in Cherries Jelly........... 214
and Gooseberry Tarts....... 220
Curry
Eggs with Rice............ 270
Lamb.................... 66
Sauce with Turkey......... 78
Custard..................... 255
Caramel with Raisins....... 256
and Fruit................ 256
Ice Cream................ 257
Soft..................... 256

Dandelion
Dill Steak Rolls.............. 55
Doughnuts
Potato.................. 289
Dried
Beans and Peas............ 131
Drying Berries............ 247
Fruit.................... 219
Fruits and Nuts............ 247
Dripping.................... 64
Duck....................... 71
with Burgundy Sauce....... 81
Roasted.................. 80
Dumplings
Apple................... 205
Apple, Baked............. 314
see Ragoût

Edible Plants................ 251
Eels, see fish
Eggs....................... 267
and Cheese Strata.......... 263
Columbus................ 271
Cooked in Maple Syrup..... 243
Curried with Rice.......... 270
Devilled.................. 270
Egg Nog, Kentucky......... 271
French Toast with Maple
Syrup.................... 243
Goldenrod Toast........... 268
in a nest................. 268
Pickled.................. 269
Scotch.................. 269
Baked in Tomatoes......... 271
Elderberries
Canned.................. 219

Farcie, Freda's Lobster......... 109
Faggots, Parsnip.............. 174
Fat, to render................ 80
Fiddleheads................. 162
A Taste of Spring.......... 162
Fig, Paste for Filling........... 248
Finnan Haddie, see fish
Fireplace Frivolites............ 339
Fish
Cod.................... 91
Codfish Cakes............. 92
Codfish in a Nest........... 92
Cod, Salt — Baked with
Cheese.................. 92
Cod, Salt — Dinner......... 91
Cod, Salt — Pie............ 93
Cod, Salt — to prepare...... 91
Eels.................... 103
Eels, Bessie's Broiled........ 104
Eels, Boiled............... 105
Eels, Fried............... 104
Eel, Pie.................. 105
Finnan Haddie............ 89
Finnan Haddie, creamed.... 90
Finnan Haddie Savory...... 89
Haddock................ 88
Haddock, Baked with Cheese 89
Haddock, stuffed........... 88
Hake Casserole............ 87
Island Style Casserole....... 90
Mackerel................. 93
Mackerel, Baked Spanish.... 94
Mackerel, Fillets and Cheese 95
Mackerel, Millie's Soused.... 95
Mackerel, Pate............ 96
Mackerel, Salt — Broiled
with Parsley Butter......... 95
Pâré, Mackerel or Trout..... 96
Pickled.................. 85
Salmon.................. 98
Salmon, Chowder.......... 99
Salmon, Croquettes........ 98
Salmon Macaroni Salad..... 99
Salmon Spoonbread........ 99
Salmon, West River Pâté.... 99
Sauce, with............... 86

Smelt.................... 100
Smelt, Broiled Stuffed....... 103
Smelt, Camp Fire.......... 101
Smelt, Creamed and Onion 102
Smelt, Du Chef............ 102
Smelt, Outdoor Grill....... 101
Tomcod.................. 93
Trout, Brook in Clam Juice 96
Trout, Fried a la Quebec..... 96
Trout, Marinated.......... 96
Trout, Pate............... 96
White.................... 87
Forcemeat
Balls for Fish Soups........ 109
Fowl....................... 71
Frappe, see Cranberry.......... 218
Fricassee
Francois Goose............ 79
Mrs. Gallant's............. 59
Fritters...................... 288
Annie's.................. 288
Carol's.................. 288
Parsnip.................. 173
Pumpkin -180
Sprout................... 144
Fruit
and Custard............... 256
Jam..................... 220

Game Bird.................. 71
Grouse, Roasted........... 83
Pigeon, Roasted........... 83
Stuffed.................. 74
Garlic...................... 252
Gin
Orange.................. 235
Ginger
To Preserve.............. 337
Gingerbread
Pear Sauce............... 230
Spicy................... 285
Gingseng................... 39, 252
Goose...................... 71
Corn or Pickle Meat........ 62
Francois Fricassed.......... 79
Hashed.................. 78
Preserved................ 80
Render Fat............... 80
Gooseberry................. 219
and Currant Tarts.......... 220
Jam..................... 220
Spiced................... 220
Grouse
to Roast.................. 83
Grunt, see Blueberry

Ham
Baked, Joan's............. 46
Baked, Verna's............. 46
Beer Glazed Slices.......... 47
and Broccili Strata.......... 142
Devilled Squares........... 47
'n' Lamb Savory........... 65
Hasenpfeffer — Rabbit......... 69
Hash
Corned Beef with Eggs...... 64
Goose.................... 78
Turkey Potato............. 78
Head Cheese, see Pork
Herbs...................... 131
History, of Prince Edward Island 9
Hocks, see Pork
Hominy, see Corn
Honey...................... 337
Horseradish................. 163
Butter, Lemon............. 327
Horseradish Sauce......... 163
Household Hints............. 37

Ice Cream
Custard.................. 257
Irish Moss.................. 126
to dry.................... 127
jelly.................... 128
Irish Stew.................. 66

Jam
Blackberry................ 210
Blackberry and Apple....... 211
Carrot to imitate Apricot Preserve................. 148
Fruit.................... 220
Gooseberry............... 220
Making.................. 208
Peach.................... 226
Pumpkin Spread for Bread... 180
Raspberry, Wild........... 236
Jelly
Blackberry................ 211
Cherries in Currant......... 214
Cranberry................ 217
Irish Moss................ 128
Making.................. 209
Rhubarb................. 237
Jolly Boys.................. 296

Kentucky Egg Nog............ 271
Kitchen Bouquet............. 252

Lamb and Mutton
Baked Stuffed Chops........ 67

Chops Cooked with Mint Sauce . . . 65
Curry . . . 66
'n' Ham Savory . . . 65
Irish Stew . . . 66
Mock Venison . . . 67
and Rosemary . . . 66
Lamb's Wool . . . 204
Lettuce . . . 163
Lemon . . . 221
Brandy . . . 223
Butter, Horseradish . . . 327
Crystalized . . . 222
Dessert . . . 221
Herbed Vinegar . . . 338
Loaf . . . 284
Pepper, Seasoned . . . 338
Sauce . . . 222
Sauce, to serve over Hot Puddings or Cake . . . 328
To Keep . . . 222
Uses . . . 221
Zest . . . 222
Liver
Chicken Pâté . . . 76
Loaf . . . 61
Mushroom Caps with Chicken Liver . . . 166
and Onions and Brown Gravy . . . 61
Lobster, see shellfish

Macaroons
Butter . . . 297
Macaroni, Salmon Salad . . . 99
Mace . . . 252
Maple (includes Syrup)
Acorn Squash Bake . . . 183
Cinnamon Buns . . . 244
Cream Candy . . . 244
Duff . . . 245
Eggs Cooked in . . . 243
French Toast with . . . 243
The Mightly Maple-More than a Sugar Bush . . . 242
Stuffed Apple to serve with meat . . . 244
Sugar . . . 243
Taffy . . . 245
Toast . . . 244
Marmalade
Making . . . 210
Orange, San Diego . . . 226
Measurements . . . 33
Meat Loaf
Celery . . . 152
Melon . . . 224
Milk
Sour . . . 260
To Sour . . . 262
Whitewash . . . 262
Mincemeat
Cookie Bars . . . 287
Green Tomato from Helen . . . 333
Oat Squares . . . 303
Mint . . . 253
Crystallized Leaves . . . 253
Mint Sauce . . . 253
Molasses . . . 294
Bran Muffins . . . 287
Candy . . . 337
Cookies, Grandmother's Soft 295
Cookies, Jackie's Soft . . . 295
Glazed Onions . . . 169
Raisin-Nut Bars . . . 336
Muffins
Fruit, Iva's . . . 288
Molasses Bran . . . 287
Potato Flour . . . 198
Spiced Gem . . . 286
Squash . . . 183
Mushrooms . . . 164
Caps with Chicken Liver . . . 166
Croquettes . . . 165
Dried . . . 166
Nanny's Stewed . . . 164
Oven Stewed . . . 165
Mussels, see shellfish
Mustard
Relish, No-Fail . . . 160
Mutton, see Lamb

Nasturtium Sandwich . . . 254
Nature's Chewing Gum . . . 249
Noodles, for soup . . . 84
Nuts
Salad Sandwiches . . . 248
Sugar and Spiced . . . 249

Oats . . . 309
Bread, Good Old-fashioned Scotch Oat . . . 306
Bread, Porridge . . . 310
Cakes, Scotch Oat . . . 292
Cookies, Helen's Old Fashioned Oatmeal . . . 291
Mincemeat Squares . . . 303
Oatmeal — Porridge . . . 310
Onions . . . 167
and Apples . . . 168
Braised . . . 168
Briased Cukes with . . . 159
Cold Cure . . . 170
and Liver with Brown Gravy 61

Molasses Glazed........... 169
and Parsnips Loaf.......... 173
and Peas, French Style...... 175
Pickled Rings............ 169
Pie, Jean-Marie's........... 169
Ragout.................. 170
Soup, French Canadian..... 170
Stuffed.................. 171
Velvet.................. 169
Warehouse Wine.......... 171
Oranges.................... 224
Ambrosia................ 225
Brandy.................. 338
Bread.................... 284
Crystallized.............. 222
Gin..................... 225
Grated Peel.............. 225
Marmalade, San Diego...... 226
Zest..................... 222
Oxtail..................... 60
Soup................... 60
Oysters — see shellfish
Noodles, for soup............ 84

Pancakes
Batter................... 258
Old Time................ 258
Potato.................. 199
Snow.................. 257
Pandowdy
Apple.................. 202
Parsnips.................. 172
Faggots................. 174
Fritters.................. 173
Murray Harbour Casserole... 173
and Onion Loaf........... 173
Parsley, Dried................ 131
Pasties, Cornish.............. 57
Pastry...................... 317
Flaky................... 317
Fool-Proof Flaky, Debbie's... 317
Whole Wheat Crust for Pies
and Tarts................ 318
To Hot Up............... 318
Pâté
Chicken Liver, Glazed...... 76
Mackerel or Trout.......... 96
Pork..................... 44
Salmon, West River........ 99
Peach...................... 226
Brandy.................. 228
Jam..................... 226
Pickled Relish, Mrs.
Doucette's............... 227
Port Wine Sauce........... 228
Salad, Anne's.............. 227
Pears...................... 228
Butter.................... 229
Gingerbread.............. 230
Prince John............... 230
Sauce.................... 229
Spiced Baked............. 231
Tourtiere, Adrianne's....... 228
Peas....................... 174
Acadian Soup............. 175
Creamed................. 175
Dried.................... 131
French Style and Onions.... 175
Soup aux Pois (French
Canadian Pea)............. 176
Split Pea Soup with Salt
Pork.................... 48
Peppers.................... 176
Sandwiches............... 177
Stuffed Sweet............. 177
Pickle or Corn Beef, Tongue or
Goose...................... 62
Pickle
Apple Chutney............ 206
Apples.................. 206
Artichokes................ 133
Beets, Spiced............. 139
Eggs.................... 269
Helen's Sweet Sliced Pickles 160
Higdom, Tomato.......... 187
India Relish.............. 161
Longfellow, Genuine....... 186
Marrow and Apple Chutney 184
No-Fail Mustard Relish..... 160
Onion Rings.............. 169
Pumpkin................. 180
String Bean.............. 137
Tomato, Green............ 186
Tomato, Green Sandwich
Spread.................. 187
Pie
Apple................... 205
Clam and Bacon........... 123
Clam, Rappie............. 120
Chicken, Old Fashioned..... 74
Cranapple................ 217
Eel..................... 105
Mom's Impossible.......... 259
Onion, Jean-Marie's........ 169
Oyster, Little.............. 115
Pastry/Crust (see Pastry)
Rappie Pie with Clams...... 120
Rum Runners Black Bottom 319
Salt Codfish............... 93
Pigeon
to Roast................. 83
Pigs in a Blanket............. 52
Planked Steak................ 54
Plum....................... 231

Conserve.................. 231
Loaf..................... 233
Puff..................... 335
Stewed.................. 232
Sugar.................... 336
Tart..................... 232
Popcorn................... 177
Pork...................... 41
Cake.................... 43
Chops, School Children's
Choice.................. 45
Cured, About............. 46
Ham, see Ham
Head Cheese............. 42
Hocks in Jelly........... 42
Pâté.................... 44
Preserving............... 42
Salt, with Split Pea Soup.... 48
Scrapple................. 43
Tourtière................ 45
Porridge.................. 310
Pot Roast, Norma's Beef in a Pot 53
Potato.................... 194
Baked, Buttery............ 197
Baking.................. 195
Balls, Bacon and.......... 200
Biscuit.................. 198
Bread................... 196
Blue.................... 194
Cakes, Irish.............. 199
Doughnuts............... 289
Hash, Turkey............ 78
Minty New.............. 197
Muffins, Flour............ 198
Pancake................. 199
Pastry.................. 196
Salad Ring............... 195
Scalloped................ 197
Soup................... 198
Stuffing................. 199
Turnip Puff.............. 191
Preserves
Cherry.................. 215
Cherry, Baked............ 215
Crabapple, Baked......... 216
Cranberry, Carol's......... 218
Plum Conserve........... 234
Prunes.................... 234
Pudding
Bread, Raisin-Almond...... 321
Corn Flake............... 320
Cottage Pudding, Marian's... 275
Fig, Steamed............. 320
Nut Cabinet.............. 321
Queen Bread............. 259
Rhubarb, Baked.......... 238
Sausage from Malpeque..... 51
Short Day's Pud........... 239
Summer Pudding.......... 240
Wild Raspberry Mold....... 236
Pumpkin.................. 178
Baked in the Shell.......... 179
Bread................... 306
Cures................... 39
Fritters.................. 180
Pecan Loaf............... 179
Pickled.................. 180
Roasted Seeds............ 179
Seeds................... 39
Spread for Bread........... 180

Queen Bread Pudding......... 259

Rabbit
Bondinettes.............. 68
Hasenpfeffer............. 69
Mexican................. 265
Supreme, from Russ........ 69
You Fool 'Em............ 68
Welsh.................. 263
Ragged Robins.............. 297
Ragoût
Acadian Chicken with
Dumplings.............. 74
Onion.................. 170
Rarebit
Mexican................. 265
Oyster.................. 116
Welsh.................. 263
Raspberry................. 234
and Apple Butter.......... 236
Cordial................. 235
and Cream.............. 234
Puréed................. 234
Shrub.................. 235
Spring Storehouse......... 237
Squares................. 299, 300
Wild................... 235
Wild Jam................ 236
Wild Pudding Mold........ 236
Relish
India................... 161
No-fail Mustard........... 160
Peach, Mrs. Doucette's
Pickled................. 227
Render
Butter.................. 272
Goose.................. 80
Rhubarb.................. 237
Baked.................. 237
Jelly................... 237
Pudding, Baked........... 238
Short Day's Pud.......... 238

Shortcake.................. 238
Rink-Tum-Diddly............ 265
Rolls (includes buns)
Cinnamon Rolls........... 286
Magic Almond............ 315
Maple Cinnamon Buns..... 244
Roly-Poly.................. 314
Apple Pudding........... 204
Roux...................... 82
Rutabegas................. 189

Sage and Onion Stuffing....... 81
Salad
Peach, Anne's............ 227
Salmon and Macaroni...... 99
Salmon, see fish
Salt Cod
see fish
Sandwich
Banana.................. 207
Chicken.................. 73
Fig Paste for Filling........ 248
Filling for Sweet Sandwiches 248
Lobster, Hot.............. 108
Nasturtium............... 254
Nut Salad................ 248
Pepper.................. 177
Sauce...................... 323
Bechamel................ 324
Blackberry................ 211
Blueberry................ 214
Brandy.................. 329
Brown Butter............. 87
Brown Sugar.............. 330
Cherry, Hot.............. 329
Chocolate for Ice Cream or
Cake.................... 328
Cream with fish........... 86
Fish, with................ 86
French.................. 327
Hard.................... 328
Horseradish.............. 163
Hollandaise.............. 326
Lemon.................. 222
Lemon to serve over Hot
Puddings or Cake.......... 328
Mint.................... 253
Mustard................. 326
Peach Port Wine.......... 228
Pear.................... 229
White................... 324
Sauerkraut
by the Jar................ 146
Cooking................. 146
Sausage..................... 48
and Apple Rings -203
Creamed Corn Hot Pot...... 157
Lobster.................. 108
Pigs in a Blanket........... 52
Pudding from Malpeque.... 51
Stuffing.................. 51
Toad in a Hole............ 51
Toast.................... 51
Upsidedown Cornbread..... 50
Savory...................... 253
Scallop
Cheddar.................. 264
Chicken 'n' Corn........... 73
Scallops, see shellfish
Scotch Eggs.................. 269
Scrapple, Pork............... 43
Shellfish
Clam and Bacon Pie........ 123
Clam and Corn Casserole.... 122
Clam, Jellied Soup......... 122
Clam, Mosser's Chowder.... 119
Clams................... 118
Clams, Deep Fried.......... 121
Clams, in Batter........... 121
Clams in Bread Crumbs..... 122
Clams, Rappie Pie Made
with.................... 120
Crab.................... 110
Crab Au Gratin............ 110
Crab Chowder............ 110
Crab, Devilled from Stanley
Bridge 111
Lobster.................. 107
Lobster — Forcemeat Balls... 109
Lobster, Freda's Farcie...... 109
Lobster, Joan's Casserole.... 108
Lobster, Hot Sandwiches.... 108
Lobster, Sausages.......... 108
Mussel Brose............. 125
Mussel, Cheesy Baked....... 126
Mussel Chowder........... 124
Mussel Stew.............. 125
Mussels.................. 124
Oysters.................. 111
Oyster Casserole from "Up
West"................... 115
Oysters, Escalloped with
Tomatoes Au Gratin........ 114
Oyster, Little Pies.......... 115
Oyster, Rarebit............ 116
Scallops................. 116
Scallops, Julie's Mornay..... 116
Scallops, Old Settlers....... 118
Shepherd's Pie............... 57
Sherbet
Apple.................. 202
Shortcake
Rhubarb................. 238
Smelt, see fish

Soup
Asparagus, Cream of........ 134
Clam, Jellie................ 122
Crackers, Souffled.......... 84
Forcemeat Balls for......... 109
From a Chicken or Turkey
Carcass.................. 77
French Canadian Onion..... 170
Lillian's Split Pea with Salt
Pork..................... 48
Minty New Potato.......... 197
Noodles for............... 84
Ox-tail.................. 60
Pea, Acadian.............. 175
aux Pois (French Canadian
Pea Soup)................ 176
Potato.................. 198
Watercress................ 192
Sour Cream or Milk........... 260, 262
Brown Bread, Sour Milk..... 307
Homemade............... 260
Spiced Beef.................. 55
Spinach..................... 180
Creamed................ 181
French.................. 182
Spoonbread, Salmon.......... 100
Spread
Pumpkin for Bread......... 180
Tomato, Green, Sandwich... 187
Squares
Black and White........... 302
Hello Dollies............. 301
Mincemeat Oat............ 303
Pineapple................ 300
Raspberry................ 299
Raspberry, Mary's.......... 300
Speckled................. 301
Tea...................... 302
Squash..................... 182
Baked Winter............. 183
Maple Acorn Bake.......... 183
Marrow and Apple Chutney 184
Muffins.................. 183
Nutmeg.................. 182
Steak, see beef
Strata
Broccoli and Ham.......... 142
Cheese and Egg........... 263
Strawberry.................. 239
Angel Delight............. 241
Caps On................. 241
Cordial.................. 240
Crushed................. 240
Cures.................... 39
Preserved in Wine.......... 241
Shortcake................ 313
Summer Pudding.......... 240
String Bean Pickles............ 137
Stuffing
Apple.................... 207
Chicken or Game Bird...... 74
Potato................... 199
Sage and Onion........... 81
Sausage.................. 51
Wild Rice................ 193
Sugar, types.................. 36
Swiss Chard................. 184
Tapioca
Apple Bake............... 204
Tarragon
Vinegar.................. 203
Tart
Blueberry................ 214
Gooseberry and Currant..... 220
Plum.................... 232
Sand, from Stanhope....... 297
Tea Parties.................. 273
Thyme (Cures)............... 39
Toad in a Hole............... 51
Toast
Cherry.................. 215
Goldenrod............... 268
French with Maple Syrup.... 243
Maple................... 244
Sausage.................. 51
Tomato..................... 185
Cauliflower Casserole....... 150
Cheese Puff............... 265
Cheesy Fries.............. 188
Du Barry................. 188
Eggs Baked in............ 271
Escalloped............... 187
Escalloped Oysters with, au
Gratin.................. 114
Green Mincemeat from
Helen................... 333
Green Tomato Pickles...... 186
Green Tomato Sandwich
Spread.................. 187
Higdom................. 187
Longfellow Pickles......... 186
Piccalilli................. 186
Sauce.................... 47
on Toast................. 188
Tongue
Corned, to cook........... 62
To Corn or Pickle......... 63
Tourtière
Acadian Pork............. 45
Adrienne's Pear........... 228
Turkey..................... 71
with Curry Sauce.......... 78

My Mother's Delight (pressed to slice) 77
Potato Hash 78
Soup from a Carcass 77
Turnip 189
and Potato Puff 191
Scalloped 190
Supreme -190
Toss Up 191

Upside Down Sausage Cornbread 50

Vegetables 129
to glaze 131
Dried 131
Stored 130
Venison, Mock
see Lamb
Vinegar
Cider, to make 203
Cucumber 159
Lemon Herbed 338
Tarragon 203

War Cake 275
Watercress 192
Soup 192
Welsh Rarebit 263
Whitewash 262
Wild Rice 192
Plain 193
Stuffing, Mrs. Doucette's 193
Wine
Strawberries Preserved in 241
Warehouse 171

Yule Season 333

Zest of Citrus 222

transcontinental
PRINTING
IMPRIMERIE GAGNÉ